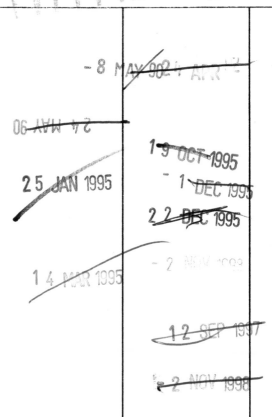

To Jane and Lucy, who started it all

Language in infancy and childhood

A linguistic introduction to language acquisition

ALAN CRUTTENDEN

At first the infant,
Mewling and puking in the nurse's arms,
And then the whining schoolboy . . .

Manchester University Press

© Alan Cruttenden 1979

Published by Manchester University Press
Oxford Road, Manchester M13 9PL

British Library cataloguing in publication data

Cruttenden, Alan
　Language in infancy and childhood.
　1. Children – Language
　I. Title
　401'.9　LB1139.L3

　ISBN 0–7190–0750–X (paperback)

Reprinted 1985

Text set in 10/12 pt VIP Times, printed by photolithography,
and bound in Great Britain at The Pitman Press, Bath

Preface

This book is primarily an introductory textbook for students who have some background in linguistics and phonetics (a glossary has been added for those who have no such background). It is intended for all students of linguistics and/or child language. It is also intended for all those concerned with language teaching or language remediation. For readers in these latter two groups the philosophy of the book is clear: greater knowledge of the facts of language acquisition will enable teachers and therapists to formulate their own tactics (the book is *not* therefore concerned with *how* to teach).

A number of textbooks on language acquisition have been published in recent years, e.g. McNeill (1970), Menyuk (1971), and Dale (1972). This book is intentionally different in its approach from any of these. It is written rather more from the viewpoint of linguistics than of psychology. Hence there is throughout an emphasis on linguistic facts, especially on the detailed order of acquisition in phonology, grammar, and, to a lesser extent, lexis. In particular, the treatment of phonology is somewhat more extensive than in previous books. (Most of the phonetic terms are explained in the glossary.)

The main aim of this book is to present the linguistic facts of language acquisition in as theoretically neutral a way as possible (of course no presentation can be *absolutely* neutral) and in some detail. Theoretical implications and issues are discussed as they arise from the facts and some major overall theories are outlined in chapter 5. There is, however, rather less discussion of theory than in comparable books, although references to more detailed treatments are always given.

The book is fairly heavily referenced because it is intended to guide those readers who wish to study particular topics in more depth. Each chapter is more or less self-sufficient, so that students interested in only one aspect of the subject may read only the relevant chapter or chapters. In this way it may be used as a mini reference book.

Chapter 7 has been written by Katharine Perera, who has also given me many detailed comments on the whole manuscript, as well as many pertinent examples which I have used. Alan Cruse has also supplied me with some data, in particular that in 1.5.

Although relatively short, the book has been a long time in the making. We have had comments from all our colleagues in the Department of General Linguistics, from members of other departments (in particular Leslie Owrid), and from many people outside Manchester (in particular Natalie Waterson, Pamela Grunwell and Frank Skitt). William Haas gave the book great encouragement when it seemed to be stumbling. To all these I give my sincere thanks, although I suspect they will often think I should have taken their advice where I have not.

I must thank all those concerned with the typing, the main burden of which has fallen on Kumiko Thomas and Nola Bowden.

Last and most importantly my thanks go to my wife, who supplied both the first informants and great encouragement, and who also found time to paint the picture on the cover and to draw the diagram on page 162.

University of Manchester, 1977   A.C.

Contents

Symbols and technical conventions   *ix*
Language development and motor development compared   *xii*
Introduction   *xiii*

1   Foundations   **1**

1.1   The neonate   1
1.2   The babbling period   2
1.3   Prosodics—variation in pitch and other factors   6
1.4   Early perception   7
1.5   First meanings   9
1.6   The one-word stage   13

2   Phonology   **16**

2.1   Development of the sound system   16
2.2   Phonemic substitution   22
2.3   Consonantal clusters   23
2.4   Stress and rhythm   24
2.5   Assimilation—the influence of one sound on another   25
2.6   Metathesis—the interchanging of sounds   26
2.7   Interaction of various factors   26
2.8   Perception of phonemic contrasts   27
2.9   Constraints on productive phonological development   29
2.10 Intonation   33

3   Grammar   **35**

3.1   Preliminaries   35
3.2   Two-word sentences   37
3.3   Syntax   48
3.4   Morphology   58
3.5   Strategies   63
3.6   Comprehension   67
3.7   Imitation   71
3.8   Parental speech   75
3.9   Discourse, conversation and register   79

4   **Lexis**   **83**

4.1   Vocabulary development   83
4.2   Which words are learnt   84
4.3   How word-meanings are learnt   85
4.4   Generalisation and differentiation   85
4.5   Relational meanings   88

5   **Some Theories**   **96**

5.1   Preliminaries   96
5.2   Behaviourist theories   97
5.3   Innatist theories   101
5.4   Cognitive theories   106
5.5   Sociological theories   110
5.6   A balanced viewpoint   113

6   **Later Development**   **115**

6.1   Phonology   115
6.2   Grammar   117
6.3   Lexis   121
6.4   Social class and language development   123

7   **Reading and Writing**   *by Katharine Perera*   **130**

7.1   Written language   132
7.2   The early stages of reading   145
7.3   The early stages of writing   152
7.4   Approaches to the teaching of reading   154
7.5   The language of reading materials   157

Glossary   *161*
References   *171*
Index   *189*

Symbols and technical conventions

Slant brackets / / enclose adult phonemic transcriptions; the type of phonemic transcription is that of Daniel Jones, *An English pronouncing dictionary*, thirteenth edition (1967), which is based on Received Pronunciation (R.P.), also called Educated Southern British. The following symbols are used:

/p/	as in *pin*	/n/	as in *no*
/b/	as in *bee*	/ŋ/	as in *sing*
/t/	as in *tin*	/i :/	as in *been*
/d/	as in *dart*	/i/	as in *tin*
/k/	as in *cart*	/e/	as in *ten*
/g/	as in *go*	/æ/	as in *pan*
/tʃ/	as in *cheese*	/ʌ/	as in *cup*
/ʤ/	as in *jay*	/ɑ :/	as in *father*
/f/	as in *fin*	/ɔ/	as in *lot*
/v/	as in *vat*	/ɔ :/	as in *caught*
/θ/	as in *thin*	/u/	as in *put*
/ð/	as in *these*	/u :/	as in *boot*
/s/	as in *sea*	/ə/.	as in *about*
/z/	as in *zoo*	/ə :/	as in *bird*
/ʃ/	as in *sheep*	/ei/	as in *pain*
/ʒ/	as in *measure*	/ai/	as in *sign*
/h/	as in *hug*	/ɔi/	as in *coil*
/l/	as in *lead*	/au/	as in *loud*
/r/	as in *red*	/əu/	as in *boat*
/w/	as in *weed*	/iə/	as in *fear*
/j/	as in *yard*	/ɛə/	as in *fare*
/m/	as in *meet*	/uə/	as in *sure*

In American English (A.E.) /ɔ/ generally falls together with /ɑ :/ so that *pot* and *father* are pronounced with the same vowel. The diphthongs /ei/ and /əu/ would be better transcribed /e :/ and /o :/ in A.E., since these vowels are generally monophthongal. In many varieties of A.E. the vowels /ə :/, /iə/, /ɛə/, /uə/ do not exist but correspond to various vowels plus /r/, or a vowel with r-colouring.

Square brackets [ ] are used for adult pronunciation when phonetic detail is required and also *for all child pronunciations*. This involves the use of a number of additional symbols from the International Phonetic Alphabet.

Change of pronunciation and the relationship between adult and child pronunciations are indicated by →.

Braces { } enclose a morphemic (or morphophonemic) transcription (see further under *Morpheme* in the Glossary).

< > marks a written form.

≡ means "corresponds to' (concerning relationships between spelling and pronunciation).

The terms 'correct', adult grammar', 'adult phonology', are not in any way meant to be prescriptive, but are useful shorthand terms whose meaning should be relatively obvious.

The word 'form' (and its adjective 'formal') is used throughout as the opposite of 'meaning'.

Quotations from child speech are generally in italics; glosses or meanings are placed in quotation marks. Occasionally technical terms and emphasised words also occur in italics, but rarely enough for this not to lead to any confusion.

Children's ages are given in the customary way, e.g. 4;1, indicating a period during the second month of their fifth year.

A guide to more technical terms in phonetics and linguistics will be found in the Glossary.

THE INTERNATIONAL PHONETIC ALPHABET Revised to 1951 (Secondary articulations are shown by symbols in brackets)

CONSONANTS

	Bi-labial	Labio-dental	Dental and Alveolar	Retroflex	Palato-alveolar	Alveolo-palatal	Palatal	Velar	Uvular	Pharyngal	Glottal
Plosive	p b		t d	ʈ ɖ			c ɟ	k g	q ɢ		ʔ
Nasal	m	ɱ	n	ɳ			ɲ	ŋ	N		
Lateral Fricative			ɬ ɮ								
Lateral Non-fricative			l	ɭ			ʎ				
Rolled			r						ʀ		
Flapped			ɾ	ɽ					ʀ		
Fricative	ɸ β	f v	θ ð | s z	ʂ ʐ	ʃ ʒ	ɕ ʑ	ç j	x ɣ	χ ʁ	ħ ʕ	h ɦ
Frictionless Continuants and Semi-vowels	w ɥ	ʋ	ɹ	ɹ			j (ɥ)	(w)	ʁ		

VOWELS

		Front	Central	Back	
Close	(y ʉ u)	i y	ɨ ʉ	ɯ u	
Half-close	(ø o)	e ø		ɤ o	
Half-open	(œ ɔ)	ɛ œ	ɘ	ʌ ɔ	
Open	(ɒ)		æ ɐ	ɑ ɒ	

OTHER SOUNDS.—Palatalized consonants: ƫ, ɖ, etc.; palatalized ʃ, ʒ: ʆ, ʓ. Velarized or pharyngalized consonants: ɫ, ɖ, ʑ, etc. Ejective consonants (with simultaneous glottal stop): p', t', etc. Implosive voiced consonants: ɓ, ɗ, etc. ɼ fricative trill. σ, ϑ (labialized θ, ð, or ʒ). ƪ, ʓ (labialized ʃ, ʒ). ɿ, ʇ, ʗ, ʖ (clicks, Zulu c, q, x). ɹ (a sound between r and l). ŋ Japanese syllabic nasal. ƪ (combination of x and ʃ). ʍ (voiceless w). ɩ, ɤ, ɞ (lowered varieties of i, y, u). ə (a variety of ə). ɵ (a vowel between ø and o). etc., or the marks ˘ or ⁀ (ts̆ or t͡s, etc.). ˜ also denote synchronic articulation (m̃ŋ̃ = simultaneous m and ŋ). ƈ, ɟ may occasionally be used in place of tʃ, dʒ, and ʒ, ʑ for ts, dz. Aspirated plosives: ph, th, etc. r-coloured vowels: ɚ, aɹ, ɔɹ, etc., or ɚ, ɑ̯, ɒ̯, etc.; r-coloured ə : ɚ or əʳ or ɹ or ɚ, or ɚ.

LENGTH, STRESS, PITCH.—ː (full length). ˑ (half length). ˈ (stress, placed at beginning of the stressed syllable). ˌ (secondary stress). ˉ (high level pitch); ˍ (low level); ˊ (high rising); ˏ (low rising); ˋ (high falling); ˎ (low falling); ˆ (rise-fall); ˇ (fall-rise).

MODIFIERS.— ˜ nasality. ͜ breath (l̥ = breathed l). ˬ voice (s̬ = z). ˈ slight aspiration following p, t, etc. ̪ labialization (n̪ = labialized n). ̪ dental articulation (t̪ = dental t). ̫ palatalization (z̫ = ʑ). ˰ specially close vowel (ḛ = a very close e). ˷ specially open vowel (e̜ = a rather open e). ˔ tongue raised (e̝ or e̞ = ẹ). ˕ tongue lowered (e̞ or e̞ = ẹ). ˖ tongue advanced (u̟ or u̟ = an advanced u, t̟ = t̪). ˗ or ‑ tongue retracted (i̠ or ɩ = ɨ, t̠ = alveolar t). ˙ lips more rounded. ˛ lips more spread. Central vowels: ï (= ɨ), ü (= ʉ), ë (= ə̈), ö (= ɵ), ë̤, ö̤. ˌ (e.g. n̩) syllabic consonant. ˆ consonantal vowel. ˌ variety of ʃ resembling s, etc.

Language development compared with motor development

Age	Motor development	Language development
0;3	Head self-supported	Babbling begins (and continues to at least 1;0)
0;6	Sits with assistance. Bouncing	
0;9	Crawling. Sitting without support. Pulls to stand but falls with bump	Babbling and intonation sound more like human language
1;0	Walks when hands are held	First words
1;3	Walks unevenly Crawls upstairs	Lexical overgeneralisation (continues to around 2;6)
1;6	Walks well Crawls downstairs (backwards)	
1;9		Two-word sentences
2;0	Runs well. Walks up and down stairs with only one foot forward at a time	Three-word sentences
2;6	Sits on pedal cycle but pushes with feet on ground	Vowel system complete for many children. Sentences of four words and more
3;0	Rides pedal cycle. Walks upstairs with alternating feet	Nominalisations
3;6		Consonantal system complete for many children
4;0	Walks downstairs with alternating feet	Syntax now generally correct although limited
5;0	Runs up and down stairs	Some children still have consonantal difficulties with (a) fricatives, (b) consonantal-clusters, (c), /r/

The chronological ages associated with the various milestones should be taken as only very general approximations. There is very considerable individual variation from the ages given. For more details of motor development, see Sheridan (1973).

Introduction

A number of points concerning the plan and orientation of the book need to be made clear. The main part of the book is organised in a fairly traditional linguistic fashion, i.e. there is a division into phonology, grammar, and lexis. While for most purposes the division is very convenient, certain topics inevitably do not fit conveniently into this plan (as of course would happen with any plan). In particular, this applies to parental speech, which concerns phonology, grammar, and lexis; and yet it seemed important to deal with all aspects of this topic together. In many ways it merited a separate chapter and yet it would have been considerably shorter than the other chapters. An uneasy compromise has given it a section of its own under grammar. To a lesser extent the same problem applied to discourse, conversation, and register, which have also been given a section under grammar. Both these topics (parental speech and discourse) are in the forefront of research in child language at the moment (e.g. Snow and Ferguson, 1977; Waterson and Snow, in press) and it should not be assumed that any attempt is being made to minimise their importance in not giving them separate chapters.

The book is divided into two by chapter 5 (which outlines some theories). The last two chapters deal with early school-age learning but in much less detail than the earlier chapters deal with pre-school-age learning. In particular they are not concerned with the methodology of language teaching or speech therapy. The approach to reading and writing in chapter 7 is necessarily different from the approach in the earlier chapters. Reading and writing are usually explicitly taught in a way that speech is not; it is therefore even more difficult to talk of any normal pattern of development—so much will depend on the teaching method adopted. The approach taken has therefore been firstly to relate the writing system to the spoken system; then to discuss the skills involved in learning to read and write; and finally to discuss some of the approaches to teaching reading.

It must be stressed again that all the chapters in the book are more or less self-sufficient. Therefore, if any reader finds chapters 1 and 2 phonetically too technical, he can start with chapter 3. On the other hand, speech therapists will have more use for chapter 2 than any other chapter in the book.

Because of the effort to adopt a neutral position, the book is very much less in the mould of transformational grammar than most of the other textbooks on the subject. The grammatical framework is largely that of Quirk *et al.* (1972) and the phonological framework that of Trubetzkoy

(1939). The generative phonology of Chomsky and Halle (1968) is largely irrelevant to early child language. No one has ever seriously suggested that deep phonology is acquired before surface phonology, although similar claims have been made for deep structure. The exact relevance of transformational-generative grammar in any of its variants is in considerable doubt (besides imposing a considerable burden of formalism on the beginner). In addition, the translation of the more traditional phonemic and grammatical approaches into generative descriptions is considerably easier than the converse.

Throughout the book there is great emphasis on usual orders of development and there is also some mention of ages of acquisition. None of this should be taken as implying either that there is an absolutely fixed order of development or an absolute age for the acquisition of a particular linguistic structure. Reference is intended only to common orders of development and common ages of acquisition. Indeed, there is currently great interest in how children differ in these matters. Nelson (1973) showed some children developing faster referentially (as shown in a vocabulary largely consisting of words for things) and others developing faster expressively (as shown in a vocabulary containing more words for social formulae and names of people). Bloom (1976) showed some children trying out new words in grammatical structures they already had; other children trying out new structures using old words. Both studies showed children advancing on one front while holding another constant. Ramer (1976) showed some children expanding their syntactic ability at a fast rate (regardless of when syntax actually started) while others developed at a slow rate.

Numerous examples have been given throughout the book. Where the examples are from published literature, the sources have been quoted. Otherwise they are from data collected from various children by the author himself or in some cases from data supplied by colleagues. Examples are generally from English, although occasional reference has been made to other languages where information was available and known to the author.

1 Foundations

This chapter describes the cries and sounds made by babies during their first months of life and the way these sounds change during the babbling period (approximately 0;4 to 0;10). It also surveys some studies of auditory perception in infants. It then considers the first meaningful expressions which children use and the development of forms and meanings during the one-word stage (approximately 0;10 to 1;7). Technical terms (e.g. those involving the organs of speech and types of articulation) are explained in the glossary.

1.1 *The neonate*

The newborn baby rapidly proclaims the importance of sound in his life by his birth cry. Usually a baby takes one or two gasping inspirations and then gives a cry which is tense, voiceless, and lasts about one second. The cry may occur before the whole body has been delivered and certainly before the umbilical cord has been cut. (Wasz-Höckert *et al.*, 1968.)

During the next few years a good deal of crying will take place. While in the later years the types and occasions of crying are fairly predictable, it has always been a matter of dispute how far children in the first months of life (particularly the first three months) have different cries under different conditions and how far such differences are recognised and responded to by babies' mothers. On balance, it seems that gross differences in types of cry are present and that at least some mothers may be sensitive to such differences. Wolff (1969) was able to identify three types of cry during the first two weeks of life. The basic type of crying is apparently a rhythmical type in which a period of silence (during which inspiration occurs) of just over half a second continuously alternates with a period of voiced expiration of about half a second. This appears to signal that a child is uncomfortable and more particularly that he is hungry; hence it is often called the hunger cry. A second type is the pain cry, which is characterised by one relatively long burst of voiced expiration of about four seconds. The third type of cry identified by Wolff is the 'mad' cry (i.e. one of exasperation, or rage, when, for example, something is taken away from him); this is identified by a temporal pattern similar to the basic or hunger cry but with considerable additional fricative noise. All three of these cries have a pitch pattern which at first rises and then falls towards the end. From the third week onwards Wolff was able to identify a 'fake cry' (at least this is what mothers identify it as); the implication is that the child has no distress but simply wants attention. The main characteristic of this cry appears to be a moan on a low level pitch interspersed occasionally with jumps to a higher pitch. It should be noted that in the early weeks children cry when in some way discontented but are not generally making any noise at all when contented (indeed, they are usually asleep during this time!).

Certain sounds which are more obviously 'segmental' occur during this period, as a by-product of crying or of bodily functions. Thus glottal stops, glottal affricates and glottal fricatives (i.e. sounds made in the larynx) occur as part of the tension associated with some of the types of crying; they also occur as part of the straining involved in defecation. Similarly labial sounds may arise simply from opening and closing the mouth during crying. A clear connection also exists between the sucking habit and the occurrence of click sounds. Milk is sucked into the mouth using a velaric ingressive airstream (i.e. a closure is made between the back of the tongue and the soft palate; and the mouth cavity is enlarged, thereby sucking milk into the mouth) before it is swallowed. The sounds which occur when air is sucked in rather than milk are generally called clicks (a labial click is similar to the mechanism of a kiss!). Some of the glottal and labial sounds have their counterparts in the phonology of English and other languages; the click sounds occur in the phonology of only a very few languages (in English they are of course used only extra-linguistically, e.g. to make horses 'geeup' and as the 'tut-tut' of disapproval).

1.2   *The babbling period*

Somewhere about the third month of life two things appear to happen about the same time, either of which might be used to define the beginning of the babbling stage. Firstly a rapid advance in the control of the articulatory apparatus occurs, (Cruttenden, 1970) of which the main sign is often the first occurrence (and in quite large numbers) of pulmonic-lingual consonants, i.e. sounds in which the airstream from the lungs is interrupted by an articulation between the tongue and the roof of the mouth. Thus plosives and nasals (and sometimes a lateral) at the dental, alveolar, palatal and velar places of articulation (i.e. sounds made with both the tip and the body of the tongue) may occur as well as a great variety of vowel-like sounds. The second important event around the third month is the discovery that sounds are fun; the genesis of sounds being used simply for pleasure may lie in a period of restlessness which often occurs just before babies begin to cry as feeding time approaches (Wolff, 1969) but this activity is rapidly transferred to other times when they are more content, e.g. immediately after food. It has been suggested (Lewis, 1936) that the pre-prandial period produces mainly apical and labial consonants (thus called discomfort sounds), because of the anticipation of food; whereas velar sounds originate in the post-prandial period (thus called comfort sounds) when children are swallowing and belching.

These two events (pulmonic-lingual articulations and pleasure in sounds) characterise the beginning of the babbling period. Other labels are often used which may refer to subparts of this period: 'cooing' presumably refers to a period when back vowels with lip rounding are frequent, 'lalling' presumably to a predominance of *l* sounds. Babbling, or playing with sounds without meaning, continues until the occurrence of the first words, and may then continue even further alongside the first words for some months. During the period before the first words (which will usually appear sometime between 0;9 and 1;3) a change of emphasis in the child's repertoire of sounds occurs, which is often called 'babbling drift' (Brown, 1958b). At the beginning of the babbling period, when pulmonic-lingual sounds first occur, they are nevertheless still heavily outnumbered by glottal and labial sounds: and the manner of articulation is more commonly continuant than plosive, e.g. [ʋ] more commonly than [b]. During the period before the appearance of the first words, plosives and nasals establish their predominance. Thus [bdgmn] become the predominating consonants. These same consonants are usually utilised in the first phonemic distinctions (see 2.1.1 below) in any language (not just

English). The child's repertoire of consonants has drifted so that it is available for the take-off into language. Throughout the babbling period it is likely that low vowels and simple open syllables (i.e. of the consonant-vowel type and without any consonant clusters) predominate. It has been suggested (Weir, 1966) that babies' babbling (and perhaps crying too) varies according to the language which their parents speak, i.e. that babbling drift is specifically in the direction of the mother-tongue. It seems likely that such language-specific variation as occurs concerns primarily prosodic characteristics, e.g. pitch, loudness, tempo, and voice-quality (see 1.3 below), although it is by no means proven that such variation does occur at all (Atkinson *et al.*, 1969).

One common view of sounds in the babbling period is exemplified by a statement from Grégoire (1937): 'The child at the height of his babbling is capable of producing all conceivable sounds.' Whether or not children have this capability, in the author's experience no children ever do so. Sounds are far more likely to be limited primarily to those mentioned above, with the addition from time to time of the odd 'exotic' sound which has a short period when it is highly favoured by a particular child and then disappears. Such a sound might, for example, be a uvular trill [R] (exotic to English ears if not to French) or a type of lateral sound made with the tip of the tongue actually out of the mouth. But such sounds never take up a central position in the sound repertoire.

1.2.1   *The functions of babbling*

Two functions of babbling have been suggested. The first and less controvertible starts from the idea of babbling being sounds for pleasure. The pleasure for the baby at first consists simply in making movements combining his breathing, laryngeal and articulatory apparatus. But the pleasure is rapidly enhanced as he discovers what sounds he can make by this means. He then gradually builds up a large number of links between tactual and kinæsthetic impressions in his vocal tract on the one hand and auditory sensations in his ears on the other (Fry, 1966). The child learns how to produce certain sounds. Such a view of babbling is supported by evidence from deaf children. In such children babbling begins about the normal age and continues for a while but then gradually fades. This is presumably because the deaf child is not hearing the auditory effects of his own articulations (or, for that matter, of others).

The other suggested function of babbling is more controversial. While at first babbling is just pleasure, proponents of this second hypothesis claim that the course of babbling is controlled by 'operant conditioning' (Skinner, 1938; Olmsted, 1966; and 5.1 below).

The suggested sequence of events is as follows (Mowrer, 1950):

(i) The sound and sounds of a mother's voice are early associated with the receipt of food.

(ii) The sounds the child first makes remind him of his mother's voice (which is associated with the 'reward' of food). He therefore seeks to make his sounds more like his mother's.

(iii) In so far as his sounds do approximate to adult sounds he is given parental approval and encouragement, and this in turn leads to further improvement.

(iv) Eventually he produces adult words, which are then associated with objects by further parental approval and training (Bullowa *et al.,* 1964).

Opponents of this application of operant conditioning theory claim that babbling has no connection with early words. They suggest that children continue to try out all possible sounds in babbling (which, as we have said above, does not seem to be the case), regardless of the language to which they are exposed, and in addition they suggest that a period of silence intervenes between the cessation of babbling and the appearance of the first words (again this does not seem to apply to a large number of children). Proponents of this theory concerning the function of babbling point to babbling drift as evidence confirming this viewpoint. But babbling drift itself has been confirmed only in its weaker form, i.e. that babbling drifts towards those sounds which are most universal in languages: and has not been confirmed in its stronger form, i.e. that babbling drifts towards the mother-tongue to which the child is exposed. Operant conditioning may account for the fact that the sound sequences of babbling gradually become more like human language. They may even account for the meanings attached to the first few words (e.g. [mama] and [dada]). But it is doubtful whether the acquisition of complex systems of word-meanings can be adequately accounted for by such a theory.

1.3   *Prosodics — variation in pitch and other factors*

It will be recalled that most early crying has a rising-falling pitch contour. Lieberman (1967) produced acoustic evidence that children's babbled utterances also have this type of contour for a long period before other patterns occur. He suggested that if we compare such a pattern in crying and babbling with a similar unmarked intonation pattern for statements in adult English (and probably in all other languages), it can be concluded that crying is the genesis of intonation. There are severe objections to such a simplistic view. Evidence was not produced by Lieberman from children's early meaningful utterances, as opposed to babbling; secondly, there are many dialects of English (for example, Belfast) which regularly have an intonation pattern with a final rise as the unmarked pattern for statements; and lastly, even if other objections are overlooked, the similarity adduced as evidence seems to be of too gross a kind (an overall rising–falling contour) to warrant such a specific and weighty conclusion (that intonation springs from crying). Certain factors in the use of pitch and loudness may be biologically conditioned. It may be, for example, that excitement will result in a higher level of pitch, extra loudness, and an increased tempo. But there is no evidence as yet to suggest that any particular pitch contour used in language or languages is innate or universal.

Many babies are excellent mimics of pitch patterns. Nakazima (1962) found that such mimicry began around eight months. One of the author's children mimicked in her babbling a pitch pattern consisting of a high-level pitch followed by a mid-level pitch. Her mother usually used this as the intonation for *all gone*; the child produced the pattern on all sorts of nonsense syllables. E. Pike (1949) noted the same sort of mimicry in her children, although in this case such a mimicked (in one case rising) pitch pattern was used for their first words. Pike and her husband controlled the intonation which they used to one of their children and found the child's patterns closely following the models she was given. Weir (1966) maintained that pitch pattern was one of the main factors which differentiated Chinese children from American children between the ages of five and seven months. Even at the age of two to three years Kirk (1973) found that children learning the Ga language of West Africa were better at imitating the tones of the language than the segments. Mandarin-speaking children master

Chinese tones well before segmentals (Li and Thompson, 1977).

Such a facility for imitating pitch does not indicate that pitch patterns are being used meaningfully. Statements abound in the psychological and linguistic literature on child language suggesting that children have control of the intonational system of their language before they produce their first words. In the main such statements stem from a confusion between mimicry and meaningful usage; and from the possible biological basis of factors like the use of high pitch and extra loudness when excited. What little evidence there is (Lewis, 1936; Raffler-Engel, 1964; Tonkova-Yampol'skaya, 1968) suggests that some (and possibly a minority) of children use contrasting intonation contours during this period (before the first meaningful expressions) in a very limited way and one which does not necessarily correspond with adult usage. At this time children obviously show considerable command of the forms of intonation but nothing like an adult command of its functions.

Somewhat later the first meaningful expressions used by children may have characteristic fixed pitch patterns associated with each of them (see Halliday, 1975) and during the one-word stage some children may begin to use the difference between fall and rise to signal different sentence functions (1.5 and 1.6 below).

1.4 *Early perception*

Recently new techniques have enabled advances to be made in the study of infants' responses to various kinds of auditory stimuli. These techniques include measuring changes in heartbeat and in electrical activity in the brain in addition to sophisticated conditioning methods, such as training babies to suck more strongly on dummies (pacifiers) when they hear a variation in sound.

Neonates respond to certain gross differences in frequency, loudness, and length of sound (Morse, 1974). Moreover frequencies within the normal speech range appear to produce quieter, more attentive behaviour, whereas those outside the normal speech range appear to produce startled behaviour. This seems to confirm the findings of Lewis (1936) that infants' smiles are confined to hearing a human voice (and not other noises) during the second month of life and that certain gross differences of voice-quality are appreciated in the following two or three months, differences like those between male and female, friendly and unfriendly, and familiar and unfamiliar. Kaplan (1969) found that babies four months old gave no sign that they were aware of the difference between a sentence said with a typical statement intonation compared with a typical question intonation, whereas at eight months they did. It must not be assumed, of course, that they attached adult meanings to these patterns. Around this age children may come to associate a certain pitch pattern with a very specific meaning in one situation (cf. item-learning of grammatical patterns in 3.1.3 below). For example, a high rise might be associated with a door about to open and someone about to come into the room where the child is (because a parent has frequently said *listen!* with this pitch pattern).

Turning from perception of prosodic characteristics to perception of segmental differences, such little evidence as there is suggests that at a very early age children can, under experimental conditions, perceive some differences between sounds which will later be used in the phonology of their language. Under such conditions infants between one and four months old can perceive voicing differences between plosives (e.g. between [p] and [b]); they can distinguish differences dependent on place of articulation (e.g. between [p], [t], and [k]) and the difference in manner of articulation between English /r/ and /l/ (Eimas *et al.,* 1971 Eimas, 1974; Eimas, 1975). Such perceptual ability as children have at this early age must not be confused with the later incorporation of sound distinctions into the phonological system. The ability to perceive a difference between two sounds when the difference is highlighted under experimental conditions is not the same as the ability to recognise that two sounds are being used systematically to make differences of *meaning.* Such experiments do, however, show that there may be a very early sensitivity to sounds which are used in language.

Many of the experiments with infants' perception have been directed to proving that early perception is *categorical.* For a proper understanding of the notion of categorical perception, a knowledge of acoustic phonetics is necessary. However, we will attempt to explain with the help of one example. The difference between [p], [t], and [k] can be shown to be related to an acoustic continuum. When adults are given a stimulus from anywhere on this continuum they always identify the sound as [p], [t], or [k]. However, when asked to say whether two stimuli are the same or different, they can recognise two stimuli as different only when they come from two different categories, even though the acoustic distance between the stimuli is the same in all cases. Thus if two stimuli of a certain acoustic distance are presented and they lie on different sides of the boundary between [p] and [t] they will be perceived as different; but if two stimuli of the same acoustic distance are presented which lie wholly within the [p] category they are not perceived as different. In other words adults do not perceive in absolute acoustic terms but according to categories which are linguistically relevant in language. Such categorical perception has been shown to apply to adult perception of many consonantal distinctions.

The experiments with infant perception have attempted to show that even at this early age perception is already categorical and so to claim that children are born with a perceptual pretuning to the sorts of differences which are linguistically relevant. So it has been shown, for example, that infants respond to the difference between an unaspirated plosive and an aspirated plosive (aspiration is the main cue distinguishing plosives in syllable-initial position in English, e.g. *bat* v. *pat*) but do not respond to the difference between an aspirated and a heavily aspirated plosive (a difference never used in languages).

There are many difficulties associated with the whole notion of categorical perception (e.g. it may sometimes apply to sound differences outside language, such as those between different musical instruments). It nevertheless does seem true that there is something about speech sounds which makes them rather special for children. Indeed, most infants, like adults, appear to process speech sounds with one side of the brain (generally the left) and non-speech sounds with the other (Morse 1974).

1.5 *First meanings*

Sometime towards the end of the first year of life children begin to produce expressions which have meaning. Babies' utterances during this year have become more like adult utterances both in their sounds and in their pitch patterns, and gradually certain sound sequences become tied to certain situations. As an illustration, here is the set of expression of an English child aged 1;1. We call them expressions rather than words because many do not have any relationship to words in the adult language. (The sign indicates an accented syllable having falling pitch.)

Expression	Gloss	Example of use
['dadɛ/ 'dada]	downstairs	I'm ready to go downstairs
	upstairs	We're going upstairs
[da 'da]	bath	That's a bath
	water	Let me splash my hand in the water
[ba 'ba]	cat, dog, small animal	That's a . . . .
[na 'na]	piano, music	I want to bang the piano [pointing to radio]
	singing	[singing to himself]
[ma 'mam]	'yum-yum'	I'm enjoying my food
[ḍai 'ḍzai]	light	That's a light [pointing to light]
[dɛ 'de]	stick	That's a stick
[gɒ 'gɒ]	watch, clock, kitchen scales	That's a . . . .
		Where is your watch? [pointing to wrist where watch is missing]
	girl	Read me the story about the girl (in picture book)
	walk	I want a walk
	sleep	I'm tired; I want to go to bed
		I'm going to sleep
		That's a bed [also any white cloth looking like a sheet]
		[Also used for playing at sleeping while cuddling a piece of cloth]
['gɑ :]	car	Show me the car in the picture book
		Take me to the car
		That's a car
['dɔ :]	door	I want to go out the door
		Open the door for me
['fiɔ :]	wind	That's the noise of the wind
	lawnmower, hoover, bicycle	Start up the machine for me
['kh̥ :/ 'kɣ :]	key	[pointing to key in keyhole]
	switch, taps on the cooker	[pointing to switch on wall but wanting the light on]

Expression	*Gloss*	*Example of use*
['ʃzː]	shoes	I want to go for a walk so put my shoes on
['dʒsː]	juice	I want some (orange) juice
['d̺ðː]	drink	I want a drink
	ring	That's a ring (toy ring)
['tðː]	flower	That's a flower
['dɒ]	(general deictic)	Look at that
['dɛ]	finished	I've finished my food
[drl 'də]	(general demand)	e.g. Make that noise which
(emphatic:	make it happen!	comes by blowing across
[drːl 'də])	do it!	the top of the bottle

The sounds used in the expressions at this stage include sounds like [s] and [ʃ] which usually occur late in phonological development. It is likely that, when this child's vocabulary explodes into a larger number of words more directly related to adult words, sounds like this will disappear for a while, later to reappear in a more normal sequence of development. The expressions are of three phonetic types:

(i) Reduplications or partial reduplications like [da 'da] and [na 'na].
(ii) Single consonant-vowel syllables like ['gɑː] and ['dɔː].
(iii) Sequences without a vowel, like ['ʃzː] and ['dʒsː].

It is to be noted that this child already has an accentual contrast between ['dada] and [da 'da]; this sort of accentual contrast is used early in syntax (see 2.10 and 3.2 below). All reduplications except ['dada] have the accent on the second syllable, which is unusual (see 2.4 below). In all the words the accent is manifested by a high falling (or alternatively rising–falling) intonation. This child does not have characteristically different pitch paterns associated with each word as Halliday's (1975) child did. For example, three expressions used by Halliday's child between 1;0 and 1;1½ were:

[nã]	(with a fall from mid level pitch to low pitch)	'Give me that'
[yi]	(with high level pitch)	'Yes, I want that'

[aː]   (with a pitch pattern starting
at a mid level, rising to a high
pitch, and returning to mid   'Yes, I want what you
again)   just offered'

So some children may make characteristic use of pitch at this time (though nothing like systematic adult usage). The amount of variation in pitch at this stage may depend on the number of attitudinal pitch patterns which adults use to their children.

Some expressions are obviously related to adult words like ['gɑː] 'car' and ['ʃzː] 'shoes' (for the overextension of their meaning see 4.4 below), others are related to adult onomatopoeic expressions like [ma 'mam] to 'yum-yum', and the origin of others is obscure, e.g. [drl 'də]. Particularly interesting is [gɒ 'gɒ] in the meaning of 'sleep' ; Halliday's (1975) child had a similar expression, [gwγi], and another child known to the author had [gɔik]. Evidently the use of an expression involving velar consonants is common when going to sleep; cf. Lewis's (1936) characterisation of velar sounds as comfort sounds made when the child is lying on his back, contented (see 1.2 above). Those expressions which are not directly related to adult words will in time disappear, unless of course they are taken over by the parents as special family words.

The expressions are obviously used with three main functions (see Halliday, 1975, and 5.5 below for a more detailed discussion of the functions of language at this age). Firstly, indicating e.g. ['tð ː], 'that's a flower'; secondly, demanding, e.g. ['dð ː], 'I want a drink'; and thirdly, expressive, e.g. [ma 'mam], 'I'm enjoying my food'. Some expressions may be used in either of the first two functions: thus ['gɑ ː] may mean 'That's a car' or 'Take me to the car'. A fourth function, that of imaginary play-acting, can be seen when [gɒgɒ] 'sleep' is used when the child is playing at sleeping while cuddling a piece of cloth.

Finally it should be mentioned that the child whose expressions have been used by way of illustration in this section was estimated to have comprehension at this time extending to around two hundred words. He also responded appropriately to simple questions in *where* like *Where's daddy's nose?* and *Where's mummy's eyes?* and commands like *Give me the ring.* Even allowing that situational clues may lead to the overestimation of comprehension, children's understanding of language at this period is already in advance of their production.

1.6 *The one-word stage*

As stated in 1.5, somewhere around the last quarter of his first year the child uses his first meaningful expressions. We may for convenience wish to call them words, although at the beginning of the one-word stage neither their phonetic form nor their meaning is quite like that of adult words. Phonetically, they appear at first to be whole units rather like animal cries; almost any sound from the adult phonemic inventory and many not in it may occur, and often in combinations looking distinctly unlike patterns of sound found in most human languages. [tð] 'that's a flower' (see 1.5 above) is more like a typical extra-linguistic noise (e.g. [f:] when hot and bothered). Semantically, the words often express a composite meaning (they are sometimes called 'holophrases'). Some indications of this meaning may come not only from the one word but also from gesture, facial expression, and action. Some writers wish to apply the term grammar to this stage; however, it seems best to reserve this term for the conveying of meaning by some formal syntactic or morphological means, e.g. order and inflection (see Dore, 1975, for a full discussion of this issue).

The child discussed in 1.5 was at the beginning of the one-word stage. At this time words are, as just stated, phonetically like animal cries. The child's vocabulary is small, and as one word is gained, another may be lost. The meanings intended (in addition to the basic lexical meanings of the words) are mainly of the interpersonal kind, e.g. indicating, or demanding, or expressive. Each interpersonal function may have an unmarked variant (Halliday, 1975), e.g. [dɒ] as a general indicator or deictic. Usually the interpersonal functions are not formally differentiated (e.g. there is no systematic marking of all questions). At the beginning of the one-word stage there is little evidence to suggest that meanings of the ideational sort (e.g. agent, possessor . . . etc. . . ., see below) are intended. It is also doubtful whether many children are using intonation contrastively in their early expressions (e.g. they do not use the difference between rise and fall to signal the difference between indicating and demanding), although as we have seen in 1.5 some children may have a fixed pitch patern for each expression.

By the end of the one-word stage a number of important changes have taken place. The child has a much larger vocabulary and may be able to sustain a simple conversation (see 3.9 below).

The phonetic make-up of words has now stabilised to something which forms the basis for phonemic development. Thus a child's words are commonly at this time composed of the consonants [bdgmn] and vowels [a] and possibly [iu]; during the one-word stage he has learnt that words are made up of a limited number of phonological units combined in different ways. He has, in other words, learnt the phonemic principle. Also by this time interpersonal functions way be marked by special vocabulary items (e.g. *what* and *where*) or by intonation (e.g. questions by a rising pitch pattern). Menyuk and Bernholtz (1969) found one child marking three functions: for example, the word *door* could have a falling pitch when a door was being 'named', a rising pitch when the child was asking a question, and a rising–falling pitch pattern for special emphasis. Moreover ideational meanings are now conveyed by a combination of action, gesture, facial expression, and other non-linguistic cues; such meanings will anticipate the two-word stage (see 3.2 below). Some of the most common which occur are (cf. Greenfield and Smith 1976):

(i) Recurrence	e.g. *more* (pointing to meat)
(ii) Negation	*no* (struggling to escape being held)
(iii) Location	*garden* (holding plant which belongs in the garden but is now indoors)
(iv) Possession	*John* (pointing to John's hat)
(v) Agent	*Mummy* (asking mummy to push a ball through a hole after the child had failed)
(vi) Action	*eat* (wanting to eat some berries that he had just picked)
(vii) Affected object	*drain* (pointing to the men in the road cleaning out a drain)

Moreover, even at this stage, there may be rules which predict which word a child will encode, when he has several different possibilities open to him. In (v) above, the child could have said *ball* or *push* instead of *mummy* (at least, he could if we assume that he knew these words). Greenfield and Smith (1976) suggest that the affected object is encoded if it is not in the child's grasp (as in (vii) above); whereas the action is encoded if the object is in the child's grasp (as in (vi) above); but after the object or action has been mentioned once, it is not used in the next utterance (this accounts for (v), because the child had previously said *push* when holding the ball himself and trying to push it through the hole).

2 Phonology

This chapter describes the development of a system of contrasts between sounds. Then it discusses the various types of relationship between the sounds used in children's words and the sounds used in the corresponding adult words. The development of the perception of sound contrasts is surveyed briefly. An attempt is then made to show some of the factors which govern the order of acquisition of sounds. Finally the development of intonation is described. Technical terms used in this chapter are explained more fully in the glossary. The reader is reminded that adult phonemic forms are enclosed in slant brackets / /, whereas all children's words transcribed phonetically are enclosed in square brackets [ ]. Reference should be made to pp. ix–xi for the meanings of individual symbols.

2.1 Development of the sound system

An important landmark is reached in a child's linguistic development when he begins for the first time to use sounds contrastively. Once he has two words in his vocabulary, say [mama] and [dada], the process of acquiring the phonological system has begun. Many early studies of the child's development failed to take account of the importance of this landmark. Irwin (1947a, 1947b, 1948), for example, in a number of studies showing s shift in the output of children's consonant and vowel sounds over the period from birth to 2;6 years, took no account of whether such sounds were used meaningfully in words or whether they occurred in playful babbling. This viewpoint on phonetic development sees such development simply as the acquisition of the motor ability to produce sounds.

The thorough studies of Trubetzkoy (1939) and his followers in the 1930s of the concept of the phoneme as a minimally contrasting unit of sound utilising various combinations of distinctive articulatory features (such as labial, apical and dorsal; and voiced and voiceless) led to a breakthrough in the study of the acquisition of phonology. This occurred with the publication in 1941 of Roman Jakobson's *Kindersprache, Aphasie, und allgemeine Lautgesetze* (not published in English until 1968).

Jakobson suggested that, regardless of what has gone on before in babbling, a child starts off speaking (meaningfully) with two consonantal units (or phonemes) and one vowel unit (as in in the suggested [mama] and [dada] above). He builds up his phonemic (as opposed to sound) repertoire by a process of binary splits. Moreover the development of the phonemic system by such splitting is basically the same in all languages and depends upon the distinctive features utilised by the phonemes. Other writers (though not Jakobson) have suggested that a period of relative silence intervenes between the cessation of babbling and the first words. Such an interval does not, however, seem crucial. Babbling and meaningful words could, and usually do, occur simultaneously; and it seems likely that the child utilises for his first phonemic distinctions precisely those sounds which have become most frequent in his babbling.

At this point it should be said that Jakobson in his book was not concerned with the age of acquisition of distinctions, but only with the order of acquisition. In fact it seems likely (Templin, 1957; Anthony *et al.,* 1971) that a child's vowel system is often complete at least by the age of 3;0, whereas consonantal distinctions are acquired more slowly and may not be complete in many cases before the age of 5;0 or 6;0.

2.1.1 *Consonantal system*

(i) Distinctions dependent on manner of articulation Early words generally have the structure of an open syllable consisting of a consonant plus an open vowel, e.g. [ma] 'more'. This syllable is often reduplicated, e.g. [mama]. The first consonantal phonemic contrast which develops is that between oral and nasal, e.g. between [mama] and [papa] or [baba]. Generally one frictionless continuant phoneme, often [l], develops at an early stage, e.g. [lala] 'light', v. [dada] 'daddy' (but some of the distinctions within the frictionless continuants occur very late). Phonemic distinctions between various places of articulation among plosives and nasals, e.g. [baba] v. [dada] and [mama] v. [nana], are likely to be made before the first fricative phoneme occurs to contrast with a plosive

or nasal, e.g. [si :] 'see' v. [ti :] 'tea' or [fu :] 'full' v. [mu :] 'cow'. The full system of fricative phonemes involves contrasts which are generally the last part of the phonemic system to develop. Phonemic distinctions based on the English affricates /tʃ/ and /dʒ/, e.g. [ti :] 'tea' v. [tʃi :] 'cheese', generally occur later than the earliest fricatives but not necessarily later than the fricatives at the corresponding place of articulation, e.g. a distinction between [ti :] 'tea' and [tʃi :] 'cheese' may occur earlier than a distinction between [ʃi :] 'sheep' and [ti :] 'tea' or between [ʃi :] 'sheep' and [si :] 'see' (this is contrary to what is predicted in Jakobson).

(ii) *Distinctions dependent on place of articulation* Looking more closely at the acquisition of contrasts dependent on place of articulation (with special reference to English), it is generally considered (following Jakobson) that distinctions between labial and apical consonants occur before contrasts involving velars, e.g. [ba] or [baba] 'baby' v. [da] or [dada] 'daddy' before [da] or [dada] v. [ga] or [gaga] 'garage', but a number of cases of velars before apicals have been reported (e.g. Weeks, 1975). Often, too, there are words which vary freely between [g] and [d] in a child's speech (see 2.1.3 below); sometimes, too, [ʔ] may be used as a ubiquitous replacement for all apical and velar (and even labial) plosives. Jakobson suggests that the first fricative phoneme to occur is generally [s], but a recent review of the evidence (Ferguson, 1973) shows that [f] occurs first at least as frequently. This first fricative phoneme occuring in contrast with the plosives may phonetically even be [h], [θ], [ʃ], or [ɬ] (this last occurs in the adult language only as a lisp). But the first contrast involving place of articulation among fricatives will usually be a labial [f] as against some form of apical, e.g. [sɔ :] 'saw' v. [fɔ :] 'fall'. The various distinctions of place among the apicals, e.g. [θɔ :t] 'thought' v. [sɔ :t] 'sort' v. [ʃɔ :t] 'short', are among the last consonantal distinctions to be acquired. The development of distinctions among the various frictionless continuants /lrwj/ varies considerably. A common pattern of development is for an [l] and/or a [w] to occur first, [w] subsequently splitting into [w] and [ɹ]; and [l] into [l] and [j], e.g. [wʌn] 'one' v. [ɹʌn] 'run' and [let] 'let' v. [jet] 'yet'. However, adult /l/ may develop differently in different syllable-positions (particularly in those accents like R.P. which have different allophones in different positions); and adult /r/ and /w/ may both occur as [ʋ] at one stage.

(iii) *Distinctions dependent on voicing*   By the use of symbols such as *p t k* Jakobson implies the priority of the fortis (voiceless) series of plosives over the lenis (voiced). Most of the evidence (e.g. Leopold, 1947; Olmsted, 1971; Cruttenden, 1970) suggests that [bdg] occur first and that the distinction between pairs of plosives is at first manifested by the occurrence of heavily aspirated forms of [ptk]. At least, this is the position in English. It must be remembered that the distinction between two series of plosives, e.g. /ptk/ and /bdg/, may be manifested by different features in different languages. The common factor in language development is that the first plosives to occur (at least in word-initial position) are voiceless, fortis, and unaspirated. In a language like English where both /ptk/ and /bdg/ have little voice in word-initial position and where the main distinction between the series in this position is aspiration, the early voiceless, fortis, unaspirated plosives seem most like adult /bdg/. However, in languages like French and Lebanese Arabic (Preston, 1971), where the main distinction between the two adult series is one of voice, the first plosives are obviously more akin to the adult language /ptk/.

In syllable-final position the distinctions between /ptk/ and /bdg/ are primarily dependent in the adult language on differences in the length of preceding vowels and continuant consonants, which are shorter before all fortis consonants including /ptk/, e.g. the vowel is shorter in *beat* than in *bead* and the nasal continuant is shorter in *lent* than in *lend*. This may be reflected in the different treatment of the members of such pairs in some children's language. Smith (1973) reports that his child omitted a lenis plosive following a nasal but omitted the nasal before a fortis plosive, thus *mend* → [mɛn] but *meant* → [mɛt]. In cases like *beat* and *bead*, where a vowel precedes the plosive, it is likely that the priority of voiceless fortis unaspirated plosives in children's language unambiguously indicates /ptk/ in all languages (including English) before the distinction of vowel length is used to clearly mark the difference between /ptk/ and /bdg/.

Thus in English a child's first plosives are generally perceived by adults as /bdg/ in initial position but /ptk/ in final position. Ferguson (1973) found that voicing in fricatives generally develops in a way analogous to the development of plosives, i.e. initial fricatives generally appear voiced but final fricatives voiceless.

It is not at the moment clear whether the development of voicing contrasts is related in any firm way to manner and place contrasts.

2.1.2   *Vowel system*

Tracing the course of development of vowel contrasts is more difficult. Vowels are by their nature not as 'discrete' as consonants and it is often difficult to determine whether a contrast is present or not; in addition the attainment of the vowel system is often complete by the age of 3;0 if not earlier and is therefore learnt at a very rapid rate. Jakobson suggests that the first vowel contrast to occur in language is that between open [a] and close (front) [i]. This is followed by a third degree of opening: [papa] v. [pepe] v. [pipi]; or by a back [pupu] thus:

$$
\left.\begin{array}{l} i \\ e \\ a \end{array}\right\} \text{ or } \begin{array}{cc} i & u \\ & \\ & a \end{array}
$$

There is little other detail in Jakobson which is relevant for English; but for French and German and other languages with front rounded vowels, he suggests that these occur only after the acquisition of the corresponding unrounded vowels, i.e. phonemes /y ø œ/ will follow /i e ɛ/. Smith (1973) suggests that the last English vowel distinctions learnt by his son were /e/v./æ/ v./ɛə/, e.g. *dead* v. *dad* v. *dared*; /ɔ :/ v./ɔi/, e.g. *ball* v. *boil*; /u :/ v./əu/, e.g. *boot* v. *boat*.

2.1.3   *Variability*

The major difficulty in interpreting Jakobson's general theory of phonemic development is that it is not clear how much free variation is allowed within each phoneme. For example, when the contrast between [b] and [d] first emerges, are we to infer from Jakobson that [g] never occurs? If so, Jakobson is wrong, because [g] and [d] are often in free variation. Or does he choose to label the distinction labial v. dental (= alveolar for English) and use the symbol *t* because the alveolar stop is the most commonly occurring variant? This seems a more likely position, although even this is not confirmed for all children. Jakobson himself suggests that often [ʔ] does duty as an indeterminate stop phoneme; Anthony *et al* (1971) suggest that [ʔ] also functions at one stage as an indeterminate fricative phoneme and that later [h] has the same function (see 2.1.1 above).

Even if we allow that Jakobson is choosing to represent the

phoneme by a symbol for the most frequently occurring variant, there are still difficulties: the first fricative phoneme may often be [s] or [f]; but is sometimes [h], [ʃ], [θ] or [ɬ]. It appears that the general notion of binary splitting and his suggested order within manner of articulation (e.g. plosives before fricatives) may be true but that within place of articulation more account must certainly be taken of free variation and individual variation.

What is more, free variation may play a crucial role in phonemic development. A common developmental pattern is exemplified in the acquisition of the adult contrast between /s/ and /ʃ/:

Stage 1   Both are pronounced [s̄], e.g. *sell, shell* → [sel]
Stage 2   [s] and [ʃ] are in free variation for both phonemes, e.g.
          sell, shell → [sel] or [ʃel] indiscriminately
Stage 3   [s] for *sell*
          [s] or [ʃ] for *shell*
Stage 4   [s] for *sell*
          [ʃ] for *shell*

The important development is between stages 2 and 3, which indicates at least the partial development of the contrast between the two phonemes (cf. Compton, 1970).

There is yet another dimension of variation: different words, all of which have /ʃ/ in the adult language, are likely to be at different stages of development in the child's language at any one time. Some adult words with /ʃ/ may be at stage 3 and some at stage 4. For example, in the words *shoe* and *sheep* a child may still be varying between [s] and [ʃ], whereas in the words *sharp* and *shop* his phoneme may have stabilised as [ʃ]. Phonemic development spreads only slowly through the words in the child's vocabulary (see in particular Ferguson and Farwell, 1975, who compare this type of development with 'lexical diffusion' in historical change; see also 2.9.1 below). It is often the case that a child's immediate imitations of adult words may be more stable than his spontaneous productions, e.g. while still varying between [s] and [ʃ] when he spontaneously produces the work *shop*, he may consistently repeat the word with a [ʃ] if asked to imitate an adult's pronunciation.

2.1.4   *Postional variation*

Consonants are generally learnt first in syllable-initial position, then inter-syllabic or word-medial position, and lastly in syllable-final position. One exception seems to be fricatives, which are used first in post-vocalic positions (Olmsted, 1971; Ferguson, 1973).

When /ptk/ develop, it is often the aspirated forms which occur first, because these phonemes are usually learnt first in word-initial position. Hutcheson (1968) gave details of the development of dark [ɫ] in postvocalic position in one dialect of English as follows: [ə] → [o] → [oɫ] → [ɫ]. This is allophonic variation (i.e. compared with clear [l] in prevocalic position) which is not phonetically motivated ('extrinsic allophones'). Allophones like [ç] and [x] in German, which are phonetically motivated ('intrinsic allophones'), probably occur earlier. Indeed, Anthony *et al.* (1971) show such phonetically motivated variation occuring where it does not occur in the adult language; palatalisation in the vicinity of a front vowel, e.g. *fish* → [fiʃ]; *finger* → [fiɲɟə]; *matches* → [matʃiẓ] (see further under 2.5 below).

2.2   *Phonemic substitution*

A phoneme of the adult system not yet present in a child's system will be replaced by a phoneme which shares features with the adult phoneme and which is already present in the child's speech. Thus the following substitutions may occur in the course of development: velar plosives replaced by alveolar plosives, e.g. *keen* → [tiːn]; fricatives replaced by plosives, e.g. *seed* → [tiːd]; palato-alveolar fricatives replaced by alveolar fricatives, e.g. *fish* → [fis].

While substitutions which occur in child speech can generally be shown to share features with the adult phoneme, it is nevertheless not always possible to predict which of a number of possible substitutions will actually occur. Thus different children may replace the adult phoneme /θ/ by either /f/ or /s/; and may replace adult English /ʃ/ by /tʃ/ or /s/, e.g. *sheep* → [tʃiːp] or [siːp]. Moreover there is often an imbalance in such substitutions, particularly among the fricatives. In the absence of labio-dental fricatives, /f/ may be replaced by [s] but /v/ by [b]; in the absence of dental fricatives, /θ/ may be replaced by [s] or [f] but /ð/ by [d], e.g. [fiŋk] 'think' but [dat] 'that'.

In many cases, of course, nothing replaces the adult phoneme. This is particularly true in word-final position (which, as we have seen, is the position where phonemic contrasts develop most slowly). Thus word-final consonants are, particularly in the very early stages, omitted altogether, e.g. [ba] 'brush', [kə:] 'comb'. In addition children may often avoid producing words which involve phonemes they have not yet mastered; it is as if they deliberately avoid 'difficult' words (see Ferguson and Farwell, 1975). For example, children who do not yet have velar plosives may attempt very few words containing velar plosives.

2.3 *Consonantal clusters*

Consonantal clusters add complications to the relationship between a child's system and the adult system. There are basically two ways in which children may simplify such clusters:

(i) One or more consonants may be omitted. In /s/ + consonant clusters, common in English and many other languages, the /s/ may be omitted, e.g. /spɔt/ → [pɔt]. In clusters of consonant + /lrwj/, also very common, it is generally the /l/ /r/ /w/ or /j/ which are omitted, e.g. /kliːn/ → [kiːn]; /twist/ → [tit]; /pliːz/ → [piːz]. In three member clusters of the type /s/ + consonant + /lrwj/ only the consonant may remain, thus /spriŋ/ → [piŋ].

(ii) A type of feature synthesis may operate, thus /sməuk/ → [m̥ouk] /sliːp/ → [ɬiːp]; /spin/ → [fin]. By feature synthesis it is implied that the child's form is taking account of at least one feature from each segment. Thus in [ɬiːp] the voiceless fricative features of [s] have been added to the laterality of [l] to give the voiceless lateral fricative [ɬ]; and in [mouk] the voiceless fricative features of the [s] have been added to the nasality of [m] to give [m̥]. As the examples show, this is particularly common with /s/ + consonant clusters; also such synthesis usually occurs later in development than omission, as mentioned under (i).

An example of the stage-by-stage development of clusters can be illustrated by the word *swim*: 1. [wim] → 2. [fim] → 3. [sfim] → 4. [swim]. In the first stage, notice that in this cluster of /s/ + /w/ it is the /s/ that is omitted, rather than the /w/. This is the more common pattern, though omission of /lrwj/ following /s/ may sometimes occur when a child has acquired an [s] as a single consonant before he has any clusters. Stage 2 may on the surface appear to be regression, but in displaying feature synthesis (voiceless friction from /s/; labiality from /w/) it shows an advance, since the child is taking some account of both segments. Stage 3 is an even more complicated hybrid: feature synthesis produces [f] but a voiceless alveolar fricative is added as well. Only by stage 4 is the cluster present.

Such processes are easier to observe in word-initial position because in other positions the interval between the appearance of single consonants and of clusters is generally much shorter.

2.4   *Stress and rhythm*

What little evidence there is suggests that children (at least in the first two years of language when their words are short and there are few suffixes) make few errors in stressing the correct syllables of words. However, the position of the stress in words may often affect the phonemic structure of the word. Thus syllables before the stress may be completely dropped, e.g. /bə'nɑːnə/ → ['nɑːnə]; Fr. Au'guste → [kus] (Roussey, 1899–1900). It is of course the case that such syllables are often the most reduced in adult English.

Unstressed syllables immediately following the stress are not generally completely dropped but may be very susceptible to assimilatory influence (see below, 2.5) from the stressed syllable, e.g. /'pensil/ → ['pupu]; /'leidi/ → ['lələ]. However, polysyllabic words may involve the dropping of unstressed syllables not immediately following the stress or at least a limitation to one unstressed syllable (which may take features from two or more of the unstressed syllables following the stress), e.g. /'krɔkədail/ → ['kaka]; /'kəːdigən/ → ['kaki]. Sometimes all unstressed syllables are replaced by one sequence. Smith's (1973) Adam at one stage used [ri] and somewhat later [in].

It seems likely that children use a syllable-timed rhythm (i.e. they use a rhythm which involves giving an equal amount of time to each syllable) in the early years of language learning, whether or not the adult language is of that sort. English is not; and is more nearly stress-timed (i.e. an equal amount of time is taken from one stressed syllable to the next, regardless of the number of syllables in between). The tendency to syllable-timing may be one influence lending to the relative preponderance (compared with the adult language,) of strong as opposed to weak forms of auxiliary verbs and pronouns.

2.5   *Assimilation — the influence of one sound on another*

Children's very early words are, as we have seen, often reduplications like [mama], [dada], [ɲẽːɲẽ] 'window' (Waterson, 1971).
This is assimilation in its extreme form, i.e. only identical consonants can follow one another and only identical vowels may follow
one another. Moreover, there may in addition be assimilation
between consonants and vowels: thus only front vowels may occur
with alveolar consonants, e.g. [titi], and only back vowels with
velars, e.g. [kuku] (cf. Fudge, 1969).

As a child's phonology develops there is a fairly rapid loosening
of the bonds of assimilation. The first bond to be untied is that
between consonant and vowel, although remnants may often
remain to a later stage, e.g. the palatalisation of consonants in the
vicinity of front vowels mentioned in 2.1.4 above, which may
remain until a time when the phonological system is in most ways
very advanced. Usually the ties between vowels in adjacent
syllables ('vowel harmony') are the next to be loosened, so that we
get forms like [babu] 'bucket' (Waterson 1971) (but cf. a different
order of development in Ross, 1937: [bɔdɔ], 'water'; [bɔgɔ],
'walk'; [bugu], 'book'). Longest to persist are, most commonly,
ties between consonants preceding and following a vowel ('consonant harmony'). This type of assimilation may last for a considerable time with many children (e.g. the first year of language
learning). In some cases it may even persist long enough for the
child to be a candidate for speech therapy.

Commonly persevering types of consonant harmony most usually involve place of articulation; and, among such changes in place
of articulation, deapicalisation is by far the most frequent (in
English, and maybe universally). The direction of assimilation, in
this type as well as in most other types, is generally regressive (as
indeed it is in historical change), e.g. *shopping* → [pɔpin]; *dog* →
[gɔgi]; *duck* → [gʌk]. Occasionally the direction of assimilation is
progressive; often because the process of deapicalisation appears
to take precedence over direction, thus *glasses* → [gɑːgi]; *good* →
[gug], or because unstressed syllables are more susceptible to
assimilation than stressed, e.g. *pocket* → [pɔpi]. Occasionally, too,
a change in manner of articulation may be involved, usually from
oral to nasal, e.g. *naughty* → [nɔːni]. In concluding this section it
must be said that these examples of assimilation exemplify rules
which apply to the whole of the phonology of a child at a particular

stage: thus alveolar plosives become velar before velar consonants in all the words which are of that form in the child's vocabulary.

2.6 *Metathesis — the interchanging of sounds*

In contrast to cluster simplification and assimilation, metathesis is a process which is not likely to be systematic; that is, metathesis will apply to individual words but there cannot be a general statement that all sequences of segments of a certain sort are metathesised. Nevertheless there are often tendencies, and one tendency which seems common in English learners (and, again, may be universal) is for an alveolar consonant to be delayed, thus *wasp* → [wɔps], *ask* → [ɑːks]. Metathesis in this last word is common also among foreign learners of English and occurs in some dialects. Other examples of metathesis are *car park* → [pɑ : kɑ :k], *hospital* → [hɔtəpəl].

Metathesis can involve an interchange between adjacent consonants in a cluster but it may also involve an interchange of consonants across a vowel, e.g. *remember* → [mərembə]. In such cases vowels in successive syllables generally remain correctly ordered so that we cannot say that the transposition of whole syllables is involved. Metathesis occurs most frequently in words of more than two syllables, where the burden on either memory or planning is obviously greater, e.g. *caterpillar* → [pætəkilə].

2.7 *Interaction of various factors*

All the factors we have discussed, with the exception of metathesis (which applies to individual words, rather than the whole system) interact in a complicated, yet regular, way to determine the relationship between a child's phonology and the adult system. Let us illustrate from one child whom we will call M.:

(A) (i) The child systematically changes the adult alveolar plosives and nasal to velar, e.g. *bean* → [bi ːŋ]; *dolly* → [gɔli].

   (ii) M. also systematically changes all adult fortis (voiceless) consonants in initial position to the corresponding lenis (voiced) consonants, e.g. *cake* → [geik].

(B) (i) M. simplifies clusters of /s/ + consonant to the consonant alone, e.g. *smoke* → [məuk].

   (ii) M. simplifies clusters of consonant + /lrwj/ to the consonant alone, e.g. *please* → [bi :z]. The /p/ has become [b] by (A) (ii).

(C) M. assimilates /kg/ to [pb] before /rw/, e.g. *green* → [bi :ŋ]. The final /n/ has changed to [ŋ] by (A) (i) above. The /r/ has been omitted by (B) (ii) above, but has nevertheless influenced the change of /g/ to [b]. This suggests that in this case M. is at least perceiving the /r/ (or at least the lip-rounding associated with /r/); this sort of evidence is often used to argue that children are perceiving more than they are producing (see 2.9 below).

Now let us consider some more complicated relationships between M.'s forms and the adult system:

(a) *queen* → [bi :ŋ]. By (A) (i) /n/ again changes to [ŋ]. By a combination of (A) (ii) and (C), /k/ becomes [b]. By (B) (ii) /w/ is omitted.

(b) *stamps* → [gamp]. By a combination of the two parts of (A), /t/ has become [g]. By (B) (i) /s/ has been omitted.

(c) *straw* → [bɔ :]. By (B) (i) /s/ has been omitted and by (B) (ii) /r/ has been omitted. By a combination of (A) (i), (A) (ii) and (C), /t/ has become [b].

It will have been noticed that the adult words *bean, green* and *queen* are all said by M. as [bi :ŋ], i.e. they have become homonyms. Many children may have a high number of such homonyms in their speech. They may often be unaware that they are producing homonyms and may react crossly if their homonyms are repeated back to them. Other children appear to monitor their own productions closely and may go to great lengths to avoid homonyms, often making a difference between two words in a way not predictable from the adult language. Thus Ingram (1975) quotes the example of a child producing words for *Mark* and *milk*. Both words had the vowel [ə] but for *milk* the child said [nək], substituting [n] for /m/ (although in all other words [n] and [m] were correctly distributed). Thus *Mark* was [mək] and *milk* [nək].

2.8 *Perception of phonemic contrasts*

The implication behind studies like Eimas *et al.* (1971) (see 1.4 above) and Smith (1973) is that perception of all phonemic contrasts is available to the child before his first words. Thus Smith reported that his child could correctly point to pictures of a *mouth* and a *mouse* before he produced any words at all. However, the cumulative evidence from Menyuk and Anderson (1969), Schvachkin (1966, 1973), Beaken (1972), Garnica (1973), and Edwards (1974) emphatically refutes this and suggests that perception of phonemic contrasts is only gradually developed. Schvachkin's (1973) children developed the ability to perceive all the phonemic contrasts of Russian between 0;10 and 1;9. But Edwards (1974) reports that children as late as 3;0 do not have complete phonemic perception. In general, however, perception of a specific phonemic contrast precedes its production. Children first achieve a perceptual contrast and then try to reproduce a similar contrast in their production.

The order of development of phonological perception appears to be very similar to that suggested for production, although there may be minor differences of order among the contrasts involved in the frictionless continuants: /mnŋlrwj/. Thus Schvachkin (1966) states that the contrast between /l/ and /r/ was early perceived, although it does not appear early in production. Edwards (1974) suggested that this distinction may be acquired earlier than the distinction between /w/ and /j/ in perception but later in production. Among the frictionless continuants it may also be true that there is often a greater interval between the acquisition of phonemic perception and phonemic production than is the case for other consonants.

All the experiments so far carried out on phonemic perception use the technique of naming items with words, sometimes invented nonsense words, distinguished only by the relevant phonemic contrast. Findings from such experiments may overrate children's perception of phonemic contrasts. It is at least doubtful whether discrimination in such a situation means that a child will register the difference as meaningful in ongoing speech (in much the same way that children imitate words better than they produce them in spontaneous speech). An analogy can be drawn with the foreign language learner who might well hear the difference between two words in isolation but is not at all adept at picking up the difference in ongoing speech (e.g. the Englishman learning the contrast between French /y/ and /u/).

2.9   Constraints on productive phonological development

2.9.1   Perceptual confusion

It must be remembered that the ability to discriminate between two sounds does not necessarily indicate that the distinction between the two sounds has been perceived as having phonemic relevance. Perception of phonemic relevance must of course presuppose discrimination between sounds, but the reverse is not true (see previous discussion in section 1.4).

It is sometimes suggested that the acquisition of productive phonemic contrasts in the speech of children is in no way dependent on any sort of perceptual confusion (e.g. Smith, 1973). In support of this position it is argued that phonemic contrasts are acquired in an 'across-the-board' fashion (the term originates in Chomsky, 1964). A phoneme, once acquired, is supposed to be produced immediately in all the words where it correctly belongs. A child might, for instance, at one stage be conflating adult English /w/ and /f/ as [w]; *wheel* and *feel*, *wall* and *fall*, *wool* and *full* are produced as pairs of homonyms. When such a child acquires the contrast between [w] and [f], it is suggested that he immediately uses [f] correctly in *feel*, *fall*, and *full*, but does not misuse it in *wheel*, *wall*, and *wool* (and that he does this without hearing any of the words pronounced again by an adult). This, if correct, would imply that even before the child produced the distinction he knew which were /f/ words and which were /w/ words and that his difficulty lay somewhere in production rather than perception. However, it is at least debatable whether children acquire phonemes in this 'across-the-board' way; it is more likely that a phoneme spreads only slowly through the relevant words in a child's vocabulary (see 2.1.3 above).

Another factor put forward against perceptual confusion as a constraint on productive phonological development is the often hostile reaction of children if their own malproductions are repeated back to them. A child who says [θiŋk] for *sink* may get cross if a parent points to the sink and says *Did you say this was a think?* Also the situation of partial development of a contrast outlined in 2.1.3 above (whereby *sell* may always begin with [s] but *shell* alternates between [s] and [ʃ]) suggests that a child may in some sense be aware of a contrast even if he does not systematically produce it.

All these arguments do not, however, prove that perceptual confusion is not a constraint on productive development. They prove only that perception of any one particular contrast precedes its production. It seems likely that failure to perceive the relevance of phonemic contrasts is at least one constraint on productive phonological development. For example, when a child has an elementary consonant system consisting of [bdglmn], he may already perceive the contrast between /ptk/ and /bdg/ but not yet perceive the phonemic relevance of the contrast between /t/ and /tʃ/.

A theory of phonological development which considers children's developing perception as important is put forward in Waterson (1971). This theory arises out of a more general theory concerning language, usually called prosodic theory (the use of the term prosodic here is not to be equated with the term as used in 1.3 above). This theory, applied to child phonology, rejects the whole notion of perception in phonemic terms. It is suggested that children perceive words as whole units. They perceive certain features of the utterance but do not seem always aware of the combinations and sequences in which such features occur. So the nasality in *window* is clearly perceived but its relationship to other features in the word is not completely clear to the child, who reproduces the word in a syllabic pattern over which he has control and says [ŋẽː ŋẽː]. Children perceive the most prominent features (nasality, for example, may be particularly prominent in some word positions) and also the broad rather than the fine distinctions (plosives are early perceived, for example, because they involve the complete cutting off of the airstream). They also perceive features which occur more than once in a word (a child may perceive and produce stops only in those words where the adult form has two stops, e.g. /biskit/ → [be ːbe] but /bærəu/ → [wæwæ]). This theory suggests that a child's early productions consist of certain basic structures which are based on the way he perceives. So Waterson's child reduced some adult words containing a nasal to a simple reduplicated structure of palatal nasal plus vowel, e.g. *window* → [ɲẽːɲẽː], *another* → [ɲaɲa] and *Randall* → [ɲaɲø]. In general, this theory is attractive in its explanation of the reordering of sounds to fit a common structure but it does involve certain difficulties. As mentioned previously, children appear to perceive their own malproductions if they are repeated back to them. Also, given that a child is confusing two features in perception, e.g. labial

friction in [f] and sibilant friction in [s], the theory does not prove
that a child's preference for one or the other in his production is
always dependent on perceptual rather than productive difficulty.
While perceptual confusion may be one restraint on productive
development, it is not proven that it is the only one. (It is only fair
to point out that Waterson herself has never said that limited
perception is the only constraint—see Waterson, 1976.)

2.9.2 *Articulatory complexity*

Just as discrimination between sounds does not necessarily imply
perception of a phonemic contrast, so the ability to produce
certain sounds does not necessarily imply their utilisation for
phonemic distinctions. In the early stages of language learning,
when their inventory of phonemes is very limited, children may
none the less be able to produce many of the sounds which they
will only later use phonemically. Thus a child not making contrast
between [θ] and [s] might pronounce the words *think* and *sink*
differently on one occasion when given sufficient prompting but
still not incorporate the distinction into his spontaneous speech
immediately afterwards.

Articulatory complexity probably does play some part in the
translation of perceived phonemic distinctions into productive
speech (maybe at the stage of planning rather than execution).
This seems to be implied by the finer control needed for many of
the consonants which often occur later in development, e.g. the
apical fricatives /θðszʃʒ/.

A theory which appears to place most emphasis on ease of
production is that of natural phonology (Stampe, 1969). This
presupposes that a child's internal representations of words exactly
correspond to adult speech, even before he produces his first
words. These first words ('post-babbling forms') appear in a form
which is easiest for the human speech capacity. By a number of
phonological processes adult words are reduced to a child form
which is nearer to this 'easiest' situation. At first there will be
many processes as everything is reduced to its simplest – then
gradually the processes will become fewer as the child's forms
come nearer the adult's. The child has to learn to suppress these
processes which reduce the adult forms. The phonological processes are of three different types. Firstly, total suppression: for
example, children have to learn to suppress the reduplication

which is characteristic of the earliest words. Secondly, limitation: children may at first suppress a process only in certain positions, and this suppression may or may not correspond to the adult language. For example, children at first generally voice plosives in initial and medial positions. They may at first learn to suppress this process only in initial position, whereas in medial position it remains unsuppressed. So adult English /pæpæ/ may on first occurrence be [baba], and then develop to [paba]. Here the tendency to voice /p/ to [b] has become limited to medial position. Thirdly, ordering: children may at first apply processes in no particular order, whereas at a later stage they may combine only in a certain order. Stampe (1969) quotes an implied example from Velten (1943). Joan Velten had two processes: (*a*) final plosives became voiceless, and (*b*) nasals became plosives. She applied these processes to the /m/ in the adult word *lamb* at first in no particular order, so /læm/ → /læp/, but at a later stage process (*a*) had to precede process (*b*). Applying (*a*) first, /læm/ was unaffected, since the /m/ had not yet become a plosive. By (*b*) /læm/ then became /læb/. The theory of natural phonology is an interesting hypothesis but has not been worked out in any great detail. Its weakness lies in its initial presupposition that the child is storing (and so presumably perceiving) words in their adult form from the very beginning. This presupposition has not been supported by studies of children's phonological perception.

2.9.3 *Phonological relevance*

What, in conclusion, can be said about the development of productive phonological control? It is not the case that children cannot discriminate at all between certain sounds, nor that they cannot produce certain sounds at all. Rather, it is that the linguistic relevance of certain distinctions between sounds is only gradually understood. At any one stage, some phonemic distinctions will not have been perceived as relevant, i.e. the child will not have learnt to pay attention to a certain sound difference as making a difference of meaning. At the same time, the relevance of some other phonemic distinctions will have been perceived but the child will not have translated such perceived distinctions into productive distinctions. Obviously, perceptual similarity (e.g. between English /w/ and /r/, which are acoustically similar) will play some part in the (slow) development of perception of phonemic contrasts but it will not be the only factor. For example functional load, i.e. the number of words which are actually distinguished by a certain distinction, may also play a part. Similarly, articulatory complexity (e.g. among the apicals /θðszʃʒ/) will play a part in determining the length of the interval between phonemic perception and phonemic production, although once again it will not be the only factor. For example, the motivation of the child towards correct pronunciation may also play a part.

2.10 *Intonation*

Children's growing ability to discriminate and produce different pitches, loudness, and voice-qualities during the first year was outlined in 1.3 and 1.4 above. Towards the end of this first year a child may be using a characteristic pitch pattern with each of his early words and expressions (see 1.5 above). During the one-word stage or early in the two-word stage he may begin to use the difference between a falling and a rising pitch pattern systematically. At first the distinction may not have an obvious parallel in adult usage. Thus Halliday (1975) reports that his child used a falling intonation for 'mathetic' utterances (commenting on his environment, something like an adult statement), e.g. `Mummy book*, and a rising intonation for his pragmatic ones (where he was demanding action, something like an adult command), e.g. *More ,meat*. Halliday's child at this stage did not even understand *yes/no* questions, so was definitely not using a rising pattern to ask questions. However, if this sort of distinction between 'mathetic' and pragmatic is typical of children, it may later change to a distinction between statement and question, once they grasp the notion of asking for information. Certainly most writers on early syntax (e.g. Klima and Bellugi, 1966) have stated that children's first *yes/no* questions are marked (only) by a rising intonation, e.g. *Daddy `go* ('Daddy's going'); *Daddy ,go* ('Is daddy going?'). The use of a falling–rising tune for emphatic contrast may be the next pitch contour to be learnt, e.g. *That not ˇyours* (Miller and Ervin, 1964, note for one child aged 2;2 that 'the fall–rise is used expressively').

It should not be assumed from what has been said that *every* child has begun to use pitch contours contrastively even by the two-word stage. During this period many children may achieve various needs and still ask questions by the use of gestures (e.g. reaching) and facial expression (e.g. by the use of raised eyebrows and wide-open eyes). Nor should it be assumed that, if a child has attained a distinction between fall for statement and rise for *yes/no* questions, he has mastered English intonation. In the adult language this distinction is generally conveyed by syntax anyway; while any pitch-contour may combine with any functional type (e.g. question, statement, command, exclamation) to give particular attitudinal overtones. How such an intonation system is acquired (not directly related to syntax, though obviously there are probabilistic connections) remains largely unstudied. Above all, statements such as 'It is widely accepted in the literature that the child effectively masters the intonation pattern of his language before he has learned any words at all' (Bever, Fodor, and Weksel, 1965) should be viewed sceptically. They probably reflect facts like (i) many children are excellent mimics of intonation; (ii) pitch height and loudness may have some sort of universal connection with emotions like excitement; and (iii) children often exhibit a wide range of voice qualities (see 1.3 above).

Intonation is of course intimately connected with accent. Accent (generally realised by a falling pitch) may differentiate various semantic types of sentence at the two-word stage, e.g. `*Daddy car* ('That's daddy's car'); *Daddy* `*car* ('Daddy's in the car'). This relates to the fact that in the first, possessive, example, the object possessed is obvious ('given'), since it is probably being pointed at, and the possessor is the important ('new') information. At this stage accentual patterns correlate regularly with the various semantic types of two-word sentences. A little later the nuclear accent becomes independently variable according to the distribution of new information in an utterance. In particular it may take account of what has been mentioned in immediately preceding utterances. Halliday's (1975) Nigel, having first said *Goat try eat* `*lid,* subsequently said *Goat* `*shouldn't eat lid.* Two main accents (generally falling pitch contours) indicate two intonation-groups and thus two sentences, e.g. `*No./* `*Car.* ('No, I don't want the lorry. I want the car') *No* `*car.* (There isn't a car here.') Indeed, at the stage of two-word and three-word sentences, intonation may be the most consistent criterion for dividing child speech into sentences.

3 Grammar

This chapter describes the beginning of word-combinations and briefly discusses the applications of grammatical theory to their description (those with no background in grammatical theory may wish to omit 3.2.3). The further development of syntax and morphology is then covered in some detail. This chapter also outlines some of the strategies children adopt in learning grammar; and the relationship of comprehension and imitation to production and to each other. Finally it discusses the nature of parents' talk to children, and the variations in children's speech according to social situation.

Grammar and syntax are regarded as beginning with the first appearance of two-word sentences (around 1;6 to 1;9) and the reader should note that phrases like 'the first year of syntax' indicate the year following this first appearance. The reader should also beware of interpreting references to the age and speed of acquisition too literally. Such references are meant to be a very rough guide for those who are new to the field; those with some experience will know that there is a great deal of individual variation (which is as yet unquantified in terms of averages and standard deviations).

3.1 *Preliminaries*

The reader should bear in mind the following distinctions, which are relevant throughout this chapter.

3.1.1 *Descriptions v. explanations*

We can write a grammar for a child's language by extracting generalisations from the data we collect and by stating rules based on these generalisations. There may well be several ways of interlocking the various generalisations or rules to give different types of grammar. We may decide that one particular grammatical description is paramount because it illuminates the way grammar is being learnt: such a grammar is then not only descriptive but also explanatory. At present *no* type of grammatical theory produces a grammar of child language which can be claimed to be explanatory to a particularly high degree.

3.1.2 *Forms v. meanings*

Some grammatical descriptions of child language give prominence to formal, i.e distributional, factors, e.g. that the child learns word classes as being in a fixed positional relationship with certain other words. Other descriptions give prominence to semantic factors, e.g. that the class of words labelled noun correlates primarily with the class of names of concrete objects. Both types of factor may be relevant to grammatical development, e.g. a child may learn to classify words into one word-class (for example the word-class of *nouns*) partly on the basis of the similarity of the things they refer to and partly on the basis of the words with which they combine (for example, that *want* is frequently followed by a noun).

3.1.3 *Item-learning v. system-learning*

A child may learn a particular utterance as appropriate to a certain situation (e.g. *Here he comes*) but may not understand the rules of sentence formation which lie behind it: he may have learnt the utterance as an unanalysed whole. Such utterances are sometimes called item-learnt (as opposed to system-learnt), or mechanical, or stereotyped, or prefabricated routines (see R. Clark, 1974).

In order to assume that the child has learnt the system behind the sentence, we would expect to find the words *here, he,* and *come (s)* in other combinations, e.g. *Here's the ball, Daddy come, He do it.* We would also expect some of these combinations to be ones which the child has probably not heard but has made up for himself; ones which are productive (or 'generated') and not simply imitations (which item-learnt utterances are). A good sign that an inflectional system has been learnt is when it is subject to overgeneralisation, e.g. the production of *goed* for *went* indicates that the system for marking the past tense has been learnt.

3.2   *Two-word sentences*

The earliest two-word sentences which children use generally belong to limited number of semantic types. This is true not only of English but of languages as disparate as Luo, Samoan, and Finnish (Bloom, 1970; Slobin, 1971; Bowerman, 1973). Some of the most common types are (and it must be remembered that the following is only a loose classification – some utterances could easily be assigned to either of two types):

(i) Possession, e.g. *Mummy shoe.* The first noun generally has the accent and is usually animate. (At this stage nouns must be defined semantically as the names of concrete visible objects; much later this word-class will become a distributionally defined one in that some words which are not the names of concrete visible objects will begin to occur in the same slots, e.g. after *the.*) A variant of this type is Recipience, e.g. *Crisp birdies,* 'Throw some crisps to the birds'. Whether this is considered a separate type must depend on the regularity with which the word-order difference is maintained.

(ii) Attribution, e.g. *Blue car.* Favourite adjectives are *big, little, pretty, poor,* and *broken.*

(iii) Recurrence, e.g. *More apple.* The label is taken from Bloom (1970).

These first three types (apart from Recipience) correspond to expanded noun phrases in the adult grammar (i.e. noun phrases which are not simply nouns or proper names).

(iv) Location. Here there are two subtypes, one consisting of noun plus noun, e.g. *Daddy car,* 'Daddy's in the car', where the accent is generally on the second noun (contrast this with Possession above); and the other of noun plus prolocative, e.g. *Cat up there.* Common prolocatives are *here* and *there* and variations of them, e.g. *in here, over there.*

(v) Nomination, e.g. *That giraffe.* This type is obviously close to (iv) and an example like *Cat up there*; both types are deictic and it is not clear that they are always to be regarded as separate types (although often the word order is different).

(vi) Negation. There are two subtypes: Non-existence, e.g. *No cheese,* 'There isn't any cheese', and Disappearance, e.g. *Allgone biscuit,* 'The biscuits are finished', although it should not be assumed from these examples that *no* always indicates Non-existence and *allgone* Disappearance.

(vii) Exclamation and Greeting, e.g. *Peepo daddy, Bye-bye Sally, Tricycle dear-dear,* 'Oh dear, the tricycle's fallen over'. This last example is obviously one which is to some extent arbitrarily assigned to this category. It might have been assigned to (viii), with *dear-dear* being regarded as an action.

(viii) Action. Here there are three subtypes: agent-action, e.g. *Mummy eat*; agent-goal, e.g. *Daddy lunch,* 'Daddy is eating his lunch' (with accent generally on the second word); and action-goal, e.g. *Make pudding.* The agent is usually animate and the goal usually inanimate. The term goal is preferred to the term affected because the goal is sometimes affected, as in *Daddy lunch,* and sometimes effected, as in *Make pudding.* The genesis of the adult categories of subject and object obviously lies in this type of utterance. The category subject, for example, will come to include more than just agents and will become distributionally defined (relative to the verb) in the same way that the class labelled noun changes from being semantically to being distributionally defined (see under (i) above).

Of these types possession, recurrence, location, and negation often occur at first in larger numbers than the other types. But the action type rapidly becomes predominant (especially when three-word sentences begin to appear). This is to be expected, as it represents what will become the most productive type of sentence structure in the adult language.

This early type of child utterance has been called telegraphic (Brown and Bellugi, 1964) because it excludes function words and morphological endings; this involves the omission of all those words which are typically unaccented in the adult language. In languages with a syllable-timed rhythm rather than stress-timed like English, there may be a lesser tendency to telegraphic speech (Omar, 1973).

Until fairly recently it was assumed that there was no grammar in early child languages but that utterances represented strings of unpatterned words. Brown (1970) points out that, if this were so, there would be no reason why such utterances should start with one word and grow gradually in length. More specifically, a close look at the two-word sentences of any one child will certainly show regular formal patterns. Items and classes of words defined semantically will regularly cooccur to produce certain meanings (i.e. the classes are defined semantically but their cooccurrence is a formal matter). Animate noun plus inanimate noun produces three possible meanings; possession, location, and agent-goal. The placing of the accent (which generally means falling pitch) on the animate noun generally identifies the possessive meaning; while accent on the inanimate noun indicates one of the other two meanings. Moreover many children operate from the very beginning with a fixed word-order (relecting the most common order in the adult language) for at least some types of sentence. Even if word-order is free when two-word sentences first appear, it usually becomes fixed fairly rapidly. Action sentences are the most likely to have a free word-order for a short period, e.g. Braine (1963b). Adult English, of course, operates with a relatively fixed word-order; however, even in languages which have a freer order than English, e.g. Russian and Finnish, children often appear to go through a phase of using a fixed order (Slobin, 1971; Omar, 1973; Bowerman, 1973, who also produces evidence from one Finnish child who did not go through such a phase).

Some formal patterns correlating with semantic types are therefore present in two-word sentences, although of course not all types are so marked, e.g. one subtype of location and the agent-goal type are formally identical, e.g. *Daddy 'car* may mean 'Daddy's in the car' or 'Daddy's polishing the car'. In any one context, of course, the sentence may be unambiguous.

Assuming, then, that children's two-word utterances are in some sense grammatical, i.e. produced according to rules, the question might be asked: why the limitation to two words? The hypothesis has often been put forward that it is due to a limitation of short-term memory. Short-term memory span is often measured by the ability to remember random digits. This ability develops fairly regularly in children: two digits at an average age of 2;6, three at 3;0, four at 4;6 (Terman and Merrill, 1967). This looks rather like the development of the mean length of utterance measured in morphemes (see 3.3.1 below). The implication is that in producing only two-word sentences a child cannot remember the first word he says beyond his second word. But the relationship between short-term memory and the production of sentences has never been clearly indicated, and it may be that the difficulty of producing longer sentences relates as much to their structural complexity as to their length.

3.2.1 *Pivots*

The present interest in children's two-word sentences started with a number of studies in the early 1960s (Braine, 1963b; Miller and Ervin, 1963; Brown and Fraser, 1963; Brown and Bellugi, 1964). The main conclusion that these studies came to was that a majority of the sentences were built by combining a few oft-repeated words in one position with a large number of other words in the other position. Braine's terms, which have become the standard terms, were *pivot* (for a word which occurs very frequently and in one position) and *open*. A child's grammar at the two-word stage can thus be described as having structures of the types: $P_1 + O$; $O + P_2$; and $O + O$ (this last accounting for those sentences which do not have a pivot). P_1 and P_2 are mutually exclusive, i.e. any one pivot occurs in only one position. Some examples of pivot sentences (from Braine's Gregory) are:

$O + P_2$	$P_1 + O$	$P_1 + O$	$P_1 + O$
do it	see boy	more taxi	allgone shoe
push it	see sock	more melon	allgone vitamins
move it	see hot		allgone egg
close it			allgone lettuce
buzz it			allgone watch

where the pivots are *it, see, more* and *allgone*. Pivots may represent various adult parts of speech, but the O class most commonly comprises adult nouns and verbs.

It has been suggested that children operate at this stage with a *pivot grammar* and that it is generative (i.e. that the child is not just producing reduced imitations of adult utterances but has word-classes which he combines himself to make new sentences). Thus unlikely sentences occur like *Two foot* (Brown and Bellugi, 1964: 149) and *Allgone vitamins*. Some writers (e.g. McNeill, 1966b) have suggested that the pivot and open classes represent the genesis of the division in the adult grammar between function and content words.

But many arguments have been produced against the notion of a pivot grammar (cf. Bloom, 1971):

(i) A proportion of two-word sentences (25 per cent in Braine's corpus) have to be fitted into the $O + O$ structure. This has to cover a motley assortment of sentences like, for Brain's Andrew, *Byebye car, Pants change, Papa away*. (*Byebye, change* and *away* are not regarded as pivots for this particular child because they occur only in a very few sentences and/or because they are not limited to one position.)

(ii) The choice of pivots seems idiosyncratic in every case. While it would not be expected that all children would have exactly the same pivots, it might be expected that each child would draw his pivots from a small set (if the grammar represents a stage on the path to adult grammar).

(iii) Pivots at the two-word stage do not correlate at all closely with grammatical words in the adult grammar. When progressing to larger sentences a large amount of reclassification would have to take place, e.g. *see* in the examples above would have to be shifted to the open class (or at least to one of the classes into which open may then have split).

(iv) Part of the definition of pivots has often been that they should not occur on their own as holophrastic (one-word) utterances. Since it is implied that they are words around which a wider class of words operates, this would seen a likely limitation on their occurrence. But it is often the case that a word like *more,* while occurring in many two-word utterances, does occur on its own.

(v) Many words, which look like pivots in that they occur a very large number of times in a child's utterances and occur mainly in one position, nevertheless occur occasionally in the other position, e.g. Braine's Andrew has a pivot *off* occurring in second position in sentences like *Boot off, Light off, Pants off,* but there is one example of *off* in first position in the corpus of Andrew's sentences: *Off bib,* and here Braine does not regard it as a pivot.

(vi) The most important objection to the notion of pivot grammar, however, must be that it does not take meaning into account. The classes pivot and open have no semantic correlates (not even a central type of correlate, which is the position in the adult language, where, for example, the class labelled noun refers centrally to a class of concrete visible objects, cf. Lyons, 1966); nor do the structures $P_1 + O$, $O + P_2$, $O + O$ have any semantic correlates. The implication is that the child is learning structures without meaning (and, moreover, structures that bear no relationship to adult grammatical structures).

These arguments suggest that the notion of pivot grammar does not stand up to rigorous linguistic analysis and is not psychologically real for the child. Nevertheless children's two-word sentences do have this *pivot look* (Brown, 1973). This pivot look appears formally to depend on two factors:

(*a*) '. . . the sharp discontinuity of combinatory potential in the child's words' (Brown, 1973). The pivots occur in many different combinations; the open class words occur in a few combinations.

(*b*) The *relatively fixed* position of pivots.

Functionally the pivot look appears to arise because of the pragmatic need of the child for certain concepts. This is confirmed by the occurrence of some pivots almost universally, e.g. *more, allgone, mummy*; and only slightly less commonly *no, want, like*. The words have, as Brown (1973) points out, a wide range of applicability: many things can be *allgone* but not many can be *green*; and *mummy* is directly involved as the listener in many of the child's utterances.

3.2.2 *Deep grammar*

Some sort of grammatical description of two-word sentences is, therefore, required which takes more account of meaning than a pivot grammar. But of course the danger is then that we ascribe too much meaning to such sentences; that a child's sentence is given the meaning of a sentence which an adult would say in a similar situation. We must have firm evidence before we ascribe a specific meaning to a child's utterance. What sort of evidence can we use?

The distributional patterns used to extract pivots (i.e. a pivot occurring in either first or final position combining with an open class in the other position) can be expanded into a rather more subtle formal anlaysis, involving not only word-order but also the cooccurrence of semantic items or classes; and accentual patterns. Where such formal patterns correlate consistently with apparent situational meanings we may assume a meaningful intention on the part of the child. (See 3.2 above.) Thus the types of meaning outlined earlier in this chapter are to be considered as part of the grammar of the child where formal exponents of these meanings are present (which is so in most cases).

Two pieces of evidence suggest that a child's sentence may often involve a meaningful linguistic intention greater than that indicated solely by their form. Firstly it is clear that children's comprehension is generally greater than their production at this stage. However, this is evidence of so general a nature that until precise comprehension of individual structures is related to the corresponding production it is difficult to apply. Secondly there is the sort of evidence from sequences of sentences referred to by Bloom (1970) and Brown (1973). The sentences must occur in immediate succession and there must be no change in the situation which produces them. For example, when a mother touches a child's glass of milk, the child may say *Baby milk* immediately followed by *Touch milk* and from this it may be inferred that the child intends a total structure of the sort: action (or verb) + noun phrase consisting of an attributive (or modifier) plus noun, i.e. that the child intends at least a three-word sentence of verb + modifier + noun. Similarly if daddy kicks the child's ball, the child may say *Daddy ball* immediately followed by *Kick ball* and from this it may be inferred that the child intends a total sentence of the sort: agent (or subject) + action (or verb) + goal (or object).

From this sort of evidence Brown (1973) suggests that a basic sentence type involved in early children's utterances is of the sort agent–action–dative–object–locative, although of course this type of sentence never occurs in full in his data, nor indeed is this type of sentence wholly constructible for *one* sequence of sentences. It depends upon putting together the evidence from different sequences. Indeed, in many cases the probable adult sentence corresponding to the child sentence would not involve all the elements. In a sentence *Daddy come* where an intransitive verb is involved, no object would be present. Similarly, even in the adult correlate of some sentences, ellipsis (leaving out items which are taken for granted by the speaker and and listener) may be in order. If daddy, mummy, an elder brother and the child are taking turns to stick stamps in a book and it comes to daddy's turn, the child may say *Daddy stick*: it is likely that an adult talking in such a situation would say something like *It's daddy's turn* or *It's daddy's turn to stick* or *It's daddy's turn to stick one* but almost certainly there would be no explicit mention of *stamp,* since the stamp has been mentioned before. The adult sentence would involve ellipsis or anaphora (reference by means of pronouns to something previously mentioned). The relationship of actual child utterances to the sort of base sentence type proposed by Brown may therefore be:

(i) An element may be omitted which would be obligatory in an adult equivalent, e.g. in an utterance like *Daddy wall* where daddy was hitting a nail into the wall, some sort of verb like *hit* would be obligatory. (Bloom, 1970, suggests that this type of omission often reflects lexical unavailability, e.g. in this case the child might not know the word *hit.*)

(ii) An element in the base sentence type may be impossible both in the child's utterance and in any corresponding adult sentence, e.g. object in *Daddy come.*

(iii) An element may be omitted in the child utterance which would also be prone to ellipsis in a corresponding adult utterance, as in the example of *Daddy stick* above.

While it may be true to say that the child's sentences are made up of various combinations drawn from the elements Brown puts together in his base sentence, many very complex questions are raised if we seek to say that all a child's utterances are in some sense derived from this base sentence. In the absence of stronger proof (and remember, we are almost entirely dependent on the evidence from sentence sequences) it seems safer to say that the child is producing bits of grammar (in the sense of correlations between forms and meanings) but that we cannot be certain that he has built up for himself any notion of a whole grammatical system in which all these bits are interrelated.

3.2.3 *Grammatical theories*

Many of the descriptions of children's early two-word sentences have been written under the influence of current adult grammatical theories (the notion of pivot grammar was of course constructed specifically for children's language). The comments at the end of the preceding section concerning proof that the child has constructed any integrated system at all apply to descriptions couched in these theories as well as to Brown's basic sentence type.

It is possible to describe child's syntax using any adult grammatical theory; the question is not whether such a description can be made but how illuminating and insightful it is. The two most influential theories in the description of child grammar have been the models provided by Chomsky (1965) and by Fillmore (1968). A detailed critique of their relevance to child grammar is given by Bowerman (1973). In 3.1.2 we mentioned the different emphasis placed on forms and meanings in grammatical descriptions of child language. Pivot grammar is obviously of the formal kind whereas Brown's basic sentence type takes more account of meaning. The relationship of forms to meanings also varies considerably in those grammatical theories which have been constructed primarily for adult language. In a case grammar, as outlined in Fillmore (1968), the base structure or deep structure of sentences is semantic and consists (in part) of a verb with a number of nouns in various (case) relationships with it. In the following three sentences: (1) *John broke the window,* (2) *A hammer broke the window,* and (3) *John broke the window with a hammer,* not only is *window* in the objective case in all three sentences and *John* in the agentive case in (1) and (3) but *hammer* is in the instrumental case in (2) and (3) even though on one occasion it occurs as surface subject and on the other occasion as a surface prepositional phrase (*with a hammer*). This sort of deep structure is, then, semantic. On the other hand, the type of transformational grammar which has been termed standard (namely, that associated with Chomsky, 1965) postulates a deep structure which is basically grammatical. A passive sentence like *John was hit by Bill* is said to have a deep structure in which *Bill* is the 'deep subject' and *John* the 'deep object'. Various rules of semantic interpretation (which have not yet been worked out in any detail) indicate how this grammatical deep structure is to be given a meaning.

It is sometimes implied that children begin their grammatical acquisition by talking deep structure directly and only later learn the transformations necessary to produce correct surface structures. It is therefore worth considering how far the deep structure of transformational-generative grammar and of case grammar is reflected in early child language. Central to the Chomsky (1965) model are the basic grammatical relations of subject–predicate (sometimes labelled VP) and, within the predicate, verb–object. Two types of evidence are discussed by Bowerman (1973) which might show that the child was operating with such relations. Firstly occurrence of more utterances of the type verb–object (e.g. *Hit ball*) than of the type subject–verb (e.g. *Daddy hit*) might show that verb–object constituted the greater unity. While the verb–object type often does predominate among English children, Bowerman found that for at least one English child and for two Finnish children subject–verb types predominated. Secondly she suggested that it might be reasonable to expect that the range of semantic functions (e.g. agent, instrument, location) performed by grammatical subjects in child language might be similar to that performed by subjects in the speech of parents to children. But subjects are almost exclusively agents in child language (at least at the two-word stage). More fundamentally this model of grammar seems inadequate for describing child language precisely because semantic notions like agent or location or possession, which seem basic to children's two-word sentences, are not basic to such a model. Other more detailed parts of this TG grammar do not accord with the facts of language acquisition. For example, children acquire the present progressive aspect of the verb in English using at first only the *-ing* ending without the *is,* e.g. they say *John going* instead of *John is going.* But according to the standard TG model, the progressive has a deep structure with both *is* and *-ing* present together; a 'movement' transformation subsequently assigns the two parts to the right position relative to the verb. Again, *wh-* questions are generally acquired by children in the form illustrated *Where you go?* i.e. with the *wh-* word at the beginning of the sentence but without the inversion of the subject and verb. The standard TG formulation suggests *You go where?* as the deep structure (or at least some sort of intermediate structure). Although it is true that some sort of simplifying process is at work in children's early syntax (obviously *Where you go?* is simpler than *Where are you going?* since it is the same as the statement form in not having inversion of subject and auxiliary verb), this simplifying process does not, in many details, seem to accord with the deep structure proposed by the standard TG model.

The apparent relevance of semantic relationships such as agent and location suggests that a case grammar like that presented by Fillmore (1968, 1971) might be more illuminating. Many of the early utterances of children may, as we have seen, be characterised by such semantic relations as agent, goal, location, and possession. But there is no exact correlation between the set of case relations formalised by Fillmore and the semantic relationships in children's speech. Fillmore's instrumental case, for example, does not appear in children's two-word sentences; his dative (or experiencer in later versions of the theory) is not the exact equivalent of children's possessive. However, there is no reason why the adult cases should be present from the very beginning; and revised versions of case grammar are constantly being produced (Wells, 1974, and Greenfield and Smith, 1976, develop versions specifically child-oriented). Children's utterances of the location, action, and possession types are certainly better characterised by a case grammar than by the Chomsky (1965) model of transformational generative grammar. (Of course the semantic interpretation which must be assigned to a grammatical deep structure may eventually characterise these notions, but as so far developed it does not.) If children's early sentences are described using a grammar based on semantic (or case) relationships of the type proposed by Fillmore, what of course remains to be explained is how adult grammatical categories such as subject are acquired (i.e. the surface as opposed to the deep grammar).

It has been suggested above (3.2) that grammatical categories like subject are distributionally defined categories which arise from the previously semantically defined categories, e.g. there are at first agents with a relationship to verbs; then agents and verbs are in a fixed word-order; then the class of words occurring before verbs enlarges to include other than agents. Thus grammatical classes arise which have a probabilistic relation to semantic classes rather than an exact correlation. Of course this example is an oversimplification of the actual processes involved; in particular it might be asked: where has the class labelled verb come from? The answer is that it arises by a similar process from the semantic class of action words.

3.2.4 *Sentence functions*

Halliday (1970) makes a distinction between the *ideational* component of language, wherein the speaker is expressing his experience of the world, and the *interpersonal,* in which he is interacting with other people. (He has a third component, the *textual,* which need not concern us for the moment.) The ideational component is largely conveyed by the internal grammatical structure of a sentence (e.g. the various semantic relationships existing between the verb and the nouns in the sentence), while the interpersonal component is conveyed by various sentence types such as statement, question, and command. All that we have discussed about two-word sentences so far has had to do with the ideational component.

Halliday (1975) suggests that in the early stages of language development these two components are not independently variable, each word, and later each combination of two words, expressing a fixed composite meaning made up of strands drawn from both components. At first such meanings are expressed by articulations (often combined with specific pitch patterns) which bear little or no relationship to adult words, e.g. [na] or [nana] 'give me that'; [gwɣi] 'I'm sleepy' (see 1.5 above). Gradually the expressions are more obviously related to adult words, and sentences appear combining two words. But the ideational and interpersonal components are still not independent systems. For Halliday's child certain structural (ideational) types were always linked with certain functional (interpersonal) types. So, for example, recurrence, e.g. *More meat,* was always combined with what Halliday calls the pragmatic function, with a meaning something like an adult command or wish, i.e. 'I want more meat'; whereas the attributive type, e.g. *Green car,* was always what Halliday calls 'mathetic' (so called because the child is using language in the process of learning about his social and material environment, i.e. it has a meaning something like 'That's a green car'). This type is only loosely related to the function called statement in the adult language because it does not communicate new information, but merely points things out which the child's listeners already know. (This is quite common in the adult language, e.g. *Look! There's a four-leafed clover!*) Moreover Halliday's child consistently used a rising intonation for the pragmatic type and a falling intonation for the mathetic type. Somewhat later Halliday's child began to vary independently structure (ideational component) and function (interpersonal component), e.g. both *More meat* and *Green car* could be either pragmatic (with rising tune) or mathetic (with falling tune).

For many children it appears that the possibility of using the same structure either mathetically or pragmatically is present somewhat earlier, at least from the beginning of two-word sentences. On the other hand a consistent difference between a rising and a falling tune is not made so early by many children; it may sometimes not occur until after the two-word stage. A combination of both these variations means that a child may use a sentence *More milk* to mean both 'Some more milk has appeared' and 'I want more milk' but the distinction will not be expressed in linguistic form in any way (and thus is not, as far as this book is concerned, grammatical).

3.3 *Syntax*

This section is concerned with the development of the major constituents of sentences—the verb phrase, the noun phrase, and the adverbial phrase—and with the development of various sentence structures and processes. The choice of items dealt with under each of these headings is necessarily selective because of the many areas of development about which little is known. Detailed discussion of morphological development can be found in section 3.4 below.

3.3.1   *Mean length of utterance*

When the characteristics of the various stages of syntactic development have been described in more detail than is available at present, and when such stages have been standardised on certain ages, it will be possible to measure the progress of individuals by reference to such a standard; it will also be possible to relate new studies of the development of particular details of syntax to such a standard.

At present we have no such standard, but a rough guide to syntactic development can be obtained by measuring the mean length of utterance (MLU). Most commonly this has been carried out by counting words. The most recent study was by Templin (1957):

Age	MLU	Standard deviation
3	4·1	1·3
3;6	4·7	1·0
4	5·4	1·5
4;6	5·4	1·3
5	5·7	1·5
6	6·6	1·3
7	7·3	1·0
8	7·6	1·6

This did not go below the age of 3;0. McCarthy (1930) produced a scale starting earlier:

Age	MLU
1;6	1·2
2	1·8
2;6	3·1
3	3·4
3;6	4·3
4	4·4
4;6	4·6

It can be seen that there are considerable differences at the points where the two scales overlap. This may in part reflect differences in child rearing which took place during the intervening years, but a larger part of the discrepancy is probably due to the varying criteria applied to the task of segmenting speech into utterances, and utterances into words.

Recently, in order to take into account developments in both syntax and morphology, morphemes have been used as the units of measurement (e.g. Brown, 1973). However, this leads to further problems concerned with alternative morphological analyses, e.g. are *doggy* and *mummy* to be counted as two morphemes each in child language? (Crystal, 1975) The problems are multiplied in languages more highly inflected than English.

Nevertheless, despite these difficulties, MLU can be used to give those with no detailed knowledge of language development some general guidelines. As Brown (1973) points out, almost every addition to grammatical knowledge increases length, e.g. correct forms of negative and interrogative sentences, embedding, and the addition of obligatory morphemes like forms of *be* before the -*ing* of a verb in the progressive tense. Brown admits that after the age of 4;0 MLU becomes less useful because it begins to vary considerably with the situation, e.g. the child will use a longer MLU when telling a story than when playing a game. Such variation also makes it impossible to talk of an average MLU for the adult language.

3.3.2 *Verb phrase*

Phrasal verbs of the sort *jump over, fall off, turn around* may occur even before two-word sentences. At this stage they must be considered to be single unanalysed expressions (adverbial phrases involving the use of the corresponding prepositions *off, over, around* do not occur until very much later).

Among the various tenses of the verb the present progressive forms in -*ing* (with the *be* forms only being added later) are generally the first to appear after the simple present (which of course will represent many of the meanings of other tenses before these occur). Some form of past tense is the next to develop, often with the regular {-D}morpheme, but sometimes past time is expressed using the adult emphatic from, e.g. *He did go*. The *did* is not accented as it is in the adult emphatic use. When simple past-tense forms do occur they are most likely to express aspectual notions, e.g. *falled* and *spilled* are likely to mean 'has fallen', 'has spilt' (Antinucci and Miller, 1976). Future time is often expressed first by *going to*; followed somewhat later by *will/shall*. Other tenses seem to occur much later, perhaps after the first year of learning syntax (i.e. children will have had two-word sentences and longer for at least a year before such tenses appear). Passives occur very much later still. If forced to use them at five and six, under 50 per cent of passive sentences are correctly formed (Hayhurst, 1969); they are, however, regularly correct by the age of 9;0 (Baldie, 1976).

The first forms of auxiliaries to occur are usually negatives, e.g. *can't, won't*, and must at this stage be regarded as unanalysed units (see 3.1.3 above). Positive auxiliaries (apart perhaps from *did* and *will* as tense markers mentioned above) generally occur first in questions, and of these *can* is frequently the most common, e.g. *Can I go out?* where the *can* is asking permission. Somewhat later auxiliaries may illustrate the first use of ellipsis in a correct adult fashion, e.g. (You didn't eat your dinner up) *I did.* Tag questions (e.g. *He's coming, isn't he?*), although often appearing in item-learnt utterances during the first year of syntax (i.e. the year after the first occurrence of two-word sentences), do not begin to occur systematically until 3;6 (Crystal, Garman and Fletcher, 1976). At the age of 5;0 many children still make errors in pronoun and modal agreement, e.g. *I can go, isn't it?*, and errors of inversion, e.g. *You can go, you can?* (McGrath and Kunze, 1973; Major, 1974), not to mention errors with 'false modals' (like *You'd better go, bettn't you?*). By the age of 6;0 pronoun and modal agreement is generally correct and by 7;0 inversion also. Apart from tags, the use of complex tenses and modals continues to give difficulty until much later: here are three sentences recorded by the author which illustrate the problem:

Age 9;3. *I don't know how you could write out a grocery list in the car.* (*could* = 'can', said when sitting next to mother in a vibrating car)
I would have done that when I was at the shop. (*would* = 'should')
He would have got up by now. (*would* = 'has probably')

3.3.3 *Noun phrase*

Demonstrative pronouns often occur at the two-word stage in the type of sentence labelled nomination; *that/those* commonly precede *this/these*. Demonstrative determiners (e.g. as in *that book*) occur much later. Replacive *one* often occurs from the beginning of two-word sentences, e.g. *Daddy one,* said where grapes were being shared out. By the sixth month of syntax one child studied by the author was regularly using *one* with adjectival modifiers, e.g. *That red one, There's a big one, That little one.* This use of *one* (and *it* and *that* as well) is more commonly referential (i.e. it refers to something in the environment) than anaphoric (i.e. referring to something already mentioned), although of course it can often be both at the same time. The pronominal quantifier *some* may also occur at the beginning of syntax (although *any* as the correct form with negatives and in questions occurs much later – see 3.3.5 below) but often as a free variant of *one,* the mass/count distinction not being made at this stage. *More* (and sometimes *another*) is also present in early two-word sentences (see 3.2 above).

Some general trends in the development of personal pronouns (which may not be completely present and correct until around the age of 5;0) are as follows:

(i) Proper names are often used by children where pronouns would be used by adults; this applies particularly to the child's own name, i.e. he at first refers to himself by his own name (Huxley, 1970; Bloom, 1970; Menyuk, 1969), e.g. a child named Johnny refers to his own car as *Johnny car* and rather than saying *You are eating your lunch* says *Mummy eat lunch. Daddy, mummy,* and *baby* appear in this and other respects to behave like proper names (Halliday, 1975). Psychologists have sometimes refered to this trend as 'talking in the third person'; linguistically speaking this is only a half-truth, since children at this stage make no distinction between first and third persons.

(ii) The first pronoun to be used productively (and not just in item-learnt utterances) is *it* in post-verbal position and with object function (Menyuk, 1969). Reference is generally to something inanimate, e.g. *Eat it,* describing a dog eating his supper. Bowerman (1973) has similar evidence for Finnish.

(iii) The second pronoun to be used productively is usually one with first person and subject function; and in pre-verb position. But the form of this pronoun is often *my* or *mine* (occasionally *me*)

(Bloom, 1970), e.g. *My did feed swans, Mine finish all my sausage, Mines eating a bit more. My* seems to represent a blend between *I* and *me*; *mine* seems to arise because of utterances like *It's mine* said by older children or parents.

(iv) All second and third person pronouns generally occur first in post-verb, object position, e.g. *Hit him* occurs before *He hits.*

(v) Second person pronouns generally occur much later than first and third person pronouns, i.e. *you* occurs (with correct reference) later than the other personal pronouns.

(vi) Singular pronouns generally precede corresponding plurals, e.g. *He goes* before *They go.*

(vii) Sometimes oblique (i.e. non-subject) forms are used systematically with subject function in pre-verb position, e.g. *Him do it* (Huxley, 1970). This generalisation stems from (*a*) the greater prominence of utterance-final forms, i.e. *him* will have been heard in utterance-final position, whereas *he* will not (except in tag questions), and (*b*) the principle commonly applied by children of one meaning = one form (see 3.5.1 below).

(viii) Certain pronominal confusions may occur. Such confusions seem to be of two types. Firstly where a pronominal function is required but the relevant adult form is not yet used by a child, he will of course use a form he already has (if he uses any pronoun at all). Confusions of this sort generally involve gender or number. *It* may in this way occasionally refer to humans, e.g. *Hit it,* meaning 'Hit him'; *her* may replace *him* or vice versa; and singular forms may have plural functions, e.g. *him* may mean 'them'. Secondly confusion may arise which results in the interchange of two forms: this generally involves confusion of person, e.g. *I carry you,* said when the child wanted to be carried, and definitely copied in the first instance from his father, who said *I'll carry you* (R. Clark, 1974). This type of confusion may be limited to item-learnt utterances but may sometimes involve the systematic interchange of *I* and *you.*

Determiners *a* and *the* may initially occur in a neutralised form which is sometimes difficult to separate from a similar reduced form of *to* and *for,* e.g. [wɔnt ə gou]. Once *a* and *the* are differentiated, children correctly use *a* for non-specific usage and *the* for specific usage but often fail (at least up to 4;0) to take the listener properly into account (Maratsos, 1974). Thus a child rushes into a a room saying *The dog just bit me* when nobody else in the room knows what dog the child is talking about. (Similarly the exact reference of the pronouns children use may be unclear to the listener: a child may come in crying. *He hit me* but no one knows who he is.) Of the predeterminers, *all* is usually the first to occur – in one child known to the author it occurred five months after the beginning of syntax in *Got all them now*.

Some adjectives (as mentioned in 3.2) may occur at the two-word stage, e.g. adjectives of size (*little, big*), of colour (*green, red*), and of affection (*pretty, poor*). Much later – say, around 3;0, when the MLU is around four words – adjectives are strung together (usually in the right order), e.g. *a nice blue tie,* or coordinated, e.g. *He's muddy and wet.* At the same time nouns are coordinated, e.g *Mummy and daddy,* and post-modification of noun phrases begins, e.g. *The man with the golden gun.*

This subsection illustrates how various factors may be interacting in language development. Purely phonetic factors, like reduction to [ə], may be relevant (in this slowing up learning); adult frequency may be relevant, e.g. plural personal pronouns are less common in the adult language than singulars; and semantic function may be relevant, e.g. *it* and *mine* as the first two pronouns obviously reflect the way in which the child relates to his environment.

3.3.4   *Adverbial phrase*

Locatives (both prolocatives like *there* and nouns with no overt preposition) occur at the two-word stage (see 3.2 above), and when longer adverbial phrases first occur after a year or so of syntax it is again locatives which appear first, e.g. *in the garden, down the road.* Time adverbs, e.g. *again,* appear during the first six months of syntax (i.e. during the six months after the first appearance of two-word sentences). An early distinction is between *now* and 'not now', a meaning which may be conveyed by a number of different adverbs, e.g. *last time, soon.* This general lack of preciseness in temporal reference applies also to *today, yesterday,* and *tomorrow,* which may at one stage be free variants; or at another there may be a contrast *today* on the one hand and *tomorrow/yesterday* on the other. A three-year-old child found playing with his father's newspaper said placatingly *It's all right, daddy, it's tomorrow's paper.*

Manner adverbs in *-ly* occur towards the end of the first year of syntax, as do adverbial phrases introduced by *for* and *to.* A number of other expressions may occur as sentence introducers or completives, but otherwise devoid of meaning at this stage, e.g. *actually, really, on purpose.* The use of such expressions obviously reflects habitual use of them by parents and they will vary accordingly. *Either* and *too* may also occur early for the same reason but not be used correctly until around 4;0.

3.3.5   *Sentence structure and sentence processes*

This section concerns the types of internal sentence structure in early syntax and also the development of various functional types like command and question. Negation is also dealt with here because the formal processes involved are similar (e.g. both question and negatives involve auxiliary verbs).

The main constitutents of English sentences are all present during the first year of syntax: verb phrases, noun phrases and adverbial phrases. Noun phrases occur both as subjects and objects; and as indirect benefactive objects, e.g. *Kick it to Jenny.* In addition nouns occur as vocatives, e.g. *Go away fly* (swatting the fly on her ear); *Pennies daddy* (asking her father to get her pennies out of her money box).

The earliest structural types are subject + intransitive verb, e.g. *Teddy sleep, Jenny crying*; subject + (be) + adjective, the copula being omitted at first, e.g. *Mummy busy, Daddy tired* (initially intransitive verbs and some adjectives may constitute a single class for the child); subject + verb + object, e.g. *Mummy buy grape* (at the two-word stage one of the constituents will be omitted; see 3.2 above); and demonstrative sentences starting with *that, those* and *there*, e.g. *That's a giraffe, There's a hole, Those a bird no*, 'That's not a bird' (with, of course, the implication of free variation at first between *that* and *those* and possibly *there* as well). Other types which may follow very quickly (i.e. after two or three months) are subject + (be) + locative, e.g. *Daddy's pen in the ear*, 'Daddy's pen is on his ear'; and subject + (be) + subject complement, e.g. *Lulu good girl no*, 'Lulu is not a good girl'. In the second half of the first year of syntax, as sentences grow in length, more complicated structural types occur, in particular sentences which include both an object and an adverb, e.g. *Johnny kiss mummy on cheek*; and sentences which include both a locative and a temporal adverb, e.g. *Johnny go home tomorrow.*

In the second year of syntax nominalisations with *to* may appear.

They may at first follow a few verbs, e.g. *like* and *want,* thus *Like to get down, Like to do some riding, Want to mend my wheel.* In this period also there may be occasional occurrences of subordinate clauses, possibly with *so, because, if* and *when* (and coordinate clauses in *but*), e.g. *My didn't have my lunch because it's not time, My will be lost if I go to sleep, My do it when my get down:* but children's understanding of the meaning of these conjunctions is often very limited at this time. They may even be into their third year of syntax before they produce types of nominalisation other than those with simple *to,* e.g. verb + *wh-* clause, as in *I show you how to do it, I remember where it is, I don't know who is it,* and verb + propositional object, e.g. *I think I can do it* (Limber, 1973). Relative clauses appear at approximately the same time. They are generally attached to the object rather than the subject and follow general words like *place, way, thing, one,* and *kind,* e.g. *This is the way you do it, That's the kind I like.* Such relative clauses are most commonly formed with no relative pronoun at all or with *that* but at first very rarely with *who* or *what.* Syntactic structures like clefting, pseudo-clefting, and extraposition (see Quirk *et al.,* 1972) will not occur until after 5;0.

In subsection 3.2.4 it was stated that meanings which were something like those of adult statement and command were used by the child from a very early stage in linguistic development; Halliday's (1975) child had a distinction at the two-word stage between mathetic (using language to learn) and pragmatic (using language to get something done): and this distinction was realised by a falling versus a rising pitch pattern.

Syntactically there is no difference in form between statement and command at the two-word stage, although a command is often expressed by the use of the word *want,* e.g. *Want crispies, Want car.* However, the difference between the two becomes marked once a child begins always to put subjects in where they are obligatory. Thus *Put kettle* at the two-word stage may be either a command to put the kettle on or a statement saying that someone has just put the kettle on. But later *John put kettle on* as a statement contrasts with *Put kettle on* as a command (*John put kettle on* might also be a vocative plus command, but this would be marked by the use of two intonation groups). Towards the end of the first year of syntax commands with *let,* e.g. *Let it stop,* and negative commands with *don't,* e.g. *Don't touch my dolly,* may also occur.

Questions involve rather more complicated syntactic processes. The development of the processes concerned has been well documented by Klima and Bellugi (1966), and what follows is largely taken from that source (including many of the examples). The first stage in the development of questions is that *yes/no* questions are asked with the use of a rising intonation only, e.g. *Fraser water? See hole? Sit chair?* At this stage children make use of gesture as well in their questioning, and it may be that some children question wholly by gesture without the rising intonation. *Wh-* questions involve simply starting a sentence with a *wh-* word without an auxiliary and without inversion, e.g. *Who that? What doing? Where milk go?* There are often cooccurrence restrictions between particular *wh-* words and particular verbs, e.g. *where* may occur only with *go*. At the second stage children continue to mark *yes/no* questions only by gesture or intonation but now freely combine any *wh-* word with any verb, e.g. *Where me sleep? Why you waking me up?* At the third stage children use auxiliaries with *yes/no* questions, e.g. *Will you help me? Does lions walk?* They also introduce auxiliaries into *wh-* questions but without inversion. A final stage correctly introduces this inversion.

Negation may be indicated initially only by gesture, e.g. a shaking of the head. The stages which Klima and Bellugi (1966) document in the development of the linguistic marking of negation correspond (i.e. occur simultaneously) with those mentioned for questions. Stage one involves the addition of *no* or *not* to the beginning or end of the sentence, e.g. *No wipe finger, More jelly no, Not a teddy bear.* Similar sentences are reported form Russian (Slobin, 1966d); from French (Grégoire, 1937) involving *pas* or *non*; from Japanese (McNeill and McNeill, 1968) involving *nai*; and from Arabic (Omar, 1973) involving /la2/or/miʃ/. Stage two involves the continuing use of *no* and *not* but also *can't* and *don't* (as simple unanalysed negatives); and the negative is now most commonly correctly placed in the sentence, e.g. *We can't talk, He no bite you, He not little he big.* By stage three the process of negation is substantially correct: more negative auxiliaries occur and must no longer be interpreted as unanalysed wholes, since corresponding positive auxiliaries also occur. Errors will continue to be made involving double marking of negation. Bellugi (1967) documents the development of negation plus *some/any* as (a) *I don't want some supper*; (b) *I don't want no supper;* (c) *I don't want any supper.*

The development of interrogation and negation suggests two general principles about the learning of syntax:

(i) Children mark these different sentence processes at first in a very simple fashion, adding syntactic variations and building up the complexity of the pattern gradually. Further evidence for this comes from the negation of sentences like *I think he will come* (Bellugi, 1967). In adult English this may be negated either as *I think he won't come* or as *I don't think he will come,* with no difference in meaning. This applies also to verbs like *think, believe, suppose,* and *expect.* With most verbs, however, there is a difference of meaning (cf. *I know he won't come* and *I don't know he will come*). Adult English generally uses the sentences with the transferred negative, i.e. *I don't think he will come.* Children, however, commonly use the other type, i.e. *I think he won't come,* following the basic principle that it is second verb which is being semantically negated.

(ii) The more syntactic frills there are, the longer it will take to acquire the correct structure, i.e. syntactic complexity will, as might seem obvious, delay the learning of correct syntax. Correct *yes/no* questions involve two processes: the introduction of an auxiliary and inversion. Besides these two processes, *wh-* questions involve a third process, namely the use of a *wh-* word at the beginning of the sentence. Thus *wh-* questions are more complex than *yes/no* questions and the correct form of this type of sentence is attained later. Bellugi and Klima (1968) noted that, even when children produced correct *wh-* questions, they still produced incorrect negative *wh-* questions, e.g. a child may produce *Why did he come?* but *Why he didn't come?* The processes involved in negative *wh-* questions are more complex than those involved in positive *wh-* questions.

Syntactic complexity is obviously a factor in the development of correct syntactic structure, but it should not be assumed from this that it is the *only* factor in the development of syntax. It is likely that a child must have reached a certain stage in cognitive development before he will even attempt to encode a meaning linguistically.

3.4 *Morphology*

We are here concerned only with the development of inflectional morphology. The acquisition of derivational morphology remains largely unstudied, although Berko (1958) found that children aged 4;0 to 7;0 were mostly unable to form agents in *-er* (from verbs): adjectives in *-y* (from nouns); and diminutive nouns ending in *-let* (from other nouns).

Three stages can be distinguished in the acquisition of an inflectional morpheme:

(i) The form of the morpheme occurs but is only a free variant of the root form without the inflection.

This stage is characterised by false analogy, i.e. forms of the morpheme are overgeneralised and used where they are incorrect, as in the third example below. Thus the English possessive morpheme {-Z} may sometimes be omitted where the adult language would have it; may sometimes occur correctly; and may sometimes be used incorrectly, e.g.

Daddy book, 'That's daddy's book'
Daddys book, 'That's daddy's book'
Kiss daddys, 'I want to kiss daddy'

(ii) At this stage the morpheme is now used correctly whenever it occurs (although overgeneralisation of one allomorph may be present, e.g. *comed,* see 3.4.1 below). There is now no false analogy. The morpheme is not, however, always used where it would be obligatory in adult speech. So, of the three examples under (i), the first two would continue to occur but the third would no longer occur.

(ii) The morpheme occurs correctly and consistently. The actual phonological form of an inflectional morpheme during these early stages may vary considerably from child to child. The possessive and plural morphemes often occur as a voiceless fricative (sometimes [s] but often [θ] or [ɬ]) in all positions (with none of the allomorphic variation mentioned in 3.4.2 below). so we get forms like [hætθ], 'hats', and [penɬ], 'pens'.

The transition from stage (ii) to stage (iii) is gradual and often spread over a considerable number of months. There is thus a problem involved in saying exactly when a child has learnt a morpheme, and any solution has necessarily to be arbitrary. One approach is to define acquisition by the occurrence of the morpheme on 90 per cent of the occasions when it would occur in the adult language (or, looking at the definition in the reverse way, that it is omitted only at most in 10 per cent of the contexts where it should be present) (Cazden, 1968; Brown, 1973).

A common order of acquisition of English inflectional morphemes is as follows (Brown, 1973):

(i) Present progressive (using-*ing* without auxiliary).
(ii) Plural.
(iii) Possessive.
(iv) Past tense (the form of this tense may be confused with the past participle, e.g. *I seen it,* and the meaning attached to the tense may be at first perfective, e.g. *spilled* = 'has spilt').
(v) Third person singular present tense.

Some correct uses of the first three morphemes on the above list may be present at the two-word stage (which is generally towards the end of the second year of life) but the first acquisition of a morpheme (using the 90 per cent criterion) may not take place until the beginning of the expansion into three-word sentences. Brown (1973) gives the age of acquisition for three children (notice that Sarah's order of acquisition differs from the usual order suggested above) as follows:

	Adam	Eve	Sarah
Present progressive	2;6	1;10	2;11
Plural	2;8	2;0	2;9
Possessive	3;4	2;0	3;0
Past	after 3;6	2;2	after 4;0
Third person sg. pres. tense	after 3;6	after 2;3	3;10

The difference in age and speed of acquisition is striking. This represents the sort of variation which must be taken into account when attempts are made to suggest a normal age at which any particular inflection or structure is acquired. MLU, measured in morphemes, was better correlated with these children's development of inflexions than was chronological age. When the MLU was 2·25 only Sarah had acquired any inflexion (the plural): when the MLU was 4·00 all three had acquired the present progressive, the possessive, and the plural. Children's earliest uses of comparative and superlative adjectives like *bigger* and *biggest* are usually equivalent to 'very big', i.e. the forms are used in an absolute sense. Sinclair-de-Zwart (1960a) studied expressions like *a pencil that is larger but thinner* and found that children understood these at the age of four, although they generally did not use them, when asked to make comparisons, until the relevant Piagetian conservation concepts including seriation (i.e. the ability to grade things according to one criterion) were attained (see 5.4 below); this might be several years later. There is further discussion of comparatives under 4.5.2. below.

Of course there are not a large number of morphological inflections in English. Slobin (1966d) quotes evidence from a Russian investigator, Gvozdev, who kept a diary of his son Zhenya's language development. Russian is a heavily inflected language and Zhenya continued to make inflectional errors up to the age of eight. Errors at this stage concerned mainly gender marking on nouns and adjectives. Errors in English irregular past tense forms by overgeneralisation (see 3.4.1 below) may occur at the age of six and beyond (many children of school age still say *meetid, choosed,* and *fighted*) but otherwise the acquisition of English inflectional morphology is generally complete much earlier.

Comparison of the evidence from English and Russian suggests that several factors determine the order of acquisition of morphemes. Most important seems to be that of concrete semantic content. Because of this, plural inflections are developed early in both English and Russian; on the other hand it is gender which causes most trouble in Russian, where the three grammatical genders have no consistent referential correlates. Brown (1973) suggests that frequency in the adult language is a minor factor in acquisition. Morphophonemic complexity (i.e. the number and form of phonemic variants within one morpheme) is obviously relevant but will generally lead to overgeneralization (see 3.4.1 below) of one form rather than delay in using a morpheme at all.

3.4.1   *Overgeneralisation*

The typical development of irregular past tenses in English involves (at least for those verbs which are of very common occurrence, which most irregular verbs are) firstly the correct production of the irregular form, e.g. *went, fell, tore.* At this time the regular form of the past tense in /t~d~id/ has not yet been learnt at all and the irregular past forms which occur must be regarded as item-learnt. Once regular forms are used, e.g. *kicked, closed,* the regular ending is generalised to the adult irregular verbs, e.g. *goed, falled, teared.* In Egyptian Arabic many irregular forms are used for noun plurals; children generalise the most common form, which is the feminine ending /-at/ (Omar, 1973).

While overgeneralisation is mostly limited to past tense and plural forms in English (e.g. *mouses*, but cf. personal pronouns 3.3.3 above, and later *gooder*, *badest*), it is naturally more widespread in those languages with a larger number of morphological inflections like Russian (Slobin, 1966d). Often, too, the generalisation involved is more complicated than in English. The singular accusative case for adult Russian inanimate nouns has four possible forms: no inflexion (masculine); *-u* (feminine); and *-o* or *-a* (neuter). The most frequent form in adult speech is the zero form (no ending); the next most frequent is the form in *-u*. It is this form in *-u* which is at first generalised to mark all singular accusative forms. Obviously the most frequent overtly marked (i.e. non-zero) form is chosen. While the general strategy involved in overgeneralisation is clear, i.e. one meaning or function is expressed by one form, the form which is generalised is not simply that which is most frequent in adult speech.

3.4.2   *Conditioned variation*

The English plural and possessive morphemes both have three principle allomorphs, /-s/, /-z/ and /-iz/ (or /-əz/), which are phonetically conditioned: /-iz/ (or /-əz/) follows the sibilants /szʃʒ tʃ dʒ/; /-s/ follows other voiceless sounds, /-z/ other voiced sounds. Similarly the past tense morpheme has three allomorphs: /-id/ (or /-əd/) following /td/, otherwise /-t/ after voiceless sounds, /-d/ after voiced. Berko (1958) tested English children's productive control over these allomorphs, using pictures involving objects and actions with nonsense names. Children aged between 4;0 and 7;0 had difficulty mainly in certain very limited areas:

(i) They were not always able to produce /-əz/ and /-əd/ forms where these were the relevant allomorphs; e.g., asked to produce a plural for /tæs/, children often produced no answer or simply repeated /tæs/, with no ending. These same children often had forms like /glɑːsiz/ in their spontaneous speech. They were obviously uncertain of the rule which applied to such words, although aware of individual plurals for individual words of this sort.

(ii) There was often difficulty with words ending in a vowel, e.g. /spəu/. Again children either produced no answer at all or simply repeated the form they had been given. The rules concerning the

occurrence of voiceless and voiced sounds in these morphemes
generally reflect more general phonological rules of the language;
thus the /kt/ in *packed* and the /bd/ in *robbed* reflect the fact that
/kd/ and /bt/ are impossible sequences in English (within one
syllable). However, following a vowel the phonology of English
allows both /s/ and /z/, e.g. *niece* /ni ːs/ and sneeze /sni ːz/. The
morphemes we are considering demand a voiced allomorph after
vowels, e.g. /spəuz/. It appears that children learn the more
general phonological patterns of their language first; if
allomorphic patterns simply reflect these more general patterns
they are easily assimilated. If, however, an allomorph is formed by
a special rule, it presents children with more difficulty.

3.5 *Strategies*

In this section we attempt to bring together some of the assumptions or hypotheses which children adopt in learning to produce
grammatical sentences. We are here concerned with how a child
learns to use grammatical patterns to encode meanings: meanings
which may be ideational and/or interpersonal (cf. Halliday, 1975;
and 3.2.4 above). Because we are concerned with how formal
patterns are learnt it should not be inferred that other factors are
subsidiary in language learning. Indeed, quite the contrary is
intended: talk of encoding a meaning implies a meaning already
present to be encoded, although of course the very process of
encoding will probably give added precision to the meaning. In
general the priority of cognitive development is certainly assumed
in what follows. (There are of course some exceptions: item-learnt
utterances, social formulae like *thank you* and difficult relational
constructions with *more*, *most*, *less*, and *least* (see below, 4.5.2)
where children may not have a complete understanding of the
constructions they utter.) Children sometimes invent idiosyncratic
words for certain concepts if they have not encountered suitable
lexical items in the speech around them. Also the development of
locative adverbials before time adverbials and before manner
adverbials must represent something in cognitive development.
Nor is frequency in adult speech completely irrelevant, although
adults' speech to children (see 3.8 below) is often tailored to take
account of both their cognitive and their grammatical development
and is not, therefore, an independent factor.

Very early on in language development children must learn certain universal principles of construction basic to all languages: they must learn that language has *double articulation* (Martinet, 1960), that a number of sound units are combined in different ways to make words (or, strictly speaking, morphemes) and that these words are then combined in different ways to form sentences. In their early expressions (see 1·5 above) there is a simple relationship of one form to one meaning without this double articulation. To understand and produce sentences, which involve double articulation, children have two difficulties to overcome:

(i) They have to realise that the shortest adult expressions (words) are made up of a limited number of units combined in different ways. Presumably children come to this realisation inductively; i.e., having learnt a few words as items, they begin to realise that similar sounds are recurring at different places in different words.

(ii) They have to learn to segment adult sentences or utterances into their constituent words. Once again, presumably, a child does this by noticing recurring similar chunks in different sentences. This ability to segment is taken for granted by adults and, although children generally learn to do it rapidly and correctly, mistakes may sometimes be made. One father reciting 'Humpty Dumpty' to a three-year-old left out the last word of each line for the child to supply: Father: . . . all the king's ——. Child: /hɔ ːsizænd/. Children may often mis-segment when an unusual allomorph is involved, so *an apple* is heard as /ə næpl/ (see MacWhinney, 1976, for a number of such examples from Hungarian).

In learning their grammar there are certain other basic assumptions which children make, basic assumptions which will in general help them in their learning, but in particular instances can be seen leading them into mistakes. We now examine some of these basic grammatical strategies (for fuller discussion of these strategies see Slobin, 1973).

3.5.1 *Formal–semantic correlations*

Correlations between form and meaning in the realm of grammar are often inexact. Such irregularities inevitably cause difficulties in language. Where the correlation is fairly clear, learning is easier.

In adult grammar many subjects are animate agents and many

objects are inanimate affected things. In early child grammar these correspondences are closer; so much so that the grammatical categories of subject and object may at first be irrelevant (see 3.2.3 above). Again, in the adult language, 'the distinction between nouns and verbs rests in the "nuclear" instances upon the distinction between "things" and "properties" in the adult world' (Lyons, 1966). The nuclear instances of the adult language become the only instances in early child grammar: thus 'children's nouns name narrow categories with characteristic visual contour and size' and 'the common notion that verbs name actions seems to be truer for the vocabulary of children than for that of adults' (Brown, 1958b). Children are not at first aware of the distinction between mass and count nouns; and all nouns are assumed to have a plural. So children use *a* with mass nouns and pluralise them, e.g. *You got a pretty hair*, *There's teas in here*. The correlations assumed by children mean that their language is in one sense more restricted than that of adults, i.e. it is more tied to meaning; but in another sense it is freer, since there are fewer grammatical rules.

Inflections which have no exact meaning are learnt late. As we saw, Russian gender is learnt late. Where morphophonemic variation is involved (i.e. where the inexactness is on the formal side), overgeneralisation leads to the child fixing on one form. Thus English past tenses *goed* and *flied*; all Russian singular accusative nouns in *-u*; and Arabic plurals in /-at/ (see 3.4.1 above). In these instances the correlations assumed by children lead to mistakes in production.

3.5.2   *Word-order*

The relevance of word-order is learnt early by most children (for one exception see R. Clark, 1974, where a child is reported as not having reliable word-order until around 3;0). Most fix on certain word-orders in their two-word sentences (see 3.2 above). Later a type of structure new to a child and reversing a standard word-order will often be misinterpreted. Passive sentences are often interpreted as active (Fraser, Bellugi and Brown, 1963).

In German the standard word-order for imperatives is verb + indirect object + direct object; in addition the two objects are differently inflected. The order: verb + direct object + indirect object occurs less commonly in the adult language. However, if commands are given to children in this second type of order, children will at one stage misinterpret them despite the presence of correct inflections (Roeper, 1973). The assumption on the part of the child that there is a standard order has overruled the meaning suggested by the inflections.

At a much later age (between five and ten) a sentence like *John is easy to please* (well known in linguistic circles!) may still be misinterpreted as meaning something like 'John is finding it easy to please other people' on the analogy of sentences like *John is eager to please* (see 6.2 below). In this sentence *John* is the subject of the phrase *eager to please*; and the meaning of a sequence noun phrase plus *be* + adjective + infinitive verb is more commonly of this second type in the adult language. *John is easy to please* is interpreted in terms of the more common meaning associated with this word-order. Assumptions about regular word-order may in this area lead to mistakes in the comprehension of sentences which children hear.

3.5.3 *Morphology and function words*

Children must learn that systematic variations or additions to a word's form may modify or add to the basic meaning of the word. It seems that children approach this part of grammar by first making the assumption that the ends of utterances and, more particularly, of words are important. Such a strategy may be forced upon them because the ends of utterances have extra prominence (Blasdell and Jenson, 1970). Such extra prominence may reflect a recency principle whereby syllables heard last in an utterance remain longest in the short-term memory before being overlaid by other syllables. Children are apt to repeat ends of utterances which they do not understand (3.7 below).

Thus children appear to learn post-modification before pre-modification. Phrasal verbs like *jump over*, *fall off*, *turn around* and expressions like *hat on*, *paper away*, *pip out* are common at the two-word stage in English (although not necessarily to be analysed as two words themselves), but the use of such particles as prepositions in phrases like *off* (*the*) *chair*, *over* (*the*) *table* first occurs much later.

The progressive tense in English first occurs with *-ing* and no auxiliary verb, e.g. *John walking*, but never *John is walk* or *John's walk*. Similarly in French the *pas* is at first used without the *ne* (Grégoire, 1937) (although this reflects an increasing tendency in the adult language anyway).

English personal pronouns are learnt first in object position, e.g. *Hit it*, *Hit him* before *It hits*, *He hits* (with the probable exception of the first person, see 3.3.3 above), and similarly in French object pronouns appear at first *after* the verb and in emphatic form, e.g. *Je frappe toi* before *Je te frappe*.

3.5.4   *Sentence processes*

Children's first assumption in this area appears to be that sentences may be modified without interruption or reordering. Thus to produce negative sentences in English the child's initial hypothesis is that he must add *no* or *not* to a positive sentence, e.g. *No he go home*; similarly with *wh-* questions, e.g. *Why he go home*? (see 3.3.5 above). It may also be assumed that two sentences in some sort of subordination relationship can be simply added together sequentially. Thus nominalisations may occur like *I want you get a biscuit for me* (R. Clark, 1974) and relative clauses like *Jane is the girl cried at school*. How long children take to attain the correct form for sentences of these types may depend on the formal complexity involved (see 3.3.5 above).

3.6   *Comprehension*

The dividing line between grammar and lexis is not always clear: this section should, therefore, be used in conjunction with 4.5 and 6.3 below. What appears in this section is selective, although the selection is principally one forced by the limited amount of information available. Comprehension has generally to be investigated in a controlled experimental situation; some parts of grammar are more amenable to such experimentation than others. Most investigations have tested children's understanding of a contrast in meaning, e.g. between singular and plural in English encoded by the plural morpheme {-Z}; but it is difficult, for example, to construct such a contrast involving the possessive morpheme. Usually either pictures or toys have been used to represent a situation relevant to the particular grammatical item to be tested; but it is not, for example, easy to construct such a situation to test comprehension of the simple past tense (the more obvious contrast is between simple or progressive present and present perfect in *has/have*). A further difficulty is that there is often no exact correlation between forms and meanings (see 3.5.1 above): there are, for example, a large number of different uses of the simple present tense in English. Thus an experiment may be testing only one meaning of a particular item.

Within the verb phrase, Herriot (1969) found that children aged three understood the present progressive, future in *going to*, and present perfect when presented with a toy performing an action given a nonsense name, although he found that varying attention could easily distort results. Carrow (1968), getting children to match sentences to pictures, suggested that comprehension of the various tenses develops similarly to their acquisition in production, i.e. the first tense to be understood (apart from the simple present) is the present progressive, followed by the simple past, the future in *will*, and the present perfect, in that order. But these were the only tenses tested, so we do not know, for example, whether the future in *going to* precedes the future in *will* as it probably does in production.

Passives of the reversible sort (e.g. *The boy was chased by the dog*) were not comprehended by children aged 3;1 to 3;7 in Fraser *et al*. (1963), nor by children with an MLU of 3·0 to 3·5 in De Villiers and De Villiers (1973). However, Slobin (1966b) and Turner and Rommetveit (1967) have shown that reversible passives are always more difficult to understand than irreversible passives (e.g. *The dog was hit by a car*), both for adults and for children. De Villiers and De Villiers (1973) found that, although children with an MLU between 1·0 and 1·5 could not comprehend passives at all, children did comprehend irreversible passives by the time their MLU was 3·0, e.g. (a) *The dog was hit by a car* is correctly understood before (b) *The boy was hit by the dog*. Children at one stage clearly expect the agent to precede the verb and the goal or affected to follow it (cf. 3.2 above). Only if this pattern produces a very unlikely meaning is the passive interpretation of the sentence considered. Thus (b) makes sense if the boy is taken as the agent and the dog the affected, i.e. the meaning becomes 'John hit the dog'; but (a) does not make sense if interpreted in this way and thus the passive interpretation is forced (cf. the interpretation of subordinate clauses in *before* and *after*, 4.5.3 below). Comprehension of reversible passives is only certain by around 7;6 (Baldie, 1976).

Distinctions within the noun phrase which have been the subject of experiments are that between *a* and *the*, which was largely understood at 3;0 (Maratsos, 1976) and *one* and *some*, which were confused at 3;5 (*some* being interpreted as 'one') but generally understood correctly at 4;0 (Tanz, 1975). Comparative adjectives are discussed under 4.5.2 below.

Fraser *et al.* (1963) showed that comprehension of the singular–plural contrast marked only by inflection (e.g. *The boy draws–The boys draw*) was more difficult for the children in their experiment (aged 3;1 to 3;7) than most of the other contrasts they tested (e.g. affirmative–negative, and singular–plural marked by *is/are*). A distinction between 'one' and 'more than one' is almost certainly made by the child at this age, otherwise children would be unlikely to use the plural morpheme so regularly (and correctly) in production as they do (see above 3.4). Fraser *et al.* suggest that children had difficulty with this distinction because it was perceptually difficult to spot (children had to match sentences produced by the experimenters with relevant pictures). The difficulty may also reflect the unreal use of the present simple tense in the sentences they used, e.g. *The boy draws, The kittens play* (more natural would be *The boy is drawing, The kittens are playing*).

We have to go back to a much earlier period to find the beginning of an understanding of the various sentence functions (see 3.2.4 above). Halliday (1975), recording a conversation between his child and his family at a time before he used two-word sentences (aged about 1;4), found that he could respond to a command (this is not to say, of course, that he could not do this even earlier); he could respond to questions introduced by *who* and *where* (and probably *what* as well); and he could respond to a statement by signalling attention and continuing the conversation. However, he could not reply to a *yes/no* question; and he could only answer questions with *who* and *what* provided he knew that the answer was already known to the questioner. Halliday suggests that the reason for these two limitations is that the child had not yet grasped that language could be used for information; the child assumed that *wh-* questions were used to introduce discussion of a shared experience. Only around the age of 1;9 did he grasp the idea that language could be informative. The understanding of questions with *when* and *how* (and almost certainly *why* as well) occurs very much later, according to Brown, Cazden and Bellugi (1968). Their data on Adam, Eve and Sarah show that sentences with these question words were not understood when their MLU was 2·75 morphemes (their age at this time varied from 1;11 to 3;1).

It is difficult to present anything as a hard fact in the development of comprehension. Not only has individual variation in children to be taken into account but methods of gathering information about comprehension vary enormously from recordings of natural conversation, through tests of productive capacity giving proof of understanding, to matching a sentence produced by the experimenter with one of a number of pictures. Results from this last type of technique (e.g. Carrow, 1968) have especially to be interpreted with caution, since so many factors (e.g. attention) can interfere with children's reaction to pictures.

The study of comprehension is important not so much for determining the order of acquisition of various structures but for observing the actual process of verbal learning as it takes place in children. In particular, it is often interesting to observe the strategies which children use to guess at the meanings of sentences which are not completely intelligible to them. Such strategies may be non-linguistic, e.g. children may assume the meaning which is most likely in a particular situation; or linguistic, e.g. in interpreting passive sentences they may use a 'canonical order strategy' which takes it as a general rule that the agent must come first. Such guessing techniques become apparent only when they lead to the wrong interpretation of sentences (as with passives). But the ability of children to guess correctly may often lead to an overestimation of their understanding of linguistic structure.

3.6.1   Comprehension and production

Lenneberg (1962) gave an example of a type of case, familiar to speech therapists, in which a child, while failing to develop any speech, nevertheless comprehended language adequately at the age of eight. Production is not a necessary condition for comprehension. On the other hand, there is no evidence that adequate productive control is ever reached without comprehension; indeed, such a situation would deny the whole concept of language as meaningful. Children's early language may include item-learnt utterances (see 3.1.3 above): that is, certain utterances appear to be learnt as relevant to a certain specific situation without understanding of the constituents of the utterance. One child said *Here he comes* regularly when anyone came through the door of the room he was in, before he used any of the three words in any other sentence. But the number of such item-learnt utterances is generally a very small proportion of a child's total output. Also, correct understanding of difficult relational concepts, like the comparative (see 4.5.2 below) and *because* (see 6.3 below), may not be present when the forms are first used. In other words, cognitive development may put limits on the understanding of some parts of grammar which children nevertheless begin to use because of their frequency in the adult language. Such a limit on understanding applies also to lexical development (see 4.5 below).

In general, however, receptive understanding of language is ahead of production; and this applies to most individual grammatical structures. Fraser *et al.* (1963) tested twelve morphological and syntactic contrasts (with children aged 3;1 to 3;7) and found comprehension in advance of production on all items. Lovell and Dixon (1967) obtained similar results for children aged 2;0 to 6;0.

For most children, during the first year of productive syntax, it can be assumed that comprehension will be some weeks ahead of production. For example, Shipley, Smith and Gleitman (1969) found that children often responded better to commands given in language a stage ahead of their productions. Children using only one-word utterances (holophrases) responded as well to two-word commands as they did to commands given in their own holophrastic form, while children at the telegraphic stage (principally using two-word sentences) responded better to commands in an adult form than in their own telegraphese.

3.7 *Imitation*

Imitation can be of many different types. A basic division is between immediate imitation, i.e. where a child repeats all or part of an immediately preceding adult utterance; and delayed imitation. Generally it is impossible to say how many utterances in any one child's speech are the result of delayed imitation, although it may occur more often than has been implied in most recent studies, with their emphasis on the creative nature of children's language. Item-learnt words and utterances are clearly the result of imitation, e.g. *Here he comes* (3.6.1 above) and the occurrence of *went* before *goed* (3.4.1 above). It may also be true that this learning of an utterance as an unanalysed whole can be a prelude to the learning of a structural type. R. Clark (1974) gives the example of *Wait for it to cool*, which her child copied and used intact for several weeks; only after this period was another adjective substituted for *cool* in this structure, yielding *Wait for it to dry*. Clark suggests that 'many, though not necessarily all, the productive rules originated as invariable routines, which were in use for some time with the original lexical items before new lexical items were inserted'. The number of rules originating in this way will obviously vary from child to child; although it may be that *covert* imitation of whole sentences plays an even greater role.

Item-learning of utterances can, then, be regarded as a type of delayed imitation where only limited understanding is at first present but where the structure may after a while become productive for the child. Although we label it as a type of delayed imitation, it is of course likely that when an item-learnt utterance first occurs it is a case of immediate imitation. It is its repetition on later occasions without an immediately preceding adult model that makes us consider it as a type of delayed imitation. We, in general, exclude item-learnt utterances from the discussion of immediate imitation with which the remainder of this section (3.7–3.7.2) is concerned.

Immediate imitations generally take the form of telegraphic utterances similar to those children use in their ordinary production. In this kind of imitation children characteristically shorten a preceding adult utterance by leaving out inflections and function words, e.g. *Fraser will be unhappy → Fraser unhappy* and *No, you can't write on Mr Cromer's shoe → Write Cromer shoe* (Brown and Bellugi, 1964). A reduction in length (measured in number of morphemes) will generally be involved to approximately that which is the average in a child's ordinary productions. In the second example above *no* and *Mr* are omitted in addition to the inflections and function words, so that the sentence length is reduced to three morphemes, which was about average for this particular child at this time. This kind of imitation generally follows the word-order of the adult model, which suggests that it involves a certain degree of comprehension, at least of the basic sentence structure.

Where the structure of a sentence is completely incomprehensible to the child, the relationship of any imitation to the preceding adult utterance is likely to be more random. Typically a number of syllables from the end of the utterance may be reproduced; if the final lexical item is one that is known to the child it may be repeated on its own. At one stage of development a child may not only fail to recognise yes/no questions but may also fail to recognise any structure in them at all, e.g. a child asked *Would you like mummy to get you an ice-cream?* replied *Cream* (when his MLU would have predicted a three-morpheme imitation). Another child who was asked, on different occasions, to 'open it' and 'eat it' imitated the utterances as [nit] and [tit]. Tag questions are particularly liable to this sort of uncomprehending echoic imitation. A child told *It's nice, isn't it?* replied [intit] (with a falling intonation). Because mothers generally grade the sentences they use to their children (see 3.8 below), this echoic kind of imitation is perhaps less common in normal situations than the telegraphic sort.

Children vary considerably in the amount they imitate (Bloom, Hood and Lightbown, 1974). Among the children who might be considered 'imitators', some appear to imitate words, while others imitate structures. But in both cases children imitate what they are in the process of learning, not what they have already learnt. Words and structures which are being imitated often appear in spontaneous speech at a slightly later time.

3.7.1 *Imitation and comprehension*

Under the section on comprehension (3.6 above) it was made clear that comprehension can proceed without any articulate speech at all. Imitation is not at all necessary for comprehension to develop. However, as has already been hinted at in the section above, the relationship between any imitation that does occur and comprehension is not a simple one.

Fraser *et al.* (963), using sentences in which children almost certainly understood the lexical items and a basic sentence structure for each sentence (although sometimes they understood the wrong structure, e.g. passive as active), found imitation ahead of comprehension on all but one of the tasks in their experiment (children aged 3;1 to 3;7). In a pair of sentences like *The sheep is jumping* and *The sheep are jumping* (in which the words *sheep* and *jump* and an actor–action relationship were understood) children more often imitated *is* and *are* than they made a correct judgement about singular and plural.

In telegraphic imitation (and obviously in echoic imitation too, where there is no comprehension at all) imitation is evidently ahead. However, Slobin and Welsh (1972) find a third type of imitation particularly illuminating, namely, a recoded imitation of a model sentence. A child hears the sentence *The man who I saw yesterday got wet* and imitates it as *I saw the man and he got wet*. The example suggests that this type of imitation occurs at a later stage of development than the types we have so far been considering. It also suggests that in this instance comprehension is ahead of imitation; the child has in some sense understood the clause but did not reproduce it. However, the imitation concerns a change in basic sentence structure (from subordination to coordination), whereas telegraphic imitation typically involves simply the repetition of the same sentence structure, which a child is probably already using in production (see next section).

The conclusion must be that, for imitation of both the telegraphic and recoded types to occur, comprehension of the basic structure of a sentence must be present. Once such imitation does occur, imitation of inflections and function words may well be ahead of their comprehension. Only in echoic imitation and item-learnt utterances is there no understanding of the basic structure.

3.7.2 *Imitation and production*

It is not suggested that imitation is ever behind spontaneous production; the question is whether and how far it is ahead. Fraser *et al.* (1963) found that their elicited imitations were generally ahead of production (children, aged 3;1 to 3;7). Slobin (1968), looking at the records of Adam between 2;3 and 2;10 and Eve between 1;6 and 2;2 (see Brown, 1973, and 3.4 above) found that 15 per cent of these children's imitations were responses to adult expansions of their own telegraphic speech (for further detail, see 3.8 below) and that half these responses added morphemes not in the original child productions but echoed from the adult expansions. One child said [pik mɑ :təu] 'pick tomato', to which a parent replied *Picking tomato up*, and the child repeated [pik mɑ :təu ʌp]. Thus imitation, even if not absolutely necessary for growth in the productive control of syntax, may have a limited facilitative effect. Slobin also found that reduced and unexpanded repetitions became less frequent towards the end of the periods studied (as would be expected as the children began to comprehend some inflections and function words).

Ervin (1964), studying the naturalistic utterances of children aged two (i.e. younger than in the experiment of Fraser *et al.*), found that their imitations were not grammatically more advanced than their other productions. Although naturalistic evidence might be assumed to be more crucial, Ervin's findings are not necessarily as irreconcilable with those of Fraser *et al.* and of Slobin as might first be thought. Ervin attempted to measure the grammaticality of children's imitations with reference to a pivot-type grammar written for their spontaneous productions and, as we have seen in 3.2.1 above, such a grammar does not adequately represent child syntax. Therefore the yardstick by which she is comparing imitation and production is suspect. In addition, as she herself says, some of the imitations were 'echoes of the final few words in sentences', i.e. were imitations of the echoic sort. It may be that at the earlier age studied by Ervin there are a larger proportion of imitations of the echoic sort (since children's understanding is extremely limited), and that this results in imitation appearing structurally less advanced than spontaneous production. As children's understanding of basic sentences increases, the telegraphic type of imitation increases; such imitations will begin to include inflections and function words not present in their productions.

The conclusion to this subsection is that children go through a stage when they are likely to add in imitation inflections and function words not present in their spontaneous productions. Otherwise basic structures will be similar in production and imitation.

3.8 *Parental speech*

The characteristics of parental speech to children obviously concern phonology, grammar and lexis. We deal with this topic in this chapter simply as a matter of convenience. For a useful introduction to parental speech see Snow (1976).

Babies are interacting with their mothers at a very early age. Trevarthen (1974) suggests that the foundations of interpersonal communication are there at birth. He found that two-month-old babies hold conversations involving rudimentary sounds and gestures and that they can actually be seen initiating a conversation.

At this age they are already beginning to understand that conversation involves taking turns. By three months old the frequency of babies' vocalisations can actually be increased by the amount of adult response (Rheingold, Gerwitz and Ross, 1959). A large part of mothers' speech to children during the first two years of life consists in speaking for the child when he has not got the relevant language to speak for himself, i.e. where the child's turn in a conversation might consist only of gesture, the mother adds the relevant language. For example, a mother will say *You want another one*? when the child's look obviously indicates that he does; and then behave as if the child himself had asked for another one. Even with children aged 2;0 mothers' speech is largely directed to keeping the conversation going (Snow, 1977). They use many turn-passing devices, e.g. [hmmm], and tag questions, but no turn-grabbing or turn-keeping devices, e.g. *well*, *but*, and pause-fillers.

Some parents modify the phonology of their words to children who are in the very early stages of language learning (i.e. during the first two years of life). Ferguson (1964) found that /t/ replaced /k/ in baby talk in English, Spanish, Marathi and Comanche. English parents may replace /r/ by /w/. Parents use patterns of assimilation which are similar to their babies' words. In Japanese /nukwi/ 'warm' is often changed to /kukwi/ by parents talking to their young children. Parents also simplify their consonant clusters: a word like *tummy* reflects this (/st/ has been reduced to /t/). They may also use reduplications like [jʌmjʌm], [dudu] and [pipi]. It is a moot point whether such baby talk is a mere repetition back to the baby of his own forms or whether it is produced by parents' own feelings of phonological simplicity; it is probably a combination of both.

Parents use a smaller vocabulary in talking to young children than to adults (Drach, 1969). Certain words are characteristic of 'baby talk' and many of them involve the ending -*y* or reduplication. Some common categories are: adjectives of endearment like *little* (or *teeny*), *nice*, and *lovely*; kin names like *mummy* and *daddy*; body parts like *footsy* and *tummy*; and names of animals and nursery games like *bow-wow* and *piggy-back*.

Supporters of innatist theories of language acquisition (see 5.3 below) have suggested that children would never be able to learn grammar from the poor data to which they are exposed (e.g. with its hesitations, false starts and repetitions) unless they came to the task very specially endowed (e.g. Chomsky, 1968; Bever, Fodor and Weksel, 1965). However, parents (and, more particularly, mothers) modify their speech to young children in many ways (compared with their speech to other adults and to older children) and thus assist them to learn grammatical structure. Some of the significant modifications are (see in particular Drach, 1969, and Snow, 1972):

(i) Mothers talk more to young children than they do to older children.

(ii) Grammatical structure is generally simpler in mothers' speech to young children (e.g. there are fewer subordinations), and the MLU is shorter and is less variable according to context.

(iii) Repetition *ad nauseam* occurs in parents' speech to young children (Kobashigawa, 1969). Such repetition varies features like intonation, rate, word-order where non-critical (cf. repetitions by mothers of subject–verb–object with different orders in Finnish: Bowerman, 1973), contraction, and ellipsis.

(iv) Rate of speech is slower to young children than to adults, and intonational patterns generally involve a wider pitch-range (Garnica, 1977).

(v) There are fewer pronouns (particularly third person pronouns) in mothers' speech to young children; mothers tend to repeat nouns.

However, mothers make no special effort to maintain formal grammatical correctness in their speech to young children, i.e. they do not attempt to speak constantly in complete sentences, with no ellipsis. Indeed, the high incidence of repetitions suggests quite the reverse. It is therefore not surprising that Bever *et al.* (1965) found that, of a total of 432 mothers' utterances they analysed, only 258 were 'fully grammatical' and of these only 46 were simple declarative sentences.

Young children appear to be receiving a set of language lessons. The short MLU suggests that mothers' speech is not encumbered by too many grammatical frills, such as morphological endings and function words. The large number of repetitions gives children additional time to work out the meaning of utterances. More particularly the type of repetition which includes a minor variation like non-critical word-order gives children important clues to constituent structure (Snow, 1972), e.g. *Daddy mend broken wheel* might be repeated as *Broken wheel, daddy mend* and a listening child would be given the clue that *broken wheel* coheres more closely than *mend broken*. This is sometimes called prompting or constituent prompting.

Mothers, then, obviously modify their speech to children. They may also grade their speech so that it is just ahead of their children's own production. Shipley *et al.* (1968) showed that children often respond best to grammar just beyond their productive capacity. Not only may children be receiving a set of language lessons, but these lessons may also be carefully graded.

Mothers may respond to their children's speech in various ways. One type of response is an expansion in which a mother imitates her child's utterances but at the same time expands it. Thus one child said *Eve lunch* and mother responded *Eve is having her lunch* (Brown and Bellugi, 1964). The mother gave a grammatically fuller sentence corresponding to the meaning of the child intended (or the meaning the mother thought the child intended). Slobin (1968) investigated those interchanges where a child in turn responded to his mother's expansions. The child in the last example might have replied to her mother: *Eve have lunch*, i.e. she may herself have partially expanded her own first utterance. Slobin found that in those cases where children did respond themselves to their mothers' expansions, at least 50 per cent of the time they responded with expanded utterances. What is more, children's responses in such interchanges were often grammatically more advanced than their free speech. Parental expansions considerably help the child's acquisition of syntax (Nelson, Carskaddon and Bonvillian, 1973). Together with various question-and-answer sequences they may be particularly helpful in leading children to their first two-word sentences (Greenfield and Smith, 1976).

Parents use other techniques in their verbal interaction with their children. They often ask questions which they themselves answer, e.g. *What's this then? It's your teddy bear!* At other times they use repetitive conversation techniques in order to teach children how to converse:

Mother: *How was school today? Did you go to assembly?*
Child: *Yes.*
Mother: *Did the preschoolers go to assembly?*
Child: *Yes.*
Mother: *Did you stay for the whole assembly or just part of it?*

[Gleason, 1973]

Most important of all, parents often demonstrate what they mean by the use of gestures and actions. A mother may repeat *Stroke your dolly's hair* several times and finally demonstrate what the action is herself.

No one type of parental behaviour can at the moment be said to have the greatest influence on language development. However, it seems of paramount importance that parents talk to their children as much as possible. If at the same time they also endeavour to make themselves understood, they will probably be forced to structure their speech to their children's advantage and to accompany their speech with gesture and action.

3.9 *Discourse, conversation, and register*

The study of the sociolinguistic development of child language has only really begun over the last few years but seems likely to be one of the major growth-points in the immediate future. It divides conveniently into a syntagmatic and a paradigmatic dimension. The syntagmatic dimension is concerned with the links between the various consecutive utterances of one child ('discourse') and the links between two or more speakers ('dialogue' and 'conversation'). The paradigmatic dimension is concerned with the way in which children vary their speech to take account of particular situations and particular listeners ('style' and 'register'). We are here of course concerned with wider characteristics of language (as we were in 3.8) rather than grammar alone.

3.9.1 *Discourse and conversation*

Under this section there is very little to say about the development of discourse: indeed, the study of discourse in the adult language is only just beginning. A brief comment on two of the most important types of discourse connectors—intonation and sentence adverbials—can, however, be made. Even at the two-word stage (see 2.10 and 3.2 above) children are generally able to place the intonational nucleus (or main accent) systematically at different points in their sentences. At this stage, however, such nucleus placement seems closely tied up with the syntax of their sentences. But at a slightly later stage of development they learn to use the location of the nucleus to mark new information (or, conversely, to make least prominent those words and phrases which are taken as given or which represent known shared information between speaker and listener). Here is one example from Halliday's (1975) Nigel, aged about one-and-a-half, taking to his father: *Goat try eat 'lid ... Man said 'no ... Goat 'shouldn't eat lid*. Nigel puts the main accent or nucleus in the last utterance on *shouldn't*, indicating that *eat lid* has already been mentioned and that *shouldn't* represents the important and new piece of meaning. At least one discourse link—placement of main accent—is, then, a device used fairly early. But the other type of discourse link mentioned—sentence adverbials—appears to be of much later occurrence. It is true that some such adverbials (e.g. *actually*) may occur even in utterances at the two- and three-word stages. But they are generally completely devoid of any meaning and form a category of optional sentence-introducers, picked up simply because of the habitual use of one or two such adverbials by adults talking to them. Conjunctional sentence adverbials (e.g. *incidentally*, *by the way*, *however*, *nevertheless*) are not used with any sort of approximation to their correct meaning until some time between 5;0 and 9;0, and in some cases even later.

Some of the very early interaction between mothers and their children has already been mentioned under 3.8. At the same time as he was learning to move the main accent up and down the sentence, Halliday's (1975) Nigel had learnt various forms of verbal interaction with other speakers. He had learnt to respond to a *wh-* question (e.g. *What are you doing?*); to respond to a command by obeying the instruction and sometimes saying what he was doing as he obeyed; respond to a statement, often repeating it but also continuing the conversation by adding his own contribution; and to initiate dialogue himself, at first only by the use of *What is that?* (Halliday, 1975: 31, 48–51). The ability to converse obviously develops in a rudimentary form very early and grows very quickly. Keenan (1974) and Keenan and Klein (1975), studying a pair of twins around three years old, noted that there is a general strategy for children's conversations: focus on the formal structure of a previous utterance and modify it (using the same lexical items) in your subsequent utterance. Such focusing takes several forms (Keenan, 1974: 177–9). The basic 'focus function' involves repetition of a constituent (e.g the twins are looking at letters in a book and one says *That 'A, 'B, that 'A,* to which the other replies *'A*). More complex 'focus functions' involve 'focus +

prosodic shift' (e.g. ˌ*Flower* as a reply to '*Flower broken*); 'focus + constituent expansion' (e.g. a reply of *Many many flowers broken* in reply to *Flower broken*); and 'focus + constituent embedding' (e.g. *I got big one* in reply to *Big one*). There is in addition a 'substitution function', exemplified by a reply of *Many moths* to *Two moths*. On some occasions one of Keenan's twins did not make an appropriate reply, in which case the speaker would keep repeating his original utterance until he did get a reply; the listener was made to attend to the speaker's utterance. In other words, egocentric behaviour was not tolerated. These conversational links between the children applied not only to meaningful speech but also to sound-play, which accounted for about a third of all utterances at 2;9 but which had virtually disappeared by 3;0. Thus sequences like the following were common:

—[ʃa] [batʃ]
—[batʃi] [bi ːtʃi] [ba ːdi] [bi ːdi] [babi]
—[ba ːdi]

It is obvious that by the age of 3;0 conversational competence is at least as well developed as other areas of language.

3.9.2   *Register*

The terms 'style' and 'register' are inconsistently used in the literature; the term 'register' is used here to cover all variations in the type of language used in response to different listeners and different situations. The earliest type of variation, pointed out by Gleason (1973), is simply that between talk and silence; children at the age of one and two may talk to their immediate family but be silent in front of strangers. A number of other variations have been observed in very young children (i.e. before the age of 3;0), many of them reported by Weeks (1971). Whisper may be used in the presence of someone sleeping, whether it is an adult taking a nap or a baby doll asleep in her cot. A loud voice may be used for correcting adults' misunderstanding, whereas a soft voice may be used for practising difficult words. A high pitch may be used when complaining or a wide voice range when story-telling.

All these registers may be necessary with any category of listener, but by the age of four many children appear to have developed clearly different registers for different sorts of listener. The most formal register is used to strangers; it obviously replaces the silence mentioned above. Thus a child uses the formality of *Thank you for having me* after visiting one of his friends' home. According to Henzl (1975), Czech children at 4;0 differentiate between the literary and colloquial registers of their language. The next most formal register is that which children use to their parents, whereas they use identifiably different and less formal registers to their peers and to babies. Their speech to their peers will abound in various sound-effects, chants, rhymes, commercials, and mimicry (this, of course, goes on well into the teens, even; see Opie and Opie, 1959). When talking to babies, children of age 4;0 use more endearments, more listeners' names, more imperatives, shorter sentences and fewer complex constructions (Sachs and Devin, 1976; Shatz and Gelman, 1973). In other words, such children's talk to babies is very like that of mothers to babies (see 3.8 above).

4 Lexis

This chapter considers the development of words and their meanings. Firstly it describes the growth in the size of children's vocabulary and some of the words which they are likely to use in the very early stages of language learning. Then follows discussion of how referential meanings are acquired and how groups of words in certain 'semantic fields' gradually become differentiated from one another. The reader may like to refer to the glossary for a discussion of the terms *reference*, *sense*, and *semantic feature* and of the difficulties in defining a *word*.

4.1 Vocabulary development

As with mean length of utterance (3.3.1 above), figures and estimates of the extent of children's vocabulary must be viewed as giving only a very gross idea of development. The difficulty of segmenting presents the same problem in counting words as it does in measuring sentence length (e.g. is *thank you* to be counted as one or two words, in the absence of *thank* and *you* in any other sentence?); in addition there is the problem of multiple meaning: are we to consider *light* in *Light the fire* and *light* in *Put the light on* as one word or two? (for further discussion of this problem, see under *word* in the glossary.) However, a gross estimate of vocabulary (based on naturalistic productive use) has been given as around 100–200 at eighteen months and around 500 at two years (Watts, 1944). At later ages it becomes difficult to measure a child's productive vocabulary by any naturalistic method, and sampling methods have therefore been used instead. Such sampling methods usually involve taking a standard dictionary or list (e.g. Thorndike and Lorge, 1944) and, by random sampling, determining the proportion of known to unknown words (see Seashore and Eckerson, 1940). The sampling usually consists in using pictures and instructions to see if the words chosen at random can be elicited from a child. There is considerable difficulty in constructing such tests in an unambiguous way. The results of some random samples are summarised in Watts (1944) and McCarthy (1954). From these it is estimated that the average child at the age of five has a productive vocabulary of at least 2,000 words and that by the age of seven that number has probably doubled. It must be remembered, of course, that the passive vocabulary of children is likely to be very much higher.

4.2   *Which words are learnt*

Usually the classes of objects first named are: items of food, parts of the body, small household and garden objects, articles of clothing, vehicles, animals, toys and things seen in pictures. Brown (1958a) discussed the words which children use to name such things. He suggested that the most usual names are not necessarily either more general or more specific: thus *car* and *fish* are likely to be used by children before *Ford* and *cod*; but *penny* or *dime* before *coin*. Nor are the most usual names necessarily the shortest: *pineapple* will be used before *fruit*. Children's names simply reflect the names most commonly given to things by adults in their conversations with children. The names which are most common are those which differentiate things just sufficiently for the most common circumstances in which they are used. We are often choosing between different fruit at mealtimes but rarely between different fish; we need to distinguish between tables and chairs for obvious reasons, so we reserve *furniture* for rather special circumstances. Children's vocabulary therefore reflects frequency in adult usage; at least, frequency in those sorts of situations and discussions which are shared with children. Such vocabulary may sometimes appear rather general (*car* and *fish*), sometimes rather specific (*apple* and *penny*); however, the fact that children's vocabulary reflects adults' does not mean that they use the words in their vocabulary with the same meanings as adults. *Apples* may at one time include oranges and *pennies* may include all coins. The development of vocabulary must not be taken to reflect semantic and cognitive development; almost all children's words will at one time or another mean something different from the meaning of the same adult word.

4.3   How word-meanings are learnt

The earliest word-meanings are learnt from non-linguistic experience. A child may learn the meaning of *flower* as something of a size to be displayed in vases, which is brightly coloured and/or which smells. It must be emphasised that this meaning will not be exactly similar to the adult meaning of *flower*. He might include as *flowers* brightly coloured leaves taken from certain trees and used decoratively indoors. Children learn their first word-meanings by attending to gross physical qualities of size, colour, and perhaps shape; and to the patterns of activity and usage associated with certain objects. It is likely that children are soon able to learn the meanings of words by making use of information obtained by linguistic induction. By knowing the meanings of surrounding words children are able to guess something about the meaning of a new word. Kol'tsova (reported in Slobin, 1966c, d) reported that children as young as 1;8 learnt the meaning of the Russian word for 'doll' more successfully if the word was presented in sentences which gave clues of this kind. Children who learnt the word in sentences like *Here is the doll*, *Give me the doll* afterwards associated only the actual doll used in the experiment with the word for 'doll', whereas those who learnt the word in sentences like *Rock the doll* and *Feed the doll* were able to generalise the word to refer to other dolls.

Children are probably not able to learn word-meanings deductively (i.e. by being given a verbal explanation) until the early school years. This seems to be due to two factors: (i) children's stock of word-meanings is not sufficient before this time to make explanation by definition and synonym possible; and (ii) it is often not until the early school years that children begin to view language as something which can be divorced from actual usage for the purpose of discussion (cf. 6.1 below). This awareness may, however, begin earlier in those families where language is talked about. So a four-year-old, stretched out on the floor, trying to extricate his toy car from under the settee, enquired: *When I'm lying down, do I say I'm not long enough, or I'm not tall enough?*

4.4   Generalisation and differentiation

Whether children's word-meanings develop from the specific to the general or from the general to the specific has been a question of perennial interest to psychologists, reflecting as it does a similar question about the way children's general sensory perception develops. McNeill (1970) has recently restated the problem in semantic feature terms: 'horizontal development' means that a child at first has an entry in his mental 'dictionary' which is not complete in terms of semantic features. The entry for *flower* may lack the specification of some features which distinguishes it from certain types of leaf; horizontal development will consist in adding more and more precise specifications to vocabulary items. If the child's semantic development is mainly of this kind, overgeneralisation of meaning is to be expected, e.g. *garden* might at one stage refer to all open-air spaces where a child can play. 'Vertical development', on the other hand, suggests that new words enter a child's dictionary complete with all the adult semantic features (i.e. having the same meaning as the adult word), and that development consists in realising that different words share the same semantic features. This type of development predicts in its extreme form that vocabulary development will proceed from more specific words to more general words; such development as we have seen in 4.2 above does not usually occur in the early stages. Vertical development may, however, be relevant at a much later stage (i.e. after the age of eleven or so) when the capacity for abstract and logical thought is developing.

Children typically go through four stages in the development of word-meanings:

(i) The very first meanings are learnt with regard to just one object or one narrowly defined situation (cf. item-learning in grammar, 3.1.3 above). A child learns *bird* as the name of one particular toy object that he possesses; or learns to say *Get down*, referring to his being allowed out of his high chair; or *shoes* is limited to a particular pair of shoes in mummy's closet (Reich, 1976). *Dog* (or *goggy*) may at this stage be just the dog in the house.

(ii) Children next go through a somewhat longer period of overgeneralisation (from approximately 1;0 to 2;6). The very first overgeneralisations are of a loose, experiential type, e.g. Bloom (1973) quotes Guillaume (1927): a French child used *nénin*, 'breast', when asking for the breast, when asking for a biscuit, and to point to a red button, an eye in a picture, and mother's face in a photograph. But overgeneralisations soon become more clearly perceptual. So *goggy* now refers to all four-legged animals, including horses and cows. E. V. Clark (1973) studied such perceptual overgeneralisations in some detail and found that the main perceptual features which form the basis for overgeneralisation are movement, shape, sound, taste, and texture. In this period *daddy* refers to all men, on the basis of some characteristic like wearing trousers, or having big feet (both to do with shape), or speaking with a low voice (sound). Some overgeneralisations at this stage may also be functional (Nelson, 1974), e.g. a child calls a soup bowl a cup, since it holds a drinkable liquid (but even this might be in part a perceptual identification). Such overgeneralisations do not occur in comprehension (Huttenlocher, 1974); this suggests that children overgeneralise in production because of their limited vocabulary.

The relationship between the various overgeneralised meanings which a child uses for one word is sometimes not at all a simple one. It may sometimes be the case that all the meanings share one or more semantic features (as when *daddy*s always have big feet) but often this is not so. The famous example of this is the one quoted by Vygotsky (1962): a child used [kwa] to mean 'duck'; then the 'pond' on which the duck floated; then for 'milk', another liquid. He also used [kwa] to refer to a coin which had a picture of an eagle on it; then to refer to any coin; and lastly to a teddy bear's eye, which looks like a coin. The associations between these meanings are sometimes loosely experiential ('duck'–'pond'), and sometimes share perceptual features ('duck'—'eagle'). Two meanings may share certain perceptual features while two other meanings share totally different perceptual features (cf. 'duck'—'eagle' with 'pond'—'milk'). This sort of relationship where a meaning is linked with at least one other meaning but where all the meanings do not share a common feature is sometimes called 'chaining'. Of course it is not unique to child language but is commonly seen in the relationship between the various meanings of a word in the adult language (see discussion under *semantic feature* in the glossary).

Another problem common in the adult language but even more difficult to deal with in child language concerns metaphor. Is a child aged 2;0 who describes the shape made by his father's knee under the bedclothes as a *mountain* just overgeneralising or, as seems more likely, making a deliberate, playful, metaphor?

(iii) Gradually usage of overgeneralised words becomes more

limited and approximates to adult usage. This process generally takes place as other words are added in the same semantic field. So in stage (ii) above *goggy* referred to all four-legged animals, including cats and horses. As the words *cat* and *horse* are added to the vocabulary *goggy* becomes more limited in its meaning. *Goggy* remains the dustbin word which is applied to all four-legged things except those which have acquired their own label. Similarly *car* might be used as the dustbin word for all (four-) wheeled vehicles, and as the words *tractor* and *bus* are added to the vocabulary the meanings of *car* become more limited.

(iv) At a much later age (Anglin, 1970, suggests that it begins between five and seven—cf. the syntagmatic–paradigmatic shift, 6.2 below—but continues up to seventeen or eighteen) children learn features which group more specific things together, e.g. the child learns the feature 'animate' as referring to a class of these more specific things (and he may for the first time use the word *animal* on occasions when he needs to refer to all animals). The difference between the overgeneralisations of stage (ii) and the generalisations at stage (iv) is between generalisation based on a failure to distinguish between objects that are perceptually similar; and generalisation which learns to treat objects which are perceptually similar as having certain features in common. Brown (1958b) calls this the difference between 'abstraction before differentiation' and 'abstraction after differentiation'.

Stage (iv) obviously relates to an increased ability to categorise and classify the world in general. While Anglin (1970) shows clearly that such development is generally from more specific to more general concepts, there must of course continue to be at least some learning of more specific items. Boys continue to add to the list of cars they can name and most children will learn the names of at least some individual flowers.

4.5 *Relational meanings*

4.5.1 *Dimensional adjectives*

Discussion in the previous sections has centred on the development of the correct referential meaning of individual words. Some areas of lexical development are amenable to a more obviously structural analysis, i.e. how meanings of related words develop relative to one another (see the discussion of the terms *sense* and *reference* in the glossary). Dimensional adjectives like *long* and *short*, *deep* and *shallow* form one such area.

E. V. Clark (1973) has used results from experiments in the area of dimensional adjectives and temporal sequencers like *before* and *after* to formulate her Semantic Feature Hypothesis. According to this hypothesis children assemble the adult meanings of words by adding semantic features (cf. McNeill's horizontal development above); the addition of such features occurs in order from most general to most specific. It is predicted from the hypothesis that children will acquire the distinction between *big* and *little* before the distinction between *long* and *short* because bigness can relate to any of three dimensions or to any combination of the three, whereas length refers to only one dimension, i.e. the most extended one. Similarly it is also predicted that the distinction between *wide* and *narrow* will occur later than that between *long* and *short* because width refers to the second most extended dimension. Such an order of development has been confirmed by Eilers *et al*. (1974).

The distinction within each of the pairs *big–little*, *long–short*, *wide–narrow* (and many others), is somewhat more complicated than it might at first glance appear. Each pair represents a pair of polar opposites. *Big*, *long* and *wide* are called positives, *little*, *short*, *narrow* negatives, since *big*, *long*, and *wide* obviously indicate more of the particular dimension being measured. But *big*, *long* and *wide* are also the unmarked members of the pairs, since such adjectives sometime indicate only the dimension we must pay attention to and make no statement about the relative extent of that dimension (this is sometimes called the 'nominal' meaning). *This river is one hundred yards wide* is not in any way a comparison with a narrow river; we cannot, for example, say *This river is two yards narrow*. *Big*, *long*, *wide*, *deep*, *high* are both the unmarked and the positive members of their respective pairs. *Long* means both (i) 'referring to the dimension of length' and (ii) 'longer than average', whereas *short* has only a meaning 'shorter than average'.

The Semantic Feature Hypothesis suggests an order of acquisition based on this linguistic analysis. The nominal meaning referring only to the dimension will be acquired first, e.g. the first meaning of *long* above. At this stage *short* and *long* (and *shorter* and *longer*, see next section) will be synonyms for the child, both with the meaning which refers only to the dimension being measured. H. H. Clark (1970) quotes an example from Donaldson (1963) in which a child was asked how he knew that Tom was four and replied, 'Because it says that Tom is four years younger than Dick.' Evidently 'four years younger' = 'four years young' = 'four years old'. At the second stage of development the meaning 'longer than average' appears, *long* and *short* still, however, remaining synonyms, both now having the possibility of this second meaning as well as the first unmarked one. It is suggested that the meaning 'longer than average' is learnt before 'shorter than average' because the positive end of such pairs is more perceptually salient. In the third and last stage of development the correct distinction is made between a pair of polar adjectives.

The sequence of development predicted by the Semantic Feature Hypothesis has only partly been confirmed by evidence from experiments and from naturalistic data. More general dimensions before more limited dimensions (i.e. *long/short* before *wide/narrow*) may be one factor influencing the order of acquisition, but there are certainly other factors. The most important of these is frequency in the language to which the children are exposed. If a child is exposed reasonably frequently to all the dimensional adjectives we have mentioned, then the Semantic Feature Hypothesis may predict the order of understanding and usage. However, particularly in the early stages of language learning, some adjectives may be used a great deal by parents and some not used at all. Some adjectives occur very commonly in adult–child interactions because of their relevance to the child's activities. One child known to the author certainly learnt the *wide–narrow* dimension before the *long–short* dimension because he was constantly pushing objects through gaps and needed to be told and to understand that some gaps were too *narrow*, and some objects were too *wide*. Additionally, some adjectives may be more restricted in their meanings in talk by parents to children than in more general adult usage, and this may affect children's learning. *Big*, for example, may be equated with *tall* (e.g. Lumsden and Poteat, 1968; Maratsos, 1973).

Nor has there been any real confirmation that children learn first the type of meaning which refers to the relevant dimension (the so-called 'nominal' meaning). Indeed, it is difficult to see how many sentences could be given such a meaning at all, e.g. *That's a big one* or *It's too narrow*. It might, however, be relevant to some areas of semantic development not so far mentioned: one child used *green* to refer to all colours, i.e. when he wished to refer to the colour of something (Cruse, 1977).

All experiments have found confusions between the various pairs. Wales and Campbell (1970) certainly found that negative adjectives (e.g. *thin, low, short*) were first learnt as synonyms for positive adjectives (e.g. *thick, high, tall*), but it is not clear from the experiment whether the meaning involved was of the nominal or the positive kind. Eilers *et al.* (1974), studying only children's understanding of the positive and negative meanings, found confusion in both directions. Brewer and Stone (1975) and Bartlett (1976) found more confusion between unmarked spatial adjectives of different dimensions than between the marked and unmarked members of one dimension, e.g. confusion between *long/wide* was more common than confusion between *long/short*. This, of course, might be expected if the distinctions between the two dimensions had not yet been learnt. It remains very likely that most children do at some stage use an adjective to indicate both ends of one particular dimension, e.g. *hot* may be used to mean both 'hot' and 'cold'. The Semantic Feature Hypothesis is a useful framework for studying the acquisition of meaning in certain semantic fields, but its predictions will undoubtedly be interfered with by other factors.

4.5.2   *Comparisons and quantifiers*

In the early stages comparatives, e.g. *shorter* and *longer*, may simply be understood as synonyms for *short* and *long*, which in turn, as we have seen in the previous section, may be synonyms themselves. *Shorter* and *longer* are next assumed to be equivalent to *shortest* and *longest* when one member of a class of objects is being singled out (Wales and Campbell, 1970, whose classes were generally made up of four or more objects). Last to be learnt is the explicit comparison of two objects as in *This pencil is longer than that one*. Of course, in all except very formal styles of the adult language, comparatives are virtually limited to this usage with *than*. Even in comparing only two items, we are likely to say *This pencil is the longest*.

The development of adjectival *less* and *more* may be essentially similar to that for polar adjectives. At first both appear to mean simply 'some'. Next both refer to the positive adjective *more*. (This applies for some children up to the age of 7;0.) At this stage a child who is asked *Which tree has more apples?* and *Which tree has less apples?* points in both cases to the tree with more apples on (Donaldson and Balfour, 1968; and Palermo, 1973). Lastly he learns to attend to both objects at the same time and compare the two. Donaldson and Balfour (1968) find similarly that at one stage *different* = 'same', although there are so many varying uses of the words *same* and *different* that it is difficult to state a simple order of development.

Donaldson and McGarrigle (1974), studying *more* and *all* in particular, suggest that while children's lexical meanings may be more general than adults' (as with *less* and *more* above), their syntactic rules may also be less precise (thus *All the cars are in their garages* may be understood as 'all the garages have cars in them', i.e. the scope of the quantifier *all* may be uncertain for children); while lexical meanings and syntactic rules are vaguer, children have on the other hand a set of what are called 'local rules' which determine meaning in any context. These 'local rules' are of a pragmatic operational sort and determine what children will pay most attention to if they are uncertain about the linguistic meaning. In the example for *all* given above, it may be that children have a local rule which says fullness takes precedence over number; thus the sentence *All the cars are in their garages* may be understood to apply correctly to a situation where all the garages are full but one car remains without a garage.

4.5.3 *Temporal relations*

E. V. Clark (1971) has charted the course of development of the conjunctions *before* and *after* between the ages of three and five. The order of occurrence of events described in clauses linked by *before* and *after* is at first understood purely in terms of the order of the clauses. Thus the following four sentences:

   (i) *He jumped the gate, before he patted the dog.*
  (ii) *Before he patted the dog, he jumped the gate.*
 (iii) *He jumped the gate, after he patted the dog.*
 (iv) *After he patted the dog, he jumped the gate.*

are all understood as indicating that the action in the first clause precedes the action in the second. In other words *before* and *after*, in so far as they have any meaning at all, are synonymous. In stage two *before* is interpreted correctly but *after* is not. *After* at this stage either continues subservient to the order of the clauses or becomes a synonym for *before*. In stage three children correctly interpret clauses linked by *before* and *after*. The stages of development are obviously similar to those for polar adjectives and support the Semantic Feature Hypothesis. At first *before* and *after* are learnt as time adverbs, perhaps indicating non-simultaneity compared with *when*, which indicates simultaneity. Then the feature [+ prior] is acquired and *before* and *after* acquire a new but still synonymous meaning. Lastly *after* acquires the meaning [− prior]. However, E. V. Clark's suggested sequence of development has not been completely confirmed by later experiments. For example, Barrie-Blackley (1973) and Coker (1975), while confirming that such sequences were often interpreted simply in terms of their order, found children making more mistakes with *before* than with *after*. Some children appear to fix on [+ prior] as Clark suggests, but others may fix on the other end of the scale. After all, it is not in this case easy to say which conjunction constitutes the positive end of the scale. It has also been suggested that some children may adopt an alternative strategy which leads them to attend to the information in the main clause before the information in the subordinate clause (Amidon and Carey, 1972). When given commands linked by *before* or *after*, e.g. *Move a blue plane before you move a red plane*, many children often do not carry out the instruction in the subordinate clause at all. Which of the two strategies most children adopt (the order-of-mention strategy or the main-clause strategy) remains for the moment a point of dispute.

Barrie-Blackley (1973) also noted that children at the age of six still did not fully understand the meaning of clauses introduced by *until*, e.g. 'Mummy lies down until Daddy comes inside'; 'Mummy doesn't come in until Daddy comes in'. A high proportion of children simply understood *until* in such sentences to mean 'and' or 'and then'.

Conflation of meaning also occurs with items like *always*, *sometimes*, and *never* (Kuczaj II, 1975). At first all three are understood either as simple negatives or simple positives (but the correct term is always present, e.g. *always* is not given the meaning 'never' unless *never* is present in the child's speech with the same meaning). At the next stage *never* is used as a simple negative, while *always* and *sometimes* are simple positives (and *usually* may be used as another simple positive). And at a later stage *sometimes* (and *usually*) will acquire separate meanings.

4.5.4 *Spatial relations*

Goodglass, Gleason and Hyde (1970) report that children learn to make the distinction between *on* and *under* before the distinction between *in front of* and *in back of* (American English = British English *behind*) which in turn occurs before the *left/right* distinction. *Up* and *down* are also among the first words with spatial meanings to be used and, as with all the relational terms which have been discussed, there may be a period when one or both words are used with both meanings, e.g. *down* may be used to mean both 'up' and 'down'. H. H. Clark (1973) postulated that in terms of the Semantic Feature Hypothesis not only would *front/back* precede *side* but *front* would precede *back* because *front* is the positive term, i.e. the face of an object which we identify first is the front; the *back* is then identified as the opposite of the *front*; and the *sides* are the faces remaining after this. The acquisition of *front* before *back* has not been confirmed in an experiment by Kuczaj II and Maratsos (1975), who found usage of the two terms arising more or less simultaneously. But they did confirm that the learning of *side* came later. Two other interesting developments are clear from this and other experiments; (i) children appear to learn the terms *front, back,* and *side* (and *left* and *right* as well) and the prepositional phrases *in front of, in back of,* and *on the side of,* firstly in relationship to their own body; (ii) 'intrinsic' uses of the terms are learnt before 'extrinsic' uses. Some things like cookers, cars, and horses have intrinsic fronts obvious either from their shape or the way they move; other things like drinking glasses, sugar lumps, and balls, have no such intrinsic front. If we use the phrases 'in front of', 'behind' and 'to the side of' with reference to such things, the meaning is generally interpreted in terms of that part which faces the speaker (or, occasionally, the listener). As might be expected, this use of *front, back* and *side* to refer to things without an intrinsic front develops later. Most children appear to have understanding and command of both types of use by the age of five. *Left* and *right* take very much longer to master. As mentioned above, they are first learnt with reference to the child's own body. It is not until after the age of nine, however, that most children master the left and right of another person's body or non-intrinsic lefts and rights like those of a road, which of course depend on the direction you are going (Parry, 1976).

5 Some Theories

Some mention has already been made of theories in various relevant sections. The operant conditioning theory of the development from babbling to the first words was mentioned in 1.2.1 above. Some theories concerning phonological development were mentioned in 2.9.1 and 2.9.2. The Semantic Feature Hypothesis was described in some detail in 4.5.1 above. This chapter considers some more general theories of language development: most of these theories take the acquisition of grammar as the central fact to be explained.

5.1 Preliminaries

Some of the general factors affecting the sequence of development have also been mentioned, in 3.5 and elsewhere. Cognitive development (see 5.4 below) is assumed to be a prerequisite for language development, e.g. the developmental sequence: space adverbials (e.g. *over there*, *on the ceiling*) before time adverbials (e.g. *yesterday*) before manner adverbials (e.g. *carefully*) probably reflects cognitive development. Linguisitc complexity is also a factor in the order and rate of development; this factor often affects not just the expression of a particular meaning in some form or another but the correct expression of the meaning. Where one meaning is encoded by one form, learning is easier than where meaning is encoded by many forms, e.g. the plural in English, which is encoded by three phonetically conditioned allomorphs /-s/, /-z/, and /-iz/ (with only a few exceptions), is learnt earlier than the plural in Arabic, where there is greater variety in the way plurals are formed (3.4 above). Frequency in the adult language is perhaps the factor whose influence on development is most difficult to quantify. Brown (1973) found that it has little influence on the order of acquisition of English inflections. But English inflections are in general all relatively frequent; it appears that it is only gross differences in adult frequency which are reflected in children's learning. For example, an auxiliary verb like *can* will be acquired before one like *need*. Lastly, perceptual prominence may also affect the order of acquisition and the approach to correct acquisition. Object pronouns may often be used in place of subject pronouns in English because they often occupy a perceptually prominent position at the ends of utterances (3.3.3 above).

Implicit in some previous sections has been the idea that there is some pressure on children to improve their language, to make their speech closer to that of the adults around them. Brown, Cazden and Bellugi (1969) and Brown and Hanlon (1970) have shown that parents' correction of children's ungrammatical sentences does not play a part in children's linguistic development. However, as Brown (1973) points out, the assumption that parental corrections might play such a role is too narrow on two counts. Firstly, it is the pressure to be more correctly and easily understood rather than the pressure to be grammatically correct which is likely to force a child to improve. Secondly, after the first year or so of talking, it is likely to be the pressure to communicate with people outside the immediate family which has most influence. Luria and Yudovitch (1971), for example, describe a case of twins whose language improved rapidly when they were separated and put into two different nursery classes.

These various factors in language learning are given a differing prominence in the different language acquisition theories which have been expounded. But such theories have often taken little account of the various experiments and data which have been published. The gulf between theory and practice in the study of language development has often been excessively wide. In this chapter we will outline some of the most influential theories and attempt a brief evaluation of them in terms of the details of development outlined in previous chapters. We divide the theories into four types: behaviourist, innatist, cognitive, and sociological (although of course such a division is bound to be something of an oversimplification).

5.2 *Behaviourist theories*

A behaviourist theory stresses the influence of the environment in the learning of language as opposed to any innate abilities a child himself brings to the task. In its extreme form it might deny that a child brings any such abilities to the task at all or, slightly less extremely, deny that we could ever know anything about such abilities even if they do exist. Although J. B. Watson is generally regarded as the originator of behaviourism, the cornerstone of behaviourist theory has been the theory of 'classical conditioning' (Pavlov, 1927). In the original experiment it was shown that dogs, who normally salivate at the sight of meat, can be made to salivate when they hear a tuning fork; in ordinary language, the dogs have been taught, or have learnt, to salivate when hearing the tuning fork. Classical conditioning can (according to some behaviourists) be made to account for some comprehension of language in humans. When a child does something wrong, he is punished and at the same time mother says *Naughty!* An association is built up between punishment and the word *naughty*, and the meaning of the word is learnt. Thus the main thrust from classical conditioning has been that language represents a 'second signal system' and that the acquisition of meanings consists in a process of pairing first and second signals (referents and words) to build up associative links.

Skinner (1938) developed a new concept of 'operant conditioning'. In this type of situation the original behaviour, instead of being an automatic reflex (like the salivation, which is an automatic response to the meat), is behaviour which at first occurs by chance but, because of the effect it has when it does occur, is likely to be repeated. Thus Skinner had rats in a cage who happened by chance to press a bar, which had the effect of giving the rats a food pellet. Rats soon learnt to deliberately press the bar. Operant conditioning can be made to account for production of human language. A child says [dada] in his babbling, daddy smiles and shows his approval (perhaps with a Smartie—the 'reward') and the child will say [dada] again. Thus the child may learn to say [dada] when daddy is around. By a process of (in this case false) 'stimulus generalisation' the child may start to use [dada] to all men, but the varying response he gets from them will teach him 'stimulus discrimination' whereby he learns to limit the expression simply to his own daddy.

So far we have dealt with the typical behaviourist approach to learning in general and attempted to show how it can be made to apply to verbal learning. But Skinner (1957) has made a more detailed attempt to explain verbal learning in terms of conditioning theory. Such an elaborate system of terminology and definition is constructed by Skinner in this book (much of its seemingly remote from actual language) that we can only summarise a few of the notions which are presented. Utterances are called 'verbal operants', and a 'functional typology' of such operants is set up which consists of four types:

(i) The *mand* (which seems to include commands and questions). this is a 'class of operant behaviours which are conditioned to the deprivation states of the individual' (and presumably rewarded by the fulfilment of the demand).

(ii) The *tact* (apparently declarative sentences), 'an operant which is conditioned to some feature of the environment and which is rewarded by social approval of some sort'.

(iii) The *autoclitic* (this seems to include grammatical notions like concord). The terms seems intended to suggest behaviour which is based upon (or 'conditioned to') other verbal behaviour.

(iv) The *intraverbal*. Another (minor) 'class of utterances which are conditioned to other verbal stimuli', but this time accounting for things like free association and alliteration.

The last two types are presumably rewarded by social approval and by the basic pleasure of verbalisation, which Skinner invokes as a reward when nothing more specific can be found.

The four types of utterance seem to be a linguistic ragbag. They are of unequal importance and refer to diverse aspects of language. While mands and tacts, if they are understood to be something like commands and statements, appear to represent the two sentence functions which occur first in child language (cf. Halliday's (1975) 'pragmatic' and 'mathetic'—see 3.2.4 above), the autoclitic has somehow to account for the whole of grammar within sentences, while the intraverbal seems irrelevant to any common use of language. All sorts of technical apparatus have to be invented to account for special situations, e.g. 'magical mands', which are mands that are not fulfilled. Such technical apparatus gives a misleading facade of scientific rigour. 'Verbal behaviour is equated with rat behaviour by virtue of the fact that the same words are used to describe both' (Chomsky, 1959).

Behaviourist approaches to language learning (of which, as we have said, Skinner represents the extreme) generally place great emphasis on the role of parental and social approval. How far such approval does play a part has already been discussed in the introduction to this chapter: parental pressures towards correct syntax are generally not very successful even when they occur

(Brown, Cazden and Belligi, 1969). But more general approval of successful communication of meaning may play a part. In the first year or so of language learning this may be parental approval (e.g. in the development of the first words from babbling), but later on it is more likely to be the approval of people outside the family circle. Even if such approval (or listener reaction) does play some part in the development of language, the terminological apparatus of conditioning theory does not seem to bring any additional illumination to how such interaction takes place.

5.2.1 *Contextual generalisation*

While social approval plays a large part in behaviourist theories of language learning, Skinner (1957) made some appeal to the notion that some parts of an utterance were conditioned to (i.e. automatically linked with) other parts. Braine (1963a, 1965) developed this notion further in his theory of 'contextual generalisation'. Braine attempts to explain the learning of grammar as dependent on two mechanisms. Firstly the location of units is learnt (i.e. word or morpheme order). More specifically, this ordering of units is learnt as applying on two levels. Within sentences it is learnt that a certain type of phrase commonly precedes another type of phrase (this is 'stimulus generalisation' because we are dealing with types of phrases and not just individual phrases); and then within phrases, it is learnt that one type of morpheme commonly precedes another type. Secondly, individual links are established between closed-class morphemes; thus *is* before a verb has an individual link with *-ing* following the verb. The links between morphemes vary in strength (i.e. they vary in the extent to which one predicts the occurrence of the other) according to the frequency of occurrence of the pair. Thus the whole theory is given a probabilistic base, i.e. it is basically a theory of how likely certain morphemes and phrases are to be followed by other words and phrases.

Various objections to this theory were put forward by Bever, Fodor and Weksel (1965a, 1965b), who asked such questions as: how does the child learn to segment utterances into morphemes and phrases? how does the child deal with different functional sentence-types like statement and question, which have different word-orders? and how does the child realise that the same order of words may represent two different structures with different meanings, e.g. *Flying aeroplanes can be dangerous*? This last query is one example of the main objection to the theory of contextual generalisation (as it is also the main objection to most behaviourist, as well as many innatist, theories), namely, that it takes no account of meaning. While contextual generalisation does incorporate structure to a limited extent (which Skinner did not), it takes no account of meaning nor does it consider situation (the physical as opposed to the verbal environment) as a factor in language learning.

5.3   *Innatist theories*

The basic position of Chomsky (1968) is that it is ridiculous to think of children as coming to language with a blank mind and then being 'conditioned' to it; there must be a very considerable innate disposition to language. Chomsky argues his innateness hypothesis on basically three counts: firstly, the existence of language universals. It is argued that the similarity in languages cannot possibly be due to anything other than a specific cognitive capacity in man. The universals of language to which Chomsky refers are of two types. Formal universals refer to the way language works, e.g. operations on sentences are structure-dependent. For example, to transform a statement into a question in English, we invert the subject and verb of the sentence (leaving aside the additional factor concerning the use of an auxiliary verb): *My brother John is a fool* becomes *Is my brother John a fool*? We must know the structure of the sentence to be able to do this; it is not a structure-independent operation like altering the order of the first two words or the last two or repeating all the syllables backwards. The other type of universal is a substantive universal. This type refers to the categories which language uses: for example, the categories noun and verb in syntax. McNeill (1966b) proposed that a child comes to the task of learning language with a language acquisition device (LAD) which has in it, among other things, a notion of a hierarchy of grammatical categories, which first shows itself in the pivot-open distinction. The pivot class splits up into the various classes of function word and the open class into nouns and verbs and, later, adjectives and adverbs. In addition the child has a knowledge of the 'basic grammatical relations' of subject–predicate, verb–object, and modifier–head (this last most often seen in the adjective + noun relationship).

The claim is of course also made that language is unique to man. While such a claim remains in many ways undisputed, nevertheless chimpanzees have recently been taught to use some of the rudiments of language. Washoe (Gardner and Gardner, 1971) has been taught one version of the American sign language (one in which a sign represents something like a word, rather than a sound). Washoe had used (by 1969, when she was four years old) a vocabulary of 85 signs and 294 different two-sign combinations (besides nearly as many combinations of more than two signs), most of which are combinations very like those which children use in their early language learning. Some were combinations which she had invented for herself like *You peekaboo me*. Sarah (Premack, 1971) learnt to associate different coloured and shaped counters with objects like bananas and pencils; with concepts like colour and size; and even with more abstract concepts like *yes/no* questions. She also responded correctly to coordinated instructions with ellipted (or deleted) subject and verb, like *Sarah insert banana pail (and) apple dish*.

It is to be noted that vocal communication was not used with either of the chimpanzees; indeed, the initial assumption of the experimenters was that previous attempts to teach apes human language had made no progress at all because of the limitations of their vocal apparatus. Using a non-vocal medium it has thus been shown that chimpanzees can be taught an elementary language system which has at least some similarities with, and some characteristics of, human language. What has been thrown in question is that man's language learning ability is qualitatively, as opposed to quantitively, different. Thus the linguistic capacity which is supposedly innate in man may be partly innate in other animals as well.

The second count on which Chomsky argues his innateness hypothesis is the fact of language learning at all. He argues that the adult speech which a child hears around him is so poorly structured and impaired in performance (by hesitations, repetitions, false starts and so on) that he could not possibly learn language unless he brought to the task a very specific capacity. In particular a child must be pre-tuned to some of the formal universals (e.g. structure-dependence) by which language operates. However, parental speech to children is, on the contrary, highly structured (see 3.8 above) and it is by no means proven that a child given sufficient examples (and seeing the meaning of such examples in situations) could not extract any of the formal universals mentioned by Chomsky.

The third and last count on which the innateness hypothesis is argued concerns the speed of acquisition of language. Language could not be learnt with the speed it is unless the child were preprogrammed to do so. The objections to this argument are much the same as those mentioned in the preceding paragraph. Parental speech in intuitively structured to provide a set of language-learning lessons (for example, the mean length of utterance of mothers' speech to a child may be about one morpheme longer than the child's own speech). Moreover language is first learnt in situations of immediacy, i.e. it is at first learnt in situations where it refers to something happening more or less at the same time and in the same place as the language is being spoken. The situation acts as a crutch to language learning: the child is often able to guess at the meaning of an adult utterance.

Arguments for innateness which relate to the way children learn language from the parental speech with which they are presented do not therefore carry much weight (other arguments based on maturation may, however, carry more weight—see below 5.3.1). The argument that linguistic universals represent something about the cognitive ability in man is, however, not so easily dismissed. Indeed, there seems no question that children come to the language learning task with some sort of innate equipment. Chomsky (1968) at one point states that it remains an open question whether a specifically linguistic ability is innate or whether language and language learning are reflections of a more general cognitive capacity; nevertheless most of his arguments seem to be implicitly presented in support of a specific linguistic ability. McNeill (1970) is even more committed to a language acquisition device. There is, however, no firm evidence to support the hypothesis of any innate, specifically linguistic, abilities. In the absence of such evidence it seems sensible to adopt the more conservative viewpoint that children must bring only certain general cognitive abilities to the task of learning language: for example, 'the ability to learn certain types of semantic or cognitive categories' (Slobin, 1966a) and the ability to symbolise such categories and the relationships between such categories.

5.3.1 *Maturation*

A rather different viewpoint on the development of language is presented in Lenneberg (1966, 1967). He compares language development with the development of other skills in man (primarily motor skills) and with the development of skills in other animals.

Language development is seen by Lenneberg as being principally due to a process of maturation. Language has the same sort of hallmarks which characterise maturational processes in animals. A sequence of milestones in the development of speech is correlated with age and with the development of other skills. Thus the majority of children begin to use single utterances or words around the age of one year and two-word utterances around the last quarter of the second year. At the one-word stage a child can usually walk a few steps, provided he is holding on to something; at the two-word stage he walks without aid, although stiffly. Language development is not very sensitive to differences of environment. The onset of language is similar in all cultures. Nor does socio-economic class affect the acquisition of the basic ability to use language (although of course it may determine that some styles are mastered better than others and it may also affect the extent of vocabulary). However, children grossly neglected and with virtually no contact with people rapidly develop language appropriate to their age when moved into a situation where they have more contact; thus, given a minimum amount of exposure to language, the amount of practice does not seem crucial. Lenneberg also argues that the development of language cannot be ascribed to the pressure of need. His evidence on this score is not convincing: he says that two-year-old deaf children learn to communicate their needs by gesture and do not have adjustment problems. But certainly many deaf children do have such problems, and autistic children (who generally have problems with language) even more so. Nevertheless Lenneberg's viewpoint on language acquisition does seem a sensible one: language appears to be dependent on a series of maturational states of readiness within the child, with the one proviso that an environment must be present giving a certain minimum level of stimulation. What such a minimum level is remains a matter of conjecture, although it might be assumed that it must at least provide an adult who talks to the child rather than just talking to others while the child is present;

and probably also an adult who in the process of talking to the child intuitively structures his language to the child's understanding.

Typical of a maturational process is a 'critical period' (e.g. Tinbergen, 1951). Provided a type of stimulation occurs during this period, a type of behaviour will be learnt; the behaviour is 'imprinted'. Lorenz (1953) reported that ducklings will learn to follow the first large moving object they see at a certain time after hatching. This is of course usually the mother duck, but by presenting himself at this period Lorenz made ducklings follow him; moreover they remained pathologically attached to humans for the rest of their life.

The question naturally follows as to whether there is a critical period for language learning in humans. Lenneberg (1966) reports that children born with normal hearing but who go deaf before the age of two develop similarly to congenitally deaf children, whereas those who go deaf after two are trained in language much more easily. This suggests a lower limit of around the age of two. But it may be considerably lower than this: Keller (1958), who lost her hearing and sight at the age of 1;7, may well have been helped to her ultimate mastery of language by the speech she had heard before her illness. Several bits of evidence suggest an upper limit of around thirteen. Lenneberg (1966) reports that for 97 per cent of humans the language function is located in the left hemisphere of the brain, and if a child receives an injury to the left hemisphere before the age of thirteen, language is often relearnt using the right hemisphere (similar relearning of other skills has been demonstrated for animals). He also reports that mongoloid children stop developing language around the age of thirteen, even when their language is still only at a rudimentary stage. Studies of 'wolf children' (i.e. children found in a wild state who had previously had little or no human contact) accord with the age of thirteen as an upper limit. Isabelle (Brown, 1958) was discovered at six-and-a-half with no language but was normal by eight-and-a-half; whereas Genie (Curtiss *et al.*, 1974) was discovered at fourteen and thereafter acquired language only very slowly. Her two-word stage lasted five months and, at the last report, she had been forming negative sentences by adding *no* at the beginning of sentences for a period of eighteen months. It is also well known that aptitude for learning a second language markedly diminishes around this age; immigrants to a new country learn to speak a second language like a native if they are under this age, whereas if they are over it they rarely do so (this is particularly true of phonology—Oyama, 1976). There is some support for the notion of a sensitive period in language learning between the ages of two and thirteen. The phrase 'sensitive period' is preferred to 'critical period', since obviously some language learning can and does take place outside the period. The limits of this period are at present in some dispute, however; Krashen (1975) favours a much earlier upper limit, contending that most of Lenneberg's evidence is as consistent with age five as with thirteen, and that the lesser ability at language learning at adolescence may be due solely to emotional factors.

Lenneberg (1966) also discusses the question of language as a specific skill. While milestones in language and speech development are generally correlated with motor development, in certain abnormal cases speech may occur without general motor development (which is generally measured by control of head, fingers and arms). Also language comprehension may develop without speech (Lenneberg, 1962, and see 3.6.1 above). But Lenneberg does not unlock a specific ability for language from other cognitive abilities, which, as we have seen in the previous section, is perhaps a more interesting question.

5.4 *Cognitive theories*

The viewpoint taken in the preceding sections has been that obviously some innate processing ability is brought to bear on all experience, including linguistic experience, and that some of this processing ability may only appear as children mature; but that there is no evidence at all suggesting some specifically linguistic innate equipment. Furth (1966) found that deaf children develop cognitively (as measured by Piagetian conservation tasks—see below) just as hearing children do, although with some retardation. Deaf children also perform comparably with hearing children on many non-verbal tests of intelligence (Reed, 1970). So language does not seem absolutely essential for cognitive growth. On the other hand there are certainly people whose mental ability is so low that they are unable to develop language. Mongoloid children rarely acquire a full use of language. Thus a minimum level of intelligence (which is presumably one factor in cognition) seems necessary for language to develop. The implication is that language is dependent on cognition but the reverse is not true. This perspective has been adopted throughout this book; cognitive development is seen as a prerequisite for grammatical and lexical development in the same way that perceptual and motor development are seen as prerequisites for phonological development.

The child, then, probably brings some innate processing ability to his cognitive growth. But what exactly is this cognition, how do we study it, and how does it develop? Most studies of cognition and cognitive development are useless for comparison with language and language development precisely because cognition is studied through language. The one framework of cognitive growth which has been arrived at least in part independently of language is that of Piaget (see in particular Piaget, 1954, and Piaget and Inhelder, 1969). The Piagetian method of studying development has essentially two variants: firstly a controlled clinical method in which children's ability to handle certain concepts is systematically explored rather as Freud explored his patients' subconsciousness (here obviously language will play a part, although only a part); this method is generally used with younger children. Secondly the measurement of performance on an experimental task such as judging whether water tipped from a wide, short glass into a narrow, tall glass remains the same in volume. Such tasks are generally called conservation tasks, since they are concerned with objects or substances retaining (or 'conserving') their properties even when they appear in a different shape, form, or position; or when they are out of sight. Once children can perform a particular conservation task they are probably able to understand the relevant concept: thus children who successfully perform a task connected with the conservation of volume are able to attend to this concept alone and not confuse it with other concepts like height. Older children (generally over five) are usually tested with such conservation tasks. In the administration of these tests language will play some part, and this has sometimes caused difficulty; but in theory at any rate Piagetian tests are not measuring language development.

In general it is the developmental stages of cognitive growth as seen by Piaget which seem most obviously to relate to language development, although in a few areas a more detailed relationship is apparent (e.g. in the development of spatial concepts and the related linguistic terms, see 4.5.4 above, and below). The first eighteen months of life are seen by Piaget as the period of the growth of 'sensori-motor intelligence'. Important developments in this period are:

(i) The coordination of a child's motor and perceptual abilities, e.g. he learns to pull an object towards him (cf. babbling as the development of motor-perceptual links—see 1.2.1 above).

(ii) The 'conservation of the object', i.e. he learns that objects remain the same in size and shape even when moved to a different place and even when out of sight.

Conservation of the object is inevitably accompanied by an elementary notion of causality, i.e. he learns that his own actions have certain effects and that two objects act on one another to produce spatial change. In short, a child in the first eighteen months takes the first steps in the construction of a model of reality and his own interaction with it. Towards the end of this period he begins to be able to represent his actions to himself before they occur. This is recognised by the appearance of the 'semiotic function' (the terms 'sign' and 'symbol' are used by Piaget and his followers in an opposite way to their general use in linguistics and philosophy and are avoided here). The semiotic function occurs in several forms:

(i) Behavioural imitation, e.g. a child imitates (sometime after the event) someone stamping her foot in rage.

(ii) Symbolic play, e.g. a child, seeing a pillow on the floor, pretends to lie down and sleep.

(iii) Drawing.

(iv) Language, which is thus seen as just one means by which a child begins to represent reality to himself.

Language, then, according to Piaget, is part of the means whereby the child is able to think about reality (its states and its actions). It follows therefore that it depends for its emergence on the construction of reality that has gone on in the first eighteen months. Detailed parallels between the construction of reality and the construction of language are not easy to draw, but some general relationships can be seen (see Wells, 1974). Many notions which seem important in early linguistic development are dependent on cognitive developments in the sensori-motor period, in particular those of agent, action, affected, location, which are obviously related to the perception of space and causality. Again, the distinction between animate and inanimate objects may relate to the early recognition of the mother as the provider of food and the comforter. A child's first smiles are usually to his mother. There is, however, one major difficulty of timing concerning the Piagetian position that language depends on the attainment of sensori-motor intelligence during the first eighteen months of life. Children's first words appear towards the end of the first year, and their one-word utterances show awareness of concepts like agent and location early in the second year (see 1.6 above). The evidence of language suggests that the attainment of sensori-motor intelligence and the related semiotic function should be placed much earlier than eighteen months.

Bruner (1975) has also formulated a theory concerning the emergence of language at this early period. Bruner's position is that grammar is acquired because of the isomorphism between syntactic categories and psychological events and processes. He suggests that grammar arises by analogy with the 'conceptual framework that is constructed for the regulation of *joint attention* and *joint activity*'. Certain routines which involve mother and child involve a sequence of experiences which are parallelled by the order of words in language. For example, the most common routine involves: 'attend to → act upon', which produces the following orders: location–feature (e.g. *There birdie*), object–name (e.g. *That lorry*) and object–act (e.g. *Daddy go*). Bruner also suggests that play draws the child's attention to situations of communication and the words that are spoken in that situation. It also enables the child to try out spoken communication in a context where it does not matter if his first attempts are unsuccessful or faulty. Bruner's theoretical position is attractive because it embeds the acquisition of language in general cognitive and social growth. Like Piaget's approach, however, it remains to be worked out in any detail (for example, it would be difficult to take a corpus of two-word sentences and explain them all within Bruner's theory). In particular, the attempt to explain word-order by isomorphism with experience runs into difficulty with those children (who may be a minority but are certainly a significant minority) whose word-order is variable in the early stages (one child is known to the author who systematically reversed subject and object even in four-word sentences but who was in other ways advanced for his age in language).

In the years following the sensori-motor period (more particularly, up to the age of seven, and called by Piaget the 'preoperational' period) the child's construction of reality and his construction of language to represent that reality continue to develop. For example, Piaget (1967) described the elaboration of spatial notions in children, and a similar order of development has been confirmed for children's understanding of spatial terms (Parisi and Antinucci, 1970). First to occur are simple locators like *in* and *on*; followed by relational terms like *in front of* and *below*; and lastly complex relational movement terms like *along* and *through*. Such an order of development is similar (though not exactly so) to that proposed by H. H. Clark (1973, and 4.5.4 above).

Around seven, Piaget suggests, children begin to develop 'operational thought', i.e. they begin to develop a certain capacity for logical thought. They can now see that if ball A is bigger than ball B and ball B is bigger than ball C, then A must be bigger than C. They begin to develop the ability to handle concepts like volume, number, weight, and quantity independently from other concepts. If presented with a similar number of counters in different shapes they will be able to say that the same number are present, whereas previously number and shape were not clearly differentiated. Piaget and his followers (e.g. Sinclair-de Zwart, 1969a; 1969b) suggest that although children may use the terminology of these concepts at earlier ages they will not necessarily understand the terms they are using. This would account for confusion between *more* and *less* (Donaldson and Balfour, 1968; and 4.5.2 above).

The interaction of cognitive and linguistic development remains to be studied in any detail, but it seems to offer a more fruitful line of enquiry than the ascription of any unique linguistic apparatus to the newborn child.

5.5 *Sociological theories*

Cognitive theories of language development (in particular, that of Piaget) view language development as waiting upon cognitive development. Conversely, language is not viewed as essential for cognitive development. But Piaget does see the symbolic function (of which language is part) as making 'thought possible by providing it with an unlimited field of application, in contrast to the restricted boundaries of sensori-motor action and perception'

(Piaget and Inhelder, 1969); language is not the means whereby a child constructs reality, but once that reality is constructed it does enable him to think about that reality more easily. Thus language is seen as relevant, though not absolutely necessary, to a child's conceptual development. The emphasis is still on the inner development of the child: thus early speech is considered by Piaget to be predominantly egocentric.

Both cognitive and sociological theories agree in rejecting an outlook which views language (and particularly grammar) as an autonomous system whose acquisition depends on innate linguistic endowment. But sociological theories differ from cognitive theories in stressing that language develops because a child has to interact with other members of society. Halliday describes language as developing to serve needs 'which exist independently of language as features of human life at all times and in all cultures' (Halliday, 1975: 32). These needs or functions are grouped under six headings:

1   Instrumental ('I want . . .').
2   Regulatory ('Do this . . .').
3   Interactional ('Hello . . .').
4   Personal ('I'm cold . . .').
5   Heuristic ('Why . . .').
6   Imaginative ('Let's pretend . . .').

These are functions of language relating to the situation in which the child finds himself. In the adult language these different functions are largely conveyed by various grammatical processes like command and question (what Halliday calls the interpersonal level of grammar).

Somewhat later the child grasps the notion that language is a thing in itself, and thus arises a seventh function, the informational. Language can be used simply for passing information to a listener. This seventh function, unlike the first six already mentioned, is conveyed in adult grammar largely by variations in internal grammatical form, e.g. what we decide to make the subject and object of the verb (Halliday calls this the ideational level of grammar). When this seventh function of language occurs to the child, he must develop grammar (i.e. sentences of two words or more and differing relationships between the words). He must develop grammar because he now almost certainly needs to combine the informational function with one of the earlier functions, e.g. he needs to impart information but at the same time question that information. Thus grammar arises for the child because of the need to 'mean more than one thing at a time' (Halliday, 1975: 48). Language evolves in the way it does because of what it has to do (i.e. first to fulfil certain needs, later for imparting information, and so that interpersonal and ideational levels of language are separately variable).

This type of theory emphasises language as learnt for purposes of interaction with other human beings (i.e. it is a sociological theory). It sees language as waiting upon cognitive development in the same way as cognitive theories do. But it sees the child as encoding his knowledge of the world for the purposes of interaction. 'The child's task is to construct the system of meaning which represents his own model of social reality. This takes place inside his own head, i.e. it is a cognitive process. But it takes place in contexts of social interaction . . . The act of meaning is a social act' (Halliday, 1975: 139–40).

This view of language development is attractive because, like the behaviourist theories outlined in 5.2, it regards the social situation as playing an important role, but, unlike behaviourist theories, it sees the child playing an active role in interacting with that situation. Grammar may indeed develop as a response to the need for utterances which combine both an interpersonal and an ideational function. It is, however, difficult to show this clearly at the two-word stage. Some children may not distinguish at all between statement and command at this time (or, in Halliday's wider terms, between the mathetic and pragmatic functions). Other children may use a certain structure always linked with a certain interpersonal function (Halliday's child at one stage always used sentences like *More meat* as requests). Yet other children may use the differences between a rising and a falling intonation to convey such differences (as Halliday's child did at a later stage). But most children at the two-word stage are not conveying by any grammatical means the difference between interpersonal functions, although they are of course displaying different ideational structures (e.g. possession, agent–action, etc., see 3.2 above). They are not combining in their grammar different interpersonal functions with ideational meanings. It seems more likely that two-word sentences arise precisely because of the necessity to convey different ideational meanings; only later are interpersonal functions marked formally in the grammar and integrated with the ideational meanings. However, this slight reinterpretation of what Halliday is saying does not necessarily detract from the validity of a functional or sociological outlook on language development.

5.6   *A balanced viewpoint*

As is often the case with theories, particularly in the social sciences, there may be at least a grain of truth in all those discussed. The problem is to find a plausible balance between them. In this section we will at least attempt to do this.

Firstly, cognition (in the sense of concepts reflecting perception, function, and other aspects of 'reality') precedes meaningful linguistic usage. Thus the correct meaningful use of a particular linguistic form or pattern must wait upon a necessary level of mental development. Before such correct meaningful usage there may, however, be 'item-learnt' or 'stereotyped' utterances which involve such forms and patterns.

Given that the necessary level of mental development has been reached, language then arises because of the need to code cognition for the purposes of communication (i.e. to 'mean'). This is a sort of behaviourist theory, but the relevant factor is communicative pressure, not linguistic correctness (except in a few minor cases like *breaked/broke*). And it is seen as an active process on the part of the child, whereby he continually revises his notions of how to communicate best. At first the communication looks extremely 'conditioned' (in the traditional sense): *more* may be conditioned to a 'deprivation' state. But as communication becomes more complicated, and linguistic forms more complex and creative, a linguistic system develops which cannot be explained in any simple behaviourist way (see Cleary, 1976).

Obviously there must be some sort of preconditioning in humans, or we would all grow up as different species. The real interest must lie in the details of the specificity or generality of the preconditioning to language. Two such more detailed questions are:

(i) Is there a specific language ability, as opposed to a more general cognitive ability? At present the answer must be 'no', or, more correctly, 'not proven'.

(ii) Is language ability (whether specific or part of a more general ability) species-specific (i.e. unique to humans)? In the light of the achievement of Washoe and Sarah, the answer to this also must be 'not proven'.

Indeed, we are a very long way from answering such questions as these, and the discussion of linguistic innateness which has dominated the last decade may turn out in the end to be the same sort of unanswerable question as that of the origin of language, which dominated the last quarter of the nineteenth century. While innateness may be an enjoyable area for speculation, child language study at the moment shows signs of returning to a more realistic study of detail, and it is hoped that some of these details are made available in this book.

6   Later Development

Chapters 2, 3 and 4 dealt with phonological, grammatical, and lexical development up to approximately the age of 5;0, although most attention was given to the period up to 2;6. This chapter looks at some of the developments in the spoken language which are still taking place during the early school years. It also briefly considers the question of the relationship between social class and language development, which has dominated much educational thought over the last few years.

It is sometimes stated or implied that language acquisition is essentially complete by the age of five (apart from vocabulary development, which obviously continues throughout life; and reading and writing). Even those who deal with children at this age may mistakenly believe that the only other area to be developed is the productive control of the more formal and complex patterns of syntax. The suggestion in this chapter is that development is incomplete in all areas of language at the time of entry into school.

6.1   *Phonology*

Templin (1957) found that the mean score on an articulation test of a carefully selected sample of sixty children at the age of 5;0 was around 75 per cent. Difficulties were more apparent in word-medial and word-final positions, and mainly concerned consonants and consonant clusters. Three areas of segmental phonology may in particular still be causing trouble at the age of five:

(i) The contrasts between dental, alveolar, and palato-alveolar fricatives, e.g. between *thumb* and *some*, and between *seat* and *sheet*.

(ii) The phoneme /r/. The contrast with /w/ may not be established and both adult phonemes may occur as [w] or [ʋ]. Alternatively such a contrast may be established but the phonetic quality of /r/ remains deviant as [ʋ].

(iii) Some consonantal clusters may not be correct, e.g. those in *please*, *last* and *Christmas*. Of course many clusters involve either an alveolar fricative or an /r/ or both, e.g. *spring*, and therefore the problem is compounded.

The development of intonation as an instrument for linking together succeeding parts of a conversation or discourse (e.g. conveying notions like what is new, what is unexpected, and what contrasts with what) remains largely unstudied. C. Chomsky (1971a) studied comprehension of contrastive stress by presenting children with pairs of sentences like: (i) *John hit Bill and then 'Peter hit him* (*him* = Bill) and (ii) *John hit Bill and then Peter hit 'him* (*him* = John), and found that this use of contrastive stress was well established by the age of six. However, Cruttenden (1974) found that when there was a more complicated interaction of intonation-groupings, placement of nucleus (main stress), and choice of tune, children's competence in this area was still developing between five and ten. The development of intonation to convey attitudinal variation, e.g. *I like his 'wife* (i.e. *but I don't like him*) compared with *I like his 'wife*, is a completely uncharted area.

Although children may operate with language which involves a certain basic structure or rule at an early age, later years may bring greater awareness of this structure or rule. Thus while children begin to use phonemic contrasts in their first words, they do not begin to be able to perform tasks which involve separating off one sound from a word until much later (Bruce, 1964; Zhurova, 1964). Children up to the age of five may have difficulty in saying what sound their name begins with or in saying what is left if a sound is taken away from a word, e.g. take the [s] away from *sink* and you are left with *ink*. Similarly, while children will generally stress noun compounds correctly when they first use them, e.g. *'greenhouse* compared with *green 'house*, they may well be twelve before they are certain enough of the stress patterns involved to be able to choose correctly between the two meanings when no clues are given in the context (Atkinson-King, 1973). Such developing awareness in phonology should be compared with that in morphology (3.4.2 above) and classification by semantic features (4.4 above).

6.2 *Grammar*

The developing awareness of linguistic structure and rules mentioned at the end of the preceding section shows itself also in
grammar. In the very early stages of syntactic development
children's grammatical categories like noun and verb, and subject
and object, appear to have high semantic correlations. Indeed, it
may well be more correct to say that children operate initially with
the cooccurrence of certain semantic classes, which rapidly acquire
fixed order (see 3.2 above) and, only later, inflectional endings.
Slowly form classes (or parts of speech) take on a life of their own
independent of semantic correlations. A stage in the development
of awareness of such classes is shown in the findings of word-
association tests which show children changing from syntagmatic
to paradigmatic responses between the ages of six and eight
(Ervin, 1961; Entwistle, Forsyth and Muuss, 1964; Entwistle,
1966). Thus in response to the word *car* said to him, a child
changes over from saying something like *fast* or *drive* to something
like *lorry*. Such paradigmatic responses occur earlier with nouns
than with verbs and adverbs.

Overgeneralisation (e.g. *comed* for *came*—see 3.4.1 above) and
difficulty with particular allomorphs (e.g. *witch–witches*, see 3.4.2
above) may continue into the early school years; otherwise we are
in this section concerned with syntax rather than morphology. As a
rough measure of grammatical development, mean length of
utterance was discussed in 3.3.1 above; it was noted there that at a
certain stage utterance length begins to vary considerably according to situation and thus becomes less useful even as a rough
measure of development. Many older surveys attempted to measure development by working out the proportion of various parts of
speech used by children. However, results vary so considerably
according to the way in which the proportions are computed
(McCarthy, 1954) that this method is virtually worthless. In any
case Templin (1957) found little difference on this count between
three-year-olds and eight-year-olds. Another type of measure
which has been popular concerns the occurrence of subordinate
clauses: Templin (1957) also used this measure and found eight-
year-olds using five times as much subordination as three-year-
olds. Within the subordinate clauses used, the proportion of
subtypes remains more or less constant: 50 per cent adverbial, 33
per cent nominal, and 15 per cent adjectival. A problem with most

other measures of syntactic development concerns the fact that children typically go through a phase of linking everything with *and* and thus it is almost impossible to delineate sentences. An approach which to some extent overcomes this problem involves a unit of measurement called the T-unit (Hunt, 1965; O'Donnell, Griffin and Norris, 1967). A T-unit is a main clause plus any subordinate clause. The average length of T-units appears to increase from about seven words at age six to about ten words at age thirteen (O'Donnell *et al.*, 1967). Loban (1963) considered the decreasing presence of 'mazes' or tangled sentences a good measure of syntactic maturity, e.g. one of his children, shown a picture, said: 'I saw a hunter programme last Sunday and he . . . and snow time he had to have a lot . . . [ə :] . . . wwwhen he . . . [ə] . . . not too many dogs, he, and that's what I think of that picture.' O'Donnell *et al.* (1967) make a similar comment about the 'decrease in use of incomplete clausal patterns'. All the measures of development mentioned are of course extremely gross but if used cautiously may be helpful in educational research.

Looking for details of more specific changes as syntax develops, we find that all that is available are gross comparisons of children at different ages. Virtually no details are known about the stages of development of individual structures in productive syntax (although some have been studied receptively, see below in this section). Menyuk (1963, 1964) found that structures used significantly more frequently at the age of six than at the age of three were passives, clauses introduced by *if* and *so*, and verb phrases involving the present perfect in *have*. There was also somewhat more frequent occurrence of reflexive pronouns, relative clauses, clauses introduced by *because* (see 6.3 below) and participal complements, e.g. *I like singing* (although no difference was found in the occurrence of infinitival complements). O'Donnell *et al.* (1967) studied children between the age of five and the age of twelve and found an increase in T-unit length in every year and a similar increase in the number of clauses within T-units. The main advances took place around six and eleven. Syntactic complexity in writing overtook that in speech at the age of twelve. There was a very frequent use of the conjunction *and* right up to the age of eleven but a decrease at the age of twelve. Favourite clause patterns at all ages were subject–verb–object, subject–intransitive verb and, to a lesser extent, subject–verb–adjective (in many styles of adult speech they may also be the most common types).

Changes particularly noticeable between five and twelve were:

(i) An increase in nominal modification. This applies to pre-nominal attributive adjective and participles; and also to post-nominal prepositional modifiers. Hall and Hall (1965) found that the ability to handle nominal modification continued to develop until fifteen. Schwenk and Danks (1974) concluded that some children may not acquire the correct normal ordering of pre-nominal adjectives, e.g. *a large red car*, until between the ages of seven and ten; however, perhaps more interestingly, they discovered that children could not vary this normal order to take account of a special context until after the age of fourteen. Thus, for instance, they did not produce *a   red large car* when comparing two large cars.

(ii) Intra-clause coordination of adjectives, nouns and predicates.

(iii) Adverbial clauses and infinitive adverbial expressions like *went out to get some more*.

As can be seen, studies of the development of productive syntax have presented us with little more than counts of the frequency of various linguistic items.

Some aspects of the development of comprehension of syntax, on the other hand, have recently been dealt with in some detail. The development of the understanding of passives was mentioned in 3.6 above. Other aspects of syntactic comprehension have been studied by C. Chomsky (1969), Kessell (1970), and Cromer (1970). The types of syntactic structures studied involve exceptions to more general rules, which children presumably learn later than the general rules themselves (cf. overgeneralisation in morphology in 3.4.1 above). Most adjectives which occur in sentences like *John is anxious to please* involve the subject of the second verb being the same as the first; thus it is John in this example who will please some other person(s). However, some adjectives are exceptions to this pattern; thus in *John is difficult to please* John is the object of *please*; other people please John. The children in C. Chomsky's (1969) experiment generally interpreted this latter type of sentence incorrectly at the age of five, whereas at nine they got it correct. Cromer (1970) reported that children's performance was more closely correlated with mental age (as measured by a Peabody Picture Vocabulary Test; Dunn, 1965) than with chronological age: thus at a mental age of 5;7 sentences of the *difficult* type were all incorrectly understood, and over 6;8 they were all correctly understood. Certainly it is likely that correlations with mental age may be more helpful than those with chronological age.

Sentences of the form *John implored Bill to buy a new hat* are generally of the sort where Bill is the subject of *buy*; it is Bill who is to do the buying. This is part of the Minimum Distance Principle (MDP) (Rosenbaum, 1967) whereby the implicit subject of an infinitive complement is the noun phrase most closely preceding it. The verb *promise* in this sort of construction, however, produces an exception to the MDP. Thus *John promised Bill to buy a new hat* involves John buying a new hat. Children go through four stages:

(i) *promise* is always incorrectly interpreted;

(ii) *promise* is sometimes correct, sometimes incorrect, but so also are other verbs which do not violate the MDP and which had been correct at stage (i), e.g. *implore* in the example above, which might at stage (ii) be interpreted as John wanting a new hat;

(iii) *promise* remains only sometimes correct, but the normal verbs are now all correct again;

(iv) all verbs, including *promise*, are now understood correctly.

C. Chomsky (1969) found a great deal of variation in the age at which children attained stage (iv): between 5;2 and 10;0. This suggests that, in this area too, mental age may be a more relevant correlation. The developmental stages involved should be compared with those involved in phonology (2.1.3 above) and morphology (3.4 above). Similar results were obtained for the verb *ask* in sentences like *John asked Bill what to do*, although the picture of development was complicated because at earlier ages children interpreted *ask* as *tell*, i.e. they imagined John commanding Bill to do something.

The other area of development investigated by C. Chomsky (1969) was the reference of pronouns. In most cases a pronominal subject of a main or subordinate clause can be coreferential with the subject of a subordinate or main clause in the same sentence. This applies to the following sentences:

(i) *If he wins the race, John will be happy.*

(ii) *John will be happy, if he wins the race.*

(iii) *If John wins the race, he will be happy.*

In all these sentences *he* and *John* can be, but do not have to be, the same person.

The exceptional type of sentence where coreference is not possible is that where there is a pronoun subject in a main clause followed by a noun subject in a subordinate clause, e.g.

(iv) *He will be happy, if John wins the race.*

Children aged five seem not to interpret the pronoun in such a sentence as coreferential with *John*. Indeed, they appear to have difficulty with the reverse problem, i.e. in interpreting *he* in sentences (i) to (iii) above as coreferential with *John*. The strategy adopted here appears to be: assume subjects are different unless the situation strongly suggests they are not.

6.3   *Lexis*

The general lines of lexical development outlined in chapter 4 obviously continue throughout the early school years and, in the case of vocabulary and very abstract meanings like that' of the word *abstract* itself, through a larger part of life. There is evidence enough that children in their early years at school have a large number of words in their vocabulary which have more limited or different meanings for them than for adults. Asch and Nerlove (1960) investigated children's understanding of words which in the adult language have both a physical and a metaphorical psychological meaning, words like *bright*, *hard* and *sweet*. Before the age of seven children generally did not use such words in the psychological sense. At the ages of seven and eight, while they often did use the words in this way, they apparently did not consider the physical and the psychological meanings as in any way related. Only at the ages of nine and ten did they begin to show any awareness of this relationship. Generally, psychological meanings of words based on tactual referents (e.g. *sweet*, *warm*, *cold*, *dry*, *hard*) are mastered before those based on visual referents (e.g. *bright*, *crooked*, *sharp*, *deep*) (Lesser and Drouin, 1975). This finding seems related to that of Anglin (1970), reported in 4.4 above, that awareness of semantic features as cross-classifying various items of vocabulary continues to develop until at least the later school years.

Similarly, some items in a child's vocabulary may not be as

clearly distinguished in meaning as in the adult language. For example, *good*, *pretty* and *happy* appear to be interchangeable synonyms for a large number of six-year-old children (Ervin and Foster, 1960); and the subtle distinctions involved in adverbial modifiers like *slightly*, *somewhat*, *quite*, *very* and *extremely* may not approximate to adult usage until the teens (Bashaw and Anderson, 1968). The development of this scale of modifiers might profitably be studied in terms of the Semantic Feature Hypothesis (see 4.5.1 above), which would predict that such adverbs would cluster as synonyms at one or the other end of the scale. *Slightly*, *quite*, *rather* and *somewhat* might be synonyms at one end and *decidedly*, *unusually*, *very* and *extremely* synonyms at the other end.

Certain relational concepts were discussed in chapter 4: e.g. quantifiers like *less* and *more*; temporal relationships like those involved in clauses linked by *before* and *after*; and spatial relationships like those involved in *in front of*, *behind* and *on the side of*. The correct use of some other relational prepositions and, more particularly, coordinating and subordinating conjunctions, may continue to develop almost into adulthood. The ubiquitous use of *and* by children in their early school years was mentioned in 6.2 above; but children many not fully understand the adversative conjunction *but* until the age of eleven or later (Katz and Brent, 1968). The common use of *or* to indicate alternatives may be acquired by 4;1 (Johansson and Sjölin, 1975) but the various more complex class relationships involved in *or* may not be comprehended until even later: on some occasions *or* may still be interpreted as *and* even among teenagers (Neimark and Slotnick, 1970). Clauses linked by *because* may be understood at first with a purely sequential meaning (Corrigan, 1975). Thus a sentence like *John hit Mary because she shouted* may be interpreted as 'John hit Mary and then she shouted'; whereas if the clauses are reversed, as in *Because she shouted, John hit Mary*, at least the temporal sequence of events may be correctly understood. Corrigan, following Piaget (1928), suggests that the comprehension and correct use of *because* develop in three stages: firstly affective uses, as in *Peter cried because Jane hurt him*; secondly causal relationships between physical events, as in *She stayed at home from school because she was sick*; and lastly logical relationships between ideas or judgements, as in *The cat is alive because she meowed*. Comprehension and use of this last type were found to be still only 50 per cent correct at the age of seven, suggesting that children have to reach the Piagetian concrete-operational (see 5.4 above) stage before they can deal with this sort of relationship. Confusion between the different uses of *because* may occur even later. A GCE 'O' level script included the following sentence (commenting on a picture of a desert scene): *The weather is very hot because of the sun and because of the people's clothes.* The conditional *if* is understood by 50 per cent of children at the age of six, while *unless* is understood only some time later than the age of nine (Legum, 1975). Children who do not understand *unless* often treat it as equal to *if.* Younger children who understand neither term may ignore the information in the subordinate clause. Lastly, concessive clauses in *although* are not understood at all at the age of six and only partially at the age of twelve (Watts, 1944; Katz and Brent, 1968). Children before this age appear to have difficulty in conceiving of exceptions to a general rule. Vygotsky (1962) maintained that causal relations develop in children's thinking before adversative relations, and this seems to be supported by their use of *because* before *although* (and before *but*). In conclusion, the understanding of most connectives is still developing between the ages of five and seven, and some are not fully understood until a much later age. (Amidon, 1976).

6.4   *Social class and language development*

In section 3.8 above it was suggested that it is vital that parents talk as much as possible to their children. It is undoubtedly true that children who have very little intercourse with adults develop language more slowly than those who do. This is amply confirmed by studies of the language of children in orphanages in the United States (McCarthy, 1954). Additionally, it is often proposed that the style of language to which children are exposed in their family and neighbourhood will crucially affect the type of language they themselves develop; and, because of this, it is proposed that lower-class children will operate under a severe handicap at school. In the United States various educational programmes have been undertaken which seek to enrich the verbal environment of lower class pre-school children, e.g. Bereiter and Engelmann (1966), which influenced the setting up of 'Operation Headstart'. In Britain the emphasis has rather been on making teachers in primary schools more aware of the problems which working-class children are likely to face.

The name particularly associated with this issue has been that of Bernstein (see in particular Bernstein, 1971), who has attempted to formalise the differences between the language of working-class children and that of middle-class children. Before outlining Bernstein's ideas some general comments must be made. (*a*) The volume of linguistic evidence produced to support the ideas has always been slender. Bernstein himself has said, 'The research was predicted on a much coarser theoretical position and this affected the nature of the data we collected, the methods of analysis and the interpretative principles' (Bernstein, 1971:17). (*b*) Bernstein's ideas have changed considerably over a period of nearly twenty years. Notions which were at first very clear-cut have become hedged around with limitations in later articles. For example, a distinction was originally made between working-class children using a 'restricted code' and middle-class children using an 'elaborated code' (for more details see the next paragraph). But later Bernstein writes: 'Because the code is restricted it does not mean that the users do not realize, at any time, elaborated speech variants, only that *such variants will be used infrequently in the process of the socialisation of the child in his family*' (Bernstein, 1971: 198). The key word here is 'infrequently', which tempers the original distinction between the uses of restricted and elaborated codes. (*c*) Bernstein's writings have often been oversimplified in textbooks and have often been used to support educational (and even political) philosophies to which he himself does not subscribe. With these provisos in mind we will attempt to outline his ideas and some of the implications which have been drawn from them.

Central to Bernstein's writings is the distinction between the restricted code and the elaborated code. Some of the differences between the two codes are: (i) syntax is more formally correct in the elaborated code, but looser in the restricted code. There are, for example, more subordinate clauses in the elaborated code, and fewer unfinished sentences. (ii) There are more logical connectives like *if* and *unless* in the elaborated code, whereas the restricted code uses more words of simple coordination like *and* and *but*. (iii) There is more originality in the elaborated code; there are more clichés in the restricted code. (iv) Reference is more explicit in the elaborated code, more implicit in the restricted code: so the restricted code uses a greater number of pronouns than the elaborated code (see the example quoted at length below). (v) The elaborated code is used to convey facts and abstract ideas, the restricted code attitude and feeling. While (i) to (iv) relate at least in part to the forms of language, (v) relates primarily to the meanings being conveyed.

Examples which show clearly all the differences between the two codes operating together are difficult to find in Bernstein's articles. One example which particularly illustrates (iv) above is quoted in Bernstein, 1971: 194. Two five-year-old children, one working-class and one middle-class, were shown a series of three pictures, which involved boys playing football and breaking a window. They described the events involved as follows:

(1) Three boys are playing football and one boy kicks the ball and it goes through the window the ball breaks the window and the boys are looking at it and a man comes out and shouts at them because they've broken the window so they run away and then that lady looks out of her window and she tells the boys off.

(2) They're playing football and he kicks it and it goes through there it breaks the window and they're looking at it and he comes out and shouts at them because they've broken it so they run away and then she looks out and she tells them off.

The elaborated code is the one which, in the adult language, would be generally associated with formal situations, the restricted code that associated with informal situations. In the earlier articles it was implied that middle-class children generally use the elaborated code (although they might sometimes use the restricted code), whereas working-class children have only the restricted code. But Bernstein later modified this viewpoint to say that even working-class children might sometimes use the elaborated code; the difference between the classes is said to lie rather in the occasions on which they can use the codes (e.g. working-class children certainly have difficulty in using the elaborated code in school). Moreover, all children can understand both codes when spoken to them.

The distinction between the restricted and the elaborated code is clearly a fuzzy one in many ways. Any one piece of speech may exemplify characteristics of both codes. There is no discrete boundary between the two. In addition, assuming that the distinction between the codes can be made, it is at least dubious whether working-class and middle-class children are consistently different in their use of the two codes. Surely we all know of some working-class homes which provide a richer language environment than many middle-class homes. As Bernstein himself points out, the number of children in the family and the family structure (e.g. whether the father is more or less authoritarian) may also be relevant. While the picture of the working-class child using restricted code and the middle-class child using elaborated code may be a convenient simplification, it must be remembered that in reality the situation is far more complicated. For example, Edwards (1976) found that there was always more variation between different tasks (e.g. narration v. explanation) than between different social classes.

Under (iv) above, one of the features of the restricted code was said to be the use of more implicit references, exemplified in particular by a more extensive use of pronominal forms. Thus an utterance like 'You do that again (and I'll . . .)' depends far more on the situational context than 'Stop kicking your foot against the table'. '. . . Context-dependent meanings are available only to *particular* types of speakers; those who share an implicit understanding of the context. Thus, context-dependent meanings could be considered *particularistic* . . .. Context-independent meanings are in principle available to all. Thus context-independent meanings could be considered *universalistic*' (Bernstein 1971: 14). Bernstein makes much of this distinction and talks of the elaborated code giving 'access to universalistic orders of meaning'. It is easy to see how such a phrase as this might be misinterpreted as indicating that children with only the restricted code are unable to understand certain types of meaning and hence are 'cognitively deprived' (i.e. their ways of thinking are limited). But elsewhere Bernstein has denied that he meant to imply this: 'Let it be said immediately that a restricted code gives access to a vast potential of meanings, of delicacy, subtlety and diversity of cultural forms, to a unique aesthetic the basis of which in condensed symbols may influence the form of the imagining' (Bernstein, 1971: 186).

Following from (ii) above, it has also been assumed that part of any 'cognitive deficit' would consist in an inability to think logically. Labov (1969) has, however, convincingly shown that young blacks in the United States, although using language which certainly seems an example of the restricted code, nevertheless display a clear ability to argue logically. One example quoted by

Labov is a boy talking about what happens after death:

> You know, like some people say if you're good an' shit, your spirit
> goin' t'heaven . . . 'n' if you bad, your spirit goin' to hell. Well, bullshit!
> Your spirit goin' to hell anyway, good or bad.
> (Why?)
> Why! I'll tell you why. 'Cause, you see, doesn't nobody really know
> that it's a God, y'know, 'cause I mean I have seen black gods, pink
> gods, white gods, all color gods, and don't nobody know it's really a
> God. An' when they be sayin' if you good, you goin' t'heaven, tha's
> bullshit, 'cause you ain't goin' to no heaven, 'cause it ain't no heaven
> for you to go to.

The speaker is here setting out 'a complex set of interdependent
propositions'; 'he can sum up a complex argument in a few words,
and the full force of his opinions comes through without qualifica-
tion or reservation'. In addition Labov notes the common faults of
so-called middle-class speech: 'Our work in the speech community
makes it painfully obvious that in many ways working-class
speakers are more effective narrators, reasoners, and debaters
than many middle-class speakers who temporize, qualify, and lose
their argument in a mass of irrelevant detail.' There is no clear
relationship between language and logical thought. (This matter
was discussed in 5.4 above, where reference was made to the
research of Piaget and Furth.)

The poor performance of lower-class children in school cannot,
then, be ascribed to any sort of cognitive or logical incapacity. It is
simply that a more formal style of language is in normal use in
school than that to which they are accustomed outside school
(although the exact characteristics of the two styles have only been
hinted at in writings about the restricted and elaborated codes).
This more formal style is accepted as the socially correct style in all
the formal situations of society, of which school is generally one.
Moreover reading and writing are almost always in this formal
style.

Furthermore the way in which children can use language for
different purposes may often be related to their family background. Tough (1973) discusses these different purposes in some
detail, and they are worth summarising:

(i) Children use language to defend their rights. A child must
learn to do this politely. In school he is not expected to say 'Give
me that one. It's mine' but 'I'd like my car now because I want to
play with it'.

(ii) Children use language for various commentaries on what's going on around them and in pictures. Commentary on his own action may help a child to concentrate his attention on a particular task. Children from many homes may never have been given encouragement to develop their facility at such commentaries.

(iii) Children use language for creating imaginary play-situations, e.g. announcing 'I'm a baddy'. Some families may only have laughed at this.

(iv) Children have to develop their conversational competence. They have to find an appropriate greeting or initiating remark. They have to develop patience while waiting their turn to speak. They have to learn to take the listener into account when giving explanations. The child who rushes in saying *It burnt me* may wrongly assume that the listener knows what *it* is. Because of the small amount of interaction between parents and children in some families, the children may never have developed these skills.

(v) The types of commands, requests, and questions children are used to may vary considerably from one home to another. A child may have difficulty in understanding and answering *wh*-questions because he has had no practice at it. He may in particular have difficulty in understanding the so-called oblique requests like *Would you like to close the door Johnny*? School-teachers may use this type of request, but children from some homes may hear it as a genuine question.

(vi) Children may use language for planning and problem-solving. The child may use language to work out that *if* he does one thing, another thing may follow or that such an event has happened *because* previously something else was done. Some adults may themselves not use language in this way and so children have no such experience.

The teacher, of course, will ask what he is to do about these problems. As stated at the outset of this section, one attempted solution which has been tried in the United States has been to devise special programmes of 'enrichment' for pre-school children. It is not a solution favoured by Bernstein: 'I have criticised the use of the concept of "compensatory education" because it distracts attention from the deficiencies in the school itself and focuses upon deficiencies within the community, family and child.' And indeed programmes of this sort in the United States have had disappointing results. In Britain it has been suggested that it is rather the schools which should in some way change, to become more accommodating towards working-class children, although detailed suggestions are difficult to find. Most children will need at least some knowledge of a more formal style, not least in reading and writing; and it will certainly help their general social and intellectual development if they can learn to use language appropriately for a wide number of purposes. Perhaps the most teachers can aim to do is to be aware of a child's difficulties in these areas and to coax him gently towards understanding and using language more diversely and more appropriately.

Bernstein has provided a framework for teachers to discuss a problem which certainly many primary school teachers are only too aware of, but that framework is simplistic and lacking in linguistic sophistication. It is one of the general aims of this book to increase teachers' detailed knowledge about language development and to enable them to formulate their own tactics for dealing with language difficulties.

7 *Reading and Writing**

In this chapter the emphasis of the book changes somewhat. So far the focus has been on the *child* as he gradually achieves mastery of the phonological, grammatical and lexical systems of English. This focus on the child is desirable because it underlines the part he plays in language learning: he is not simply imitating an adult model but constructing at each stage sets of rules which accord with his level of cognitive development. The focus on the child also makes it possible to draw attention to the remarkably similar stages of language acquisition which have been observed in children learning to speak different mother tongues. (See, for example, 1.3, 2.4, 3.2, 3.3.5, 3.4.1, 3.5.2 and 4.4 above.) Such a focus is possible because there is a considerable body of research which charts the stages and processes of language acquisition from birth to school age.

When we consider the child extending his language ability as he learns to read and write, however, it is no longer so feasible to focus on the child. This is chiefly because there is no body of research, comparable to the early language acquisition literature, which records the stages children go through as they learn to read. A great deal of reading research focuses on teaching methods and materials; there is much less on the way the child himself tackles the task. This different research emphasis highlights an important difference between learning to talk and learning to read: we tend to think of oral language being learnt and of written language being taught. This distinction is understandable when we consider that all normal children learn to speak without apparent difficulty and with no formalised teaching, whereas many normal children learn to read only with great difficulty and after extensive teaching. And, of course, before the advent of universal education, children who were not taught to read did not generally learn to read by themselves.

There are, however, some suggestions that the distinctions which have been made between learning to speak and learning to

* This chapter is by Katharine Perera

read are not so great as they might at first sight appear. For example, there is considerable evidence that mothers are skilful language teachers (see 3.8 above), so the idea that children learn to speak without being taught is probably mistaken. Then, again, it is possible to consider the teaching of reading as an attempt to control and grade the complexity of the written language presented to the child, in just the way that adults control the complexity of their oral language when speaking to the young child, so that he can induce the system for himself. Such a consideration of the similarities between the *processes* of learning to speak and learning to read suggests that it is worth examining some of the differences between spoken and written language in order to find the source of the discrepancies in children's ability to master the two systems. (It is immediately noticeable, for example, that adults seem to have intuitive knowledge of the best ways of simplifying and grading their spoken language to children, whereas even extensive research investigations have not revealed the ideal forms of written language to present to children when they begin to learn to read. See 7.5 below.) Therefore the emphasis in this chapter will be less on the child as a learner and more on the nature of what he has to learn, the English writing system.

Although it is necessary to change focus, it is felt that some account of what the child has to master in moving from the spoken to the written language is appropriate here, for several reasons. Firstly, there is currently a great deal of interest in the relationship between the spoken and written language and in how the child's knowledge of *speech* can best be utilised in the teaching of reading (Kavanagh and Mattingly, 1972). Secondly, children are normally taught to read shortly after they have acquired all the basic grammatical structures of the spoken language, so reading becomes the next major chronological stage in the growth of their language abilities. And thirdly, once it is mastered, the written language itself becomes a powerful agent in the development of the child's spoken language. This is most obvious in the growth of vocabulary; there is also evidence that learning to read increases the child's command of the more complex grammatical structures (O'Donnell *et al.*, 1967; Richardson, 1977); there is even the possibility that some children find the written language a help in completing their mastery of the phonological system, as in the pronunciation of consonant-clusters, for example (Allerton, 1976).

In order to fulfil the aim of giving a brief account of what the child has to master when he learns to read, the major part of this chapter is concerned with the characteristics of written language in general and of the English writing system in particular. Then it moves on to discuss the initial stages of the reading process, considering which aspects of the written language appear to cause most difficulty and what can be learnt from children's reading errors, ending with a range of views on the best age for learning to read. This is followed by a short section on learning to write. After this there is an examination of the principles behind the methods most commonly used in the teaching of reading, and a discussion of how far they take into account the nature of the written language and of the English writing system. Finally, this chapter considers the different ways in which the written language is simplified and graded for presentation to beginning readers.

7.1 *Written language*

7.1.1 *Characteristics of writing systems*

The writing system that would be ideal for the learner would have the following characteristics:

(i) It would have a small number of visually distinct symbols. This would mean that recognising and reproducing the symbols would not impose a heavy burden on the memory.

(ii) The symbols would represent units of the spoken language which the speaker readily perceives as units. (For example, there is evidence that syllables are more easily perceived than phonemes. See this section, below.)

(iii) The writing system would be able to express many of the features of the spoken language (such as stress and intonation—see 7.1.3 below) so that the learner would be aware of the relationships between speech and writing.

(iv) The written symbols would represent features of the spoken language in a consistent and predictable manner.

(v) The system would be stable and conservative so that it was comprehensible from one region to another and from one century to another.

It is immediately obvious that no real writing system has all these features. Indeed, some of them are mutually exclusive: for example, maximum expressiveness (iii) is not consistent with a small number of symbols (i); and regularity (iv) is incompatible with stability (v). (Writing systems can be comprehensible across geographical and historical distances only by *not* reflecting all the regional and diachronic sound changes which occur in the spoken language. Thus no writing system can be a consistent and predictable counterpart of the sound system for every speaker of the language. For example, the initial teaching alphabet, i.t.a., which was devised to represent English phonemes in a consistent way, has a high level of regularity for R.P. speakers but not for speakers with a regional accent. The i.t.a. symbol <ω> represents the phoneme /u/ and occurs in words such as *book*, *took*, *full*, and *put*. The i.t.a. symbol <ꝏ> represents the phoneme /u ː/ and occurs in words such as *tooth*, *roof*, *June* and *fruit*. For R.P. speakers this representation is consistent and predictable, but many people pronounce *book* and *took* with the phoneme /u ː/ and *tooth* and *roof* with the phoneme /u/, so for them the regularised alphabet is still arbitrary; see Trudgill, 1975.)

The characteristics of an ideal writing system, outlined above, are found to varying degrees in real writing systems. There are three major types of writing system and each has its own strengths and weaknesses. The three types are the *morphemic*, the *syllabic* and the *alphabetic*. (A morphemic writing system is more usually referred to as *logographic*; however, since the symbols represent morphemes rather than words, *logographic* is rather a misleading term.) A simplified, and therefore not wholly accurate, description of these systems is that in a morphemic script each symbol represents a morpheme, in a syllabic script each symbol represents a syllable, and in an alphabetic script each symbol represents a phoneme. Chinese languages are written in a morphemic script; Japanese in a script which combines syllabic and morphemic symbols; and most other languages, including English, Russian and Arabic, in alphabetic scripts.

A morphemic script has a symbol for every morpheme, so it is obviously burdensome to learn. To read even a simple text it is necessary to know about one thousand characters (Martin, 1972). Because there are so many characters (an average Chinese dictionary will contain about eight thousand), they have to be calligraphically complex. The two thousand Chinese characters that have recently been simplified consist, on average, of nine strokes each, while the unsimplified characters have an average of fifteen strokes each (French, 1976). Thus the system is even harder to learn to write than to read. However, it has three advantages: firstly, morphemes are easily perceived units so no special linguistic awareness is needed to move from oral to written language; secondly, the written language has such a slight relationship with the pronunciation of the spoken language that it is highly stable: people who speak different Chinese languages are able to communicate in writing when their spoken languages are mutually unintelligible (in the same way that French, German and English mathematicians are able to understand each other's written calculations even if they cannot identify the numbers when they are spoken); and thirdly, the elements of a text are so highly differentiated that the written form is less liable to ambiguity than the spoken. Carroll (1972) comments, 'Chinese speakers, even speaking the same dialect, frequently have to write out characters in the air in speaking to one another, to avoid ambiguity, or even complete confusion' (p. 108).

A syllabic script uses far fewer symbols than a morphemic system; the Japanese Hiragana and Katakana syllabaries both have forty-six symbols, plus a few diacritics to express, for example, the voicing of a consonant. Like morphemes, syllables seem to be easily perceived units. Savin and Bever (1970) found that students given a listening task responded more quickly to whole-syllable targets than to single-phoneme targets, regardless of whether the syllables were meaningful or not. It is also noticeable that, when literate adults are faced with an unfamiliar word in a text, they sound it out syllable by syllable rather than letter by letter. So a syllabic script appears to combine the virtues of economy and of congruence with the reader's linguistic perceptions. However, it does not seem to give rise to an ideal writing system, because it causes a great deal of ambiguity. Partly because of the high number of homographs that arise with a syllabic script, the Japanese use a considerable number of morphemic characters, *Kanji*, to supplement their script, and so its fundamental economy is lost. (There are 1,850 Kanji characters specified for regular use, and they constitute 25–35 per cent of any text in standard written Japanese; Sakamoto, 1975.)

An alphabetic script is very economical to learn to use because the number of phonemes in any language is always so much smaller than the number of syllables or morphemes. But the analysis of words into their constituent phonemes is a difficult task which requires a high degree of linguistic awareness. Writing of alphabetic systems, Mattingly (1972) says, 'It would seem that the price of greater efficiency in learning is a required degree of awareness higher than for logographic [morphemic] and syllabary systems, since . . . phonological segments are less obvious units than morphemes or syllables' (p. 144). Another disadvantage of an alphabetic script arises from its close relationship to the sound system of the language: the sounds of a language inevitably change; a writing system is inherently conservative; so even an orthography which originally had a regular and close correspondence to the phonemes of the language will, over the years, lose its high level of regularity, since it fossilises an earlier sound system and does not reflect subsequent sound changes. (For a fuller discussion of different types of writing systems see French, 1976, and Haas, 1976.)

It has recently been suggested that a morphemic writing system is preferable to an alphabetic system. For example, Smith (1973) says, 'It is frequently asserted that, since the English language is written in alphabetic symbols, the alphabetic system must be the basis of reading. This is rather like the argument that hotel guests should pay for the telephone answering service, even if they don't make use of it, just because it is there' (p. 116). He goes on to suggest that readers of English perceive words as unanalysed wholes (as if they were Chinese characters), not as combinations of letters representing separate sounds. Rozin *et al.* (1971) conducted an experiment in which nine seven-year-old children, who had completely failed to learn to read English orthography, were taught to read thirty Chinese characters with English words as oral counterparts. Commenting on the success of this experiment, Smith (*op. cit.*) says, 'Readers do not use (and do not need to use) the alphabetic principle or decoding to sound in order to learn or identify words' (p. 105). Three brief comments can be made here:

(i) People need to be able to read *and* write. It is obviously silly to have one writing system for readers and another for writers, and the alphabetic system is undoubtedly simpler than the morphemic for the *writer*, even if this is not true for the *reader*. (It is easier to recognise one thousand characters than to reproduce them.)

(ii) If the target vocabulary for a literate adult were only thirty words it would be unnecessary to learn twenty-six letters and the rather complex rules for their combination; it would clearly be more economic to memorise thirty whole words as units. But as the target vocabulary is several thousand words, the economy of the alphabetic principle can be seen to be a valuable asset, not to be lightly discarded.

(iii) An alphabetic system gives the reader a clue to the pronunciation of a word he has not met before. It is true that the clues are not often sufficient to make correct pronunciation guaranteed. For example, if the reader comes across the unfamiliar word *carina* presumably his grapho-phonemic knowledge suggests three possible pronunciations: /ˈkærinə/, /kəˈriːnə/ and /kəˈrainə/. This is not a clear-cut solution to the decoding problem but it is at least a start. In the Chinese writing system a very large number of basic character shapes have to be mastered before any kind of prediction about the sound and meaning of a new character can be attempted. (Many Chinese complex characters contain one element that hints at the sound and another element that hints at the meaning, but this information is available only to the reader with knowledge of many characters.)

7.1.2   *The English writing system*

Although English orthography has the advantage, shared by all alphabetic systems, that it uses a small number of symbols which themselves give the reader some guidance as to the pronunciation of an unfamiliar word, nevertheless it is not so regular a system—and therefore not so economical for the learner—as, for example, Finnish. There are four major reasons for the irregularity of English orthography:

(i) Sound changes have meant that pronunciations that were once distinct have coalesced, with the result that there are now two different spellings for the same sound, e.g. in sixteenth century London *meet* was pronounced with a vowel near Cardinal No. 1, [iː] and *meat* with a vowel near Cardinal No. 2, [eː]. Later, the first vowel became a little lower and the second a little higher so that the forms became homophonous, with their different histories preserved in the spelling (Strang, 1970).

(ii) The writing system does not have enough symbols. The principle of an alphabetic script is that one symbol should represent one phoneme. As British English has (roughly) forty-four phonemes and only twenty-six letters, it is obvious that this principle cannot be fulfilled. Twenty-one consonant letters represent twenty-four consonant phonemes. However, the letters <c>, <q> and <x> do not have distinctive grapho-phonemic value because they could be replaced variously by the letters <s>, <k>, <kw>, <ks> and <z>. Thus only eighteen letters are actually representing the twenty-four phonemes. This means that six consonant phonemes have composite or variable representation. The phonemes /tʃ/, /θ/, /ð/ and /ŋ/ are spelt, fairly regularly, <ch>, <th> and <ng>; /ʃ/ is spelt <sh> (*shore*), <ch> (*chef*), <s> (*sure*), <ti> (*nation*), <si> (*mansion*), <ci> (*special*); /ʒ/ is spelt <s> (*measure*), <si> (*vision*), <z> (*seizure*), and <ge> (*beige*).

The position is more complex for the vowels, where there are only five vowel letters and twenty vowel phonemes. Accordingly, vowel sounds are represented by single vowel letters, e.g. <a> (*cat*); by doubled vowel letters, e.g. <ee> (*see*); by combinations of separated vowel letters, e.g. <a–e> (*made*); by combinations of two or three vowel letters, e.g. <ou> (*out*); by combinations of a vowel and a consonant letter, e.g. <aw> (*saw*), <oy> (*boy*), <al> (*calm*), <ig> (*sign*); and by combinations of vowel letters with two or more consonant letters, e.g. <ough> (*though*). There are, on average, seven spellings for every vowel phoneme.

Letters represent different sound values according to their immediate graphemic environment and the learner has the problem of deciding whether two letters form one of the combinations listed above, representing only one phoneme, or whether there are two separate graphemes, representing two phonemes. For example, <sh> represents /ʃ/ in *dishevel* but /sh/ in *disharmony*; <ea> represents /iː/ in *beating* but /iːæ/ in *beatitude*.

(iii) The third reason for the irregularity of English orthography is the very large number of loan words that have been introduced over the centuries. For example, Greek words containing the Greek letter *phi*, /f/, were transliterated into English using the letters <ph>, e.g. *philosophy, photograph*. Thus the number of spellings of the phoneme /f/ was increased. French words containing the digraph <ch> were introduced into English and they retained the /ʃ/ pronunciation they had had in French, e.g. *charade, chauffeur*. In this way the number of pronunciations of the digraph <ch> was increased.

These brief examples illustrate the important fact that English grapho-phonemic relationships are complex in two directions: one phoneme may have many spellings and one grapheme may represent many phonemes. (This contrasts with a language like French where one phoneme may have many spellings but each grapheme represents one phoneme in a fairly consistent way.)

(iv) So far we have been considering an alphabetic script as one in which the symbols represent phonemes. It is, however, more accurate to say of English (and of many other alphabetic languages) that the representation is sometimes phonemic and sometimes *morphophonemic*. That is, there are in English many morphemes which each have only one written form, regardless of how they change phonologically according to their position within a word. For example, the morpheme *photo* has the graphemes <ph-o-t-o> representing the phonemes /fəutəu/. In the word *photography* the pronunciation of the first vowel changes from /əu/ to /ə/ and the pronunciation of the second vowel changes from /əu/ to /ɔ/ but the *spelling* of the vowels remains the same as in *photo*. Similarly, the morpheme *critic* has the graphemes <c-r-i-t-i-c> representing the phonemes /kritik/. In the word *criticise* the pronunciation of the second <c> changes from /k/ to /s/ but, again, the spelling is unchanged. In a *phonemic* script (e.g. Finnish) every phonological alteration is matched by a graphemic alteration; in a *morphophonemic* script, morphemes retain visual identity regardless of changed pronunciation. English is not completely consistent in this respect (e.g. *pronounce* does not retain its visual identity in *pronunciation*) but there are very many morphemes which do conform to this principle.

The irregularity of the English spelling system is generally thought to be a nuisance. However, it does have two important advantages. Firstly, it reduces the risk of ambiguity: English has more than 1,000 homophones but only about 160 homographs (Whitford, 1966). Secondly, the retention of visual identity of the morpheme, regardless of its pronunciation, enables the skilled reader to extract meaning from the text very rapidly, without the need for full decoding to sound, which slows down the reading process considerably. (Average skilled readers read silently at a rate of 300–400 words per minute, roughly twice the speed of speech.) For example, the spelling <criticise> enables the skilled reader to recognise the morpheme *critic* as one unit, whereas the phonemic spelling *<critisize> would suggest, unhelpfully, a relationship with the morpheme *size* and disguise the presence of the morpheme *critic*. Perhaps the clearest example of the aid that the morphophonemic principle affords to the skilled reader is found in the spelling of /s/ and /z/ in word-final positions. With very few exceptions, the spelling <-s> is reserved for the morpheme {PLURAL} and the morpheme {THIRD PERSON SING. PRES. TENSE}, e.g. *days* and *lacks*. The <-s> spelling is used regardless of the pronunciation, which may be /s/ or /z/. In addition, almost all other words which end in /s/ or /z/ have a different spelling of the phoneme so that they do not have a plural or third-person-verbal appearance. The alternative spellings of /s/ are: <-ss> (*cross*), <-se> (*lapse*, cf. *laps*), <-ce> (*presence*, cf. *presents*), and <-x> (*lax*, cf. *lacks*). The alternative spellings of /z/ are <-zz> (*jazz*) and <-ze> (*daze*, cf. *days*). So this apparent irregularity of spelling helps the reader by indicating possible word-classes and, hence, relationships with other parts of the sentence. It is this aspect of the English writing system which led Chomsky (1970) to assert, 'Conventional English orthography in its essentials appears to be a near-optimal system for representing the spoken language' (p. 4).

Nevertheless, it must be recognised that these features are an advantage only for a skilled reader; they are undoubtedly a source of difficulty for the learner.

So far, the term *irregular* has been used in the description of the English writing system. This, of course, is a pejorative term and many linguists would prefer the word *complex*. Whether the system is regarded as confused and irregular or complexly regular depends on the kinds and numbers of rules that are permitted in its description. For the Bullock committee (Department of Education and Science, 1975) 'regularity' means a one-to-one correspondence between sounds and symbols, so they comment on the 'evident irregularity in the phoneme-grapheme relationship of the English writing system' (p. 87). On the other hand, Wijk (1966) claims that the 'vast majority of English words, about 90–95 per cent of the total vocabulary, do in fact follow regular patterns in regard to their spelling and pronunciation' (p. 8). To achieve such a high estimate of regularity requires the application of many simple rules or fewer complex ones. A study by Berdiansky *et al.* (1969) attempted to assess the orthographic regularity of 6,092 frequently used one- and two-syllable words. One hundred and sixty-six spelling rules were needed to account for 90 per cent of the items, leaving 10 per cent as irredeemably irregular. (However, if principles of conditioned phonological variation had been taken into account, fewer rules would have been needed.) Obviously, the economy of the alphabetic principle is undermined for the learner when it entails the mastery of a large or complex set of rules. Another approach to the problem of the description of the English writing system has been taken by Albrow (1972). He has shown that English spelling is generally systematic or, rather, *polysystemic*. That is, that there are many sub-systems which together constitute the whole system. So there is one sub-system for grammatical words and another for lexical words; one for native words and another for Romance words, and so on. Rules are established for each sub-system, not for the system as a whole. It can be convincingly argued that the polysystemic nature of English orthography is positively advantageous for the skilled reader because it supplies him with information about words at many linguistic levels (e.g. phonemic, morphemic, syntactic, etymological, etc.). But, since you cannot assign a word to a sub-system until you know the word, the rules governing the sub-systems are of no help to the beginner as he tackles each new word. (Nevertheless, an understanding of these rules might well enable teachers to group words to be taught in such a way that children could more easily induce the generalisations for themselves.)

Since any orderly and revealing account of the English writing system involves the formulation of rules of one kind or another, it seems worth taking a brief look at the nature of such rules. Rather than simply list spelling rules from 1 to 166 (or whatever number is needed) it is probably more helpful to consider rules as belonging to groups, according to the linguistic level at which they operate. A few examples must suffice to illustrate this notion:

(i) Some rules can be related to phonological conditioning, e.g. when a velar plosive is preceded by a nasal, the nasal is always /ŋ/. Yet it is always written with the letter <n> and not the digraph <ng> (e.g. *uncle, ankle, anger*). This is because there is, in English, no contrast between /ŋk/ and /nk/ or between /ŋg/ and /ng/. The digraph <ng> is reserved for those positions where there is the possibility of phonological contrast (e.g. *sun* and *sung*).

(ii) There are rules that govern the permissible sequences of letters. (These could be called *graphotactic* rules, by analogy with *phonotactic* rules.) The most obvious example is that <q> is always followed by <u> (e.g. *quick*). There are many others. For example, many letters are never, or hardly ever, doubled. They are

<a, h, i, j, k, q, u, v, w, x, y>. (Some exceptions are *bazaar, radii, chukker, vacuum*.) In consonant clusters, plosives following <s> will be written <p, t, c, k> or <qu>, not <b, d> or <g> (e.g. *spin, stun, scan, skii, squirm*, not **sbin*, etc.). This is a graphotactic rule since, *phonetically*, the plosive sound which follows the /s/ has some of the qualities of both the voiced and voiceless members of the pair (i.e. the contrast between, for example /t/ and /d/ is neutralised in this position), so the systematic use of letters representing the voiceless alternatives is purely conventional.

(iii) Rules can also be established concerning the effect of letter-position within words. This conditions both the occurrence of letters and grapho-phonemic correspondences.

(a) *Occurrence of letters*. The following letters rarely occur at the ends of words: <j, q, v> (exceptions: *raj* and *spiv*). When the sound /dʒ/ occurs at the end of a word it is represented by <-ge> or <-dge> (e.g. *cage, cadge*). When /v/ occurs in final position, it is spelt <-ve> (e.g. *have, live*).

(b) *Grapho-phonemic correspondences*. The phonemic value of some graphemes alters according to their position within a word, e.g. at the beginning of a word <gh> ≡ /g/ (e.g. *ghost*), while at the end of a word <gh> ≡ /f/ or zero (e.g. *rough, though*). At the beginning of a word <x> ≡ /z/ (e.g. *xylophone*) but at the end of a word <x> ≡ <ks> (e.g. *box*).

(iv) There are spelling rules concerning word formation in polymorphemic words, e.g. final <e> on a verb is removed before the addition of <-ing> (e.g. *come, coming*).

(v) Many rules are morphophonemic (see p. 138 above), e.g. the regular past tense morpheme is spelt <ed> regardless of whether it is pronounced /t/, /d/ or /id/ (e.g. *liked, tried, wanted*).

(vi) Word-class can also affect phoneme–grapheme relationships. For example, word-initial <th> ≡ /ð/ only in grammatical words; in lexical words it always corresponds to /θ/ in this position (e.g. *this* and *thimble*). Only grammatical words have only two letters; lexical words have three or more (exceptions: *go, ox*). This means that a lexical word with the structure CV must have a digraph to represent the vowel, e.g. *bee* (cf. *be*), *sew* (cf. *so*), *two* (cf. *to*).

An awareness of the nature of the written language is a

prerequisite for an understanding of the reading process. There is little doubt that different writing systems affect markedly the ease with which beginners learn to read. For example, the majority of Japanese children can recognise 85 per cent of the Hiragana symbols, and read words written in them, at the age of five, before they go to school and without formal instruction (Sakamoto, 1975). Although the Hiragana script is not ideal for the *skilled* reader (in fact, Japanese adults need twice as long to read a text written solely in Hiragana as they do to read it in the normal combination of Hiragana and Kanji), it clearly has advantages for the *learner*. A similar point has been made about i.t.a. by Warburton and Southgate (1969) in their evaluation of the medium for the Schools Council: 'There is no evidence whatsoever for the belief that the best way to learn to read in traditional orthography is to learn to read in traditional orthography. It would appear rather that the best way to learn to read in traditional orthography is to learn to read in the initial teaching alphabet' (pp. 234–5). The more fully the nature of the English writing system is understood, the more possible it should be for teachers to simplify and grade the examples of the written language they present to their pupils in a helpful and revealing way.

7.1.3   *The relationship between spoken and written English*

(In this section, references to *speech*, *writing*, *spoken language*, etc., apply to English and not necessarily to other languages.)

Speech is, physically, a string of sounds uttered in a temporal sequence. The beginning reader has to learn that marks on paper—letters—represent some aspects of those sounds. The letters do not, of course, represent speech itself. There are many features of the spoken language which have no written counterpart. For example, when we listen to a person speaking, it is impossible not to be aware of the *pitch* of the voice (which, in an adult, generally indicates the sex of the speaker); of *voice-quality* (which may broadly suggest the speaker's age); of a regional or R.P. *accent*; and of the *speed* and *volume* of his speech. None of these features is represented in the standard writing system. (Strip cartoons frequently use expanding letters to indicate increasing volume.)

All normal speech is uttered not in a monotone but using the range of pitch-levels and pitch-movements which together constitute the system of intonation tunes (see 1.3, 2.10 and 6.1 above, and the glossary). Intonation has three main functions:

(i) It indicates the grammatical structure of an utterance by dividing it into grammatically relevant word-groups.

(ii) It is sometimes the sole means of marking the grammatical function of an utterance. For example, *You've finished* is marked in speech as a statement by a falling tone and as a question by a rising tone.

(iii) It conveys the attitude of the speaker. For example, *You are clever* may express grudging admiration, in which case it will have an intonation pattern like this: *You 'are ˇclever*; or it may express heavy sarcasm, in which case it will have a pattern like this: *'You are clever.*

Intonation is not directly expressed in writing, so these three functions have to be fulfilled in other ways:

(i) Grammatical structure: punctuation marks are used to indicate some structural units. Sentence-boundaries are marked by full stops, question marks and exclamation marks; smaller, grammatically relevant word-groups are not so systematically delineated. For example, although adverbials at the beginning of a sentence are frequently separated from the rest of the sentence by a comma (e.g. *Nevertheless*, I shan't go), many complex sentences have no internal punctuation marks to indicate their structure, e.g. *A doctor John Brown knew bought the car*. The grammatical structure of this sentence is immediately apparent in speech but is perhaps less clear in writing.

(ii) Sentence function: statements are marked by full stops, questions by question marks and exclamations by exclamation marks. Commands with the grammatical form of imperatives (with no expressed subject) end with a full stop if they are calm in tone, e.g. *<Be careful.>* represents *Be ˎcareful,* and with an exclamation mark if the tone is excited, e.g. *<Be careful!>* represents *Be ˇcareful*. Commands with the grammatical form of questions end with a question mark if they are polite or tentative, e.g. *Would you shut the door*?, and with an exclamation mark if they are forceful, e.g. *Will you go away*!

(iii) Speaker's attitude: this is very difficult to convey in writing. O'Connor and Arnold (1973) comment, 'One measure of a writer's success is his ability to solve the problem of suggesting the exact meaning he has in mind even though he has no direct method of conveying intonation' (p. 5).

Having indicated those features of speech which are represented either indirectly or not at all in writing, we can now consider what features writing does represent. The spaces between groups of letters indicate word-boundaries. (There is a clearer demarcation of words as units in writing than there is in speech, where strings of words are uttered as a phonological continuum.) The letters themselves represent phonemes (in a rather complex way—see 7.1.2 above). Apart from the complexities of correspondence between graphemes and phonemes that we have already discussed, it is noticeable that the writing system represents words in their citation forms, as if they were items of equal status on a list, and only rarely uses altered spellings to show the elisions and weak forms which are an essential characteristic of all normal speech. For example, the sentence *One or two of them are coming* will probably be pronounced /wʌn ə tu ː ə ðəm ə kʌmiŋ/ so the written forms <or>, <of> and <are> all correspond to the sound /ə/. Gimson (1970) comments that in speech the weak forms of grammatical words 'show reductions of the length of sounds, obscuration of vowels towards /ə, i, u/, and the elision of vowels and consonants' (p. 263). He lists nineteen highly frequent words which have over 90 per cent unaccented occurrences with a weak form. Of these nineteen words, only *shall* has an abbreviated written form.

So far, this chapter has outlined the major features of correspondence and divergence between speech and writing as physical systems. The relationship between spoken and written English as a whole is more complex. It has been shown that written symbols do not represent speech itself but only some aspects of it. Similarly, written language is not simply spoken language written down. (A study of transcripts of spontaneous spoken language illustrates this.) Characteristically, spoken language is produced spontaneously, rapidly, in interaction with one or more people in a shared physical environment. In contrast, written language is more often planned; it is produced more slowly; the writer generally has no present audience and his eventual readers are unlikely to read his writing in the exact setting in which he wrote it. These situational differences lead to considerable differences in the type of language which most typically occurs in the two media. Spoken language is characterised by false starts, mazes, hesitations, back-trackings and interpolations. These features are generally avoided in the final version of a piece of writing (though there will be plenty of them in the rough drafts). In speech there is a tendency towards simple sentences and coordinated constructions, with a high level of redundancy, whereas writing is more likely to contain complex sentences and subordinated constructions, with a lower level of redundancy. Because speech usually occurs face to face, it is accompanied by facial expressions, gestures and exophoric references. So spoken language can be elliptical, incomplete and non-specific in reference without losing any communicative value. The same is not true of writing. The spoken utterance *She left that there, so . . .* would need to be rendered in writing in some way like this: *Jane left the vacuum-cleaner right in the middle of the room, so no wonder someone tripped over it.*

In view of the complexity of the relationship between the spoken and the written language, it is not surprising that children do not always see the connection between the two forms. There is clear evidence of this when children who are otherwise competent readers read aloud word by word, in a stilted monotone.

7.2 *The early stages of reading*

7.2.1 *The abilities the learner needs*

Having considered the nature of the written language, its relationship with speech, and the characteristics of English orthography, we can now attempt to identify the abilities that are needed to learn to read and write. One set of abilities is needed to move from printed language, via sound, to meaning and another set of different but related abilities is needed to move from meaning to written language. The skills involved in writing are considered in 7.3 below. (It is assumed in this chapter that decoding to sound is involved in the early stages of reading; that is, that the child needs to say the words in order to get meaning from the printed text. This is a contentious issue, however. For a range of viewpoints see Conrad, 1972; Massaro, 1975; and Smith, 1973.)

Identifying and separating the various abilities that are involved in learning to read and write is not meant in any way to suggest that these abilities are acquired in a discrete way or in serial order;

nor is it intended to indicate any kind of teaching syllabus; rather, it might provide a basis for understanding the task that confronts the learner.

Before the child can learn to read or write he needs to understand that language, which so far he has known only in its oral form, has a written form too. He needs an awareness that the marks he sees—or makes—on a page represent the spoken language in some way and that they are scanned systematically from left to right and from top to bottom of the page. He also needs some knowledge of the technical terms that are used to talk about the written language, such as *letter* and *word*. That such an understanding has to be developed has been clearly shown by Reid (1966) and Downing (1969). Reid, for example, in interviews with five-year-old children, found that some of them thought numbers constituted writing; many called letters words (e.g. ' "You say one word at a time . . . m—u—s—t. *m* is a word, *u* is a word." '); some thought names were not words, and one had decided that capital letters were used for writing about big things. Vernon (1957) uses the phrase 'cognitive confusion' to describe the uncertainty about the nature and purpose of writing that is evident in children who have failed to learn to read, and Vygotsky (1962) says, 'Our studies show that it is the abstract quality of written language that is the main stumbling block' (p. 99).

In addition to some understanding of the nature and purpose of written language, the learner needs abilities at four levels: (i) the letter, (ii) the word, (iii) the sentence, and (iv) the discourse.

(i) *Letter level*. He must be able to discriminate between different letter shapes. This involves responding to significant differences such as those between <a> and <o>, and ignoring insignificant ones, such as those between <a>, <ɑ>, <A>, etc.

He must be able to associate the letters with the phonemes they generally represent, not just in one-to-one correspondences, but also the frequently occurring digraph-phoneme relationships, e.g. <sh> $\equiv$ /ʃ/, <ee> $\equiv$ /iː/

(ii) *Word level*. He needs to learn that the position of letters within words has significance for their phonemic value. For example, final <e> after a consonant is usually silent (e.g. *made*).

He needs the ability to blend phonemes into words. This entails the understanding that all spoken words are analysable into strings of separate sounds which are in themselves meaningless.

Faced with a multi-syllabled word, he has to be able to divide it appropriately into syllables. (That this can be a problem even for adults is illustrated by the mispronunciaton of unfamiliar words such as *awry* and *potsherd*, which, if wrongly syllabicated, are pronounced /ˈɔːri/ and /ˈpɔtshəːd/ rather than /əˈrai/ and /ˈpɔtʃəːd/.)

He has to be able to place the stress on the right syllable, as this conditions the phonemic value of the vowel graphemes. Contrast ˈapple and appˈrove; ˈconcert and conˈcern.

He needs to be able to recognise on sight those frequently occurring words which are not susceptible to analysis using his knowledge of either grapheme–phoneme correspondences or orthographic conventions, e.g. *any*, *does*, *once*, *two*.

(iii) *Sentence level*. He needs the ability to read all the words in a sentence quickly enough to be able to synthesise the sentence-meaning. The meaning of a sentence is more than the sum of the meanings of the words it contains. Reading words as if they were separate items on a list will not lead to an understanding of the sentence as a whole. Therefore, those groups of words which together form a grammatical construction, such as a noun phrase or a verb phrase, must be processed together so that the grammatical relationship between them is recognised. This is why reading speed is important; if individual words are read very slowly and falteringly, the first words in the group have faded from short-term memory before the last words have been read and there is then no possibility of perceiving their grammatical relationships, or of understanding the whole sentence. Quite apart from the fact that there is no point in reading without comprehension, the understanding of one part of a sentence in itself facilitates the reading of the next part, since the more information the reader has, the more accurately he can predict what is to come.

(iv) *Discourse level*. He has to be able to relate the meaning of one sentence to another, to subsequent sentences and to his own experience so that he recreates a cohesive and meaningful discourse.

7.2.2   *Sources of difficulty in reading*

Studies show that children experience most difficulty not at the level of identifying individual letters or at sentence or discourse levels but rather at letter-group and word levels.

It is well known that young children frequently confuse letters that have the same shape but a different spatial orientation, e.g. <b, d, p, q>. (This is not surprising, since physical objects the child knows, such as mugs and chairs, do not change their identity when they are turned around or upside down.) But Gibson *et al.* (1962) found that this confusion has largely disappeared by the age of seven or eight. Summing up the evidence on letter-errors, Shankweiler and Liberman (1972) conclude, 'There is considerable agreement that after the first grade, even those children who have made little further progress in learning to read do not have significant difficulty in visual identification of individual letters' (p. 299).

Although individual letter-shapes are generally accurately recognised, problems are caused by the more complex grapheme–phoneme relationships. These occur particularly in the spelling of the vowel phonemes (see 7.1.2 above), and Shankweiler and Liberman (*ibid.*) suggest that orthographic complexity is an important reason why their subjects made more errors reading vowels than consonants. This conclusion is strengthened by the fact that their experiment revealed a scale of difficulty among the vowels themselves that correlated highly (0·83) with orthographic variability. For example, in the word-list they used, the letter <i> always corresponded to the sound /i/ and there were only 7 per cent errors made on that vowel; in contrast, the following seven patterns all represented the sound /u :/ <u>, <o>, <oo>, <ou>, <oe>, <ew>, <ui>, and 26 per cent of the responses to this vowel were wrong. Their results also suggest that the position of a letter in a word affects its chances of being read accurately, since they found more errors made on consonants in final position than in initial position.

In order to establish correspondences between graphemes and phonemes, the child, who can *see* individual graphemes on the page, needs to be able to *hear* individual phonemes in spoken words. This is not easy. There are two sources of difficulty. Firstly, there is some evidence that the young child's perception of speech might be more narrowly *phonetic* than the adult's. Read (1975) studied some children who, having been taught some basic phoneme–grapheme correspondences, independently developed their own spelling systems before they went to school. He found their unconventional spellings revealed some surprisingly systematic patterns of sound representation. For example, words such as *tray*, *try* and *dragon* were spelt <chray>, <chri>, and <jragon>. Read's explanation for this is that /t/ and /d/ tend to be affricated when they occur before /r/ and the children seem to have perceived this affrication and tried to express it in their spelling. Chomsky (1970) makes a similar observation about his five-year-old daughter. 'She objected to using the same symbol for the two stops [plosives] in the word *cocoa*. It turned out, on investigation, that the difference in aspiration between the initial and medial /k/, a difference that is barely perceptible to the adult ear, seemed to be sufficiently significant to require a different symbolisation' (p. 17). A pre-school child known to the writer was playing the game of 'I spy' and said he could see something beginning with /t/. When everyone had failed to guess the answer, he announced that it was *chair*. Apparently he was able to analyse the initial affricate /tʃ/ into two distinct elements. The child who has such phonetic, rather than phonemic, perceptions does not have the same phonemic system as the adult. Therefore even those relationships between phonemes and graphemes that are completely regular and predictable for the adult may seem arbitrary to the child. For example, for an adult, the spellings <pat> and <spat> are perfectly regular. But if the child perceives the two /p/ sounds as different because of the absence of aspiration in the second one, then it will be hard for him to realise there is a regular correspondence between the letter <p> and the sound /p/.

The second source of difficulty for children in becoming aware of the phonemes of speech is that, when they hear words in the spoken language, they perceive them as unanalysed wholes. It requires considerable linguistic awareness to be able to divide a word appropriately into meaningless segments (see 6.1 above). Zhurova (1964) carried out some experiments with four- to six-year-old children in order to discover whether they could separate sounds in words. She found that it was clearly an age-related ability but that appropriate teaching could speed up the developmental process. Subjects were asked to give the first sound in the names of various animals in a folk-story; typical exchanges went like this:

Experimenter: What's the first sound in your name?
Subject: *Bel-ka* [squirrel] . . . No, not like that . . .
  Belka . . . How does it go? . . . I can't do it.
Experimenter: *B—b—belka*
Subject: B—b . . . right?

It is noticeable how much easier the children found it to divide words into syllables than into phonemes.

Another source of difficulty that occurs at word-level is the blending of separately pronounced sounds into a whole word. (The child will obviously find such blending difficult if he has not yet developed the awareness of the phonemic structure of words that was discussed in the last paragraph.) A study by Chall *et al.* (1963) suggests that the ability to blend sounds into words develops with age. In their experiment they found that six-year-old children made only 25 per cent correct responses to the Roswell-Chall Auditory Blending Test, whereas nine-year old children achieved an average score of nearly 63 per cent. Many infant teachers have certainly had experience of the child who carefully and accurately sounds out /d—ɔ—g/ several times and then, after a furtive glance at the picture, says triumphantly *puppy*.

To sum up, these are the aspects of early reading that seem to cause most difficulty: learning complex and variable grapheme–phoneme correspondences (particularly the vowels); analysing spoken words into phonemes; and blending separate phonemes into whole words.

Some scholars, notably Frank Smith and Kenneth Goodman, are highly critical of pedagogic emphasis on letters and words, believing that children should 'read for meaning'. A typical statement is this one from Smith (1973): 'Children learn to read only by reading ... This means not forcing a child to read for words when he is, or should be, reading for meaning; not forcing him to slow down when he should speed up' (p. 195). And Goodman (1972) says, 'Teaching kids to match letters to sounds is not related to the end, which is comprehension' (p. 1261). Without doubt, children read with greater fluency—and enjoyment—when they understand what they are reading, but it is unlikely that this can happen without accurate *word*-reading. Shankweiler and Liberman (1972) tested children of varying ages on the Gray Oral Reading Test, which measures fluency and accuracy of reading connected text. They compared the results with the scores their subjects obtained on word-lists and found correlations of above 0·7. They comment, 'One often encounters the claim that there are many children who can read individual words well yet do not seem able to comprehend connected text ... Our experience suggests that the problem is rare, and that poor reading of text with little comprehension among beginning readers is usually a consequence of reading words poorly (i.e. with many errors and/or at a slow rate)' (p. 294).

7.2.3 *Error analysis*

As young children's errors in speech reveal the grammatical generalisations they have made (see 3.4.1 above), so the errors they make in reading give some indication of how they tackle the task and what the process means to them. Studies of reading errors by Clay (1969), Goodman (1969) and Weber (1970) are among several which reach the conclusion that children are aware of the developing grammatical and semantic structure of the passage they are reading. If they make an error it is likely to be grammatically appropriate to the preceding context. (Most errors which are grammatically appropriate are also semantically acceptable.) An error which makes sense is generally unnoticed by the child; however, if an error makes nonsense of the passage, the child is more likely to try to correct it spontaneously. Such studies suggest that written material that is predictable in linguistic structure will be easier for children to read than books where the language is stilted and unnatural, making it difficult for the learner to predict what word might come next.

7.2.4 *Optimal age for learning to read*

There is an amazingly wide range of opinions about the age at which children will learn to read most successfully. Some people advocate teaching children as young as two-and-a-half, e.g. Doman (1965), Söderbergh (1971). Referring to such studies, Carroll suggests that the transfer from spoken to written language may be easier when the experience of acquiring the spoken language is still recent (Kavanagh and Mattingly, 1972). The Bullock Report (D.E.S., 1975) suggests, 'Children with a mental age of four-and-a-half to five can quite happily learn to read if they are given learning experiences which match their individual needs' (p. 100). Zhurova's study (see 7.2.2 above) suggests that children cannot readily perceive the separate sounds in words until they are six, and Conrad (1972) has conducted experiments which lead him to believe that the child's phonological short-term memory is not sufficiently developed until the age of six. In Iceland children start school at seven if they have already learned to read, otherwise they must wait until they are eight. Huey (1908) believed that reading instruction should be delayed until the age of ten, to ensure that the child had fully acquired the phonological system of the language. Unlike learning to speak the mother-tongue, there appears to be no upper age-limit for learning to read.

In practice, of course, for the majority of children reading instruction begins within a year or so of the beginning of formal education. There is a widespread and continuing trend, both in Europe and the United States, towards an earlier start in the formalised teaching of reading. For example, in a survey of kindergartens in the United States in 1961–62 it was found that 25 per cent of them taught reading to some children; this figure had become 83·9 per cent by 1967–68 (Downing, 1973).

7.3   *The early stages of writing*

7.3.1   *The abilities the learner needs*

As in the analysis of the abilities required for reading (7.2.1 above), the separating and listing of the abilities needed for writing are not intended to suggest that they are either learnt or taught serially, as discrete skills. Again, the analysis can be made at the levels of (i) the letter, (ii) the word, (iii) the sentence and (iv) the discourse.

(i) *Letter level*. The pupil has to learn the physical shapes of the letters and the movements necessary to make them. These movements have to be repeated until the formation of each letter is rapid, fluent and automatic.

He has to learn the correspondences between phonemes and graphemes.

(ii) *Word level*. He needs to learn orthographic conventions, e.g. that initial /ʤ/ may be spelt <j> but that final /ʤ/ must be spelt <dge> or <ge>, e.g. *cadge, cage*.

He has to learn by heart how to spell those frequently occurring irregular words which cannot be written correctly from sound even if all the phoneme–grapheme correspondences and orthographic conventions have been mastered, e.g. *of, one, said, was*.

He needs to be able to recognise proper nouns so that he can write them with an initial capital letter.

He has to think of words as discrete units so that he can leave a space between them in writing. (That children are not always aware of the position of word-boundaries is illustrated both by research studies (e.g. Downing and Oliver, 1973) and by teachers' observations. For example, a child asked his teacher how to spell the word /'hæpiri/. Questioning revealed that he wanted to write *Many happy returns*.)

(iii) *Sentence level*. He has to learn to think of sentences as units so that he can begin them with a capital letter and end them with a full stop, question mark or exclamation mark.

(iv) *Discourse level*. Having mastered the fairly mechanical abilities in (i)–(iii), the writer has to learn to represent ideas in written rather than spoken language. (That writing is not merely speech written down has been illustrated at 7.1.3 above.) Although the foundations of this can be laid in the infant school (even young children will shape a narrative using formulaic expressions such as *once upon a time* and *happily ever after* to mark beginning and end), many writers feel that the mastery of the written language is a lifelong task. However, some basic skills—such as the avoidance of exophoric reference—have to be mastered if the writer is to create original written language that will be understood by the reader.

It is worth noting that the term *writing* is used to cover every aspect from the formation of letter-shapes to the creation of works of literary merit. This can lead to misunderstanding and confusion. For example, Professor Edmund Leach, writing in the *Observer*, suggested that the effort spent on the teaching of reading and writing was wasted because 'Typewriters provide a much more efficient means of recording speech than any calligraphy'. Apart from the fact that no typewriter is as portable as a pen, this statement is obviously mistaken, since a typewriter renders unnecessary only the formation of letter-shapes, replacing none of the other skills involved in writing.

7.3.2 *When writing is taught*

Some people advocate teaching writing before formal reading instruction begins (Spalding, 1957; C. Chomsky, 1971). It is suggested that the kinaesthetic experience of forming the letter-shapes facilitates letter-recognition in reading. Also the child is able to learn some basic phoneme–grapheme correspondences and acquire a small sight vocabulary before he begins to read, so his first reading books can be less elementary and therefore more interesting. By being helped to write about his own interests and experiences the child is learning something of the nature and purpose of written language in a very direct way.

Other people believe that children should learn to write rather later. They suggest that young children may not have the physical control and coordination necessary to form letters. In addition, the task is initially very slow and laborious and may lead to frustration and boredom.

A compromise position is found in the use of the Schools Council *Breakthrough to Literacy* materials (Mackay *et al.*, 1970). Each child has a folder containing cards printed with words which are used frequently in children's writing, grammatical morphemes, e.g. <ing> and <ed>, and punctuation marks. There are also blank cards on which the teacher can write the child's more personal choice of vocabulary. The child composes his 'stories' by placing the appropriate word-cards in the right order in a cardboard frame called a Sentence Maker. He is thus able to experience the satisfaction of using written language to express his own ideas without having to struggle to write the letters or spell the words. He is even given help in the processes of word-formation and in the recognition of word-boundaries.

7.4 *Approaches to the teaching of reading*

In one sense it is true to say that there are as many approaches to the teaching of reading as there are teachers. There are, however, some generalisations that can be made. This section will very briefly consider phonic and whole-word methods and eclectic and language-experience approaches. (A useful account of the terminology is given in Southgate and Roberts, 1970.)

7.4.1 *Phonic method*

This method emphasises the phonemic structure of spoken words and the way graphemes represent this structure in writing. A *synthetic* phonic approach begins with individual letters and the sounds they represent and builds up to whole words. An *analytic* phonic approach starts with regularly spelt words and breaks them down into their grapho-phonemic components.

Advantages

(i) The method exploits fully the economy of an alphabetic script.

(ii) It leads naturally into the teaching of writing and spelling.

(iii) There is evidence that children recognise words by their component letters, particularly the initial letter, not by overall configuration (Marchbanks and Levin, 1965), so a method which emphasises letter recognition capitalises on this mode of identification.

(iv) An awareness of phoneme–grapheme correspondences lessens the burden on visual memory.

(v) Phonic knowledge provides a means of tackling an unfamiliar word (Jeffrey and Samuels, 1967).

Disadvantages

(i) The analysis of spoken words into phonemes is difficult (see 7.2.2 above).

(ii) It is difficult to pronounce some phonemes in isolation without distortion, so /k-æ-t/ easily becomes /kə-æ-tə/.

(iii) The blending of phonemes into words is difficult (see 7.2.2 above).

(iv) Phoneme–grapheme correspondences in English are complex (see 7.1.2 above).

(v) A number of highly frequent words in English are not susceptible to phonic analysis, e.g. *one*, *many*.

(vi) At best, phonics is a heuristic device; it does not provide the spoken word, rather it gives clues to its pronunciation. (For example, if a child meets the unfamiliar word <parrot> and has sufficient phonic knowledge he will be able to say /pærɔt/; only if he knows the name of the bird already will he be able to make the change to /pærət/.)

7.4.2 *Whole word method*

This method (sometimes called a look-and-say, or sight method) emphasises the visual shape of the written word without analysing it into smaller components. (In other words, written words are treated as if they were the unanalysable characters of a morphemic writing system, such as Chinese.)

Advantages

(i) The method makes no demands on linguistic awareness, since no analysis is required.

(ii) It is a good method for reading irregular words.

(iii) It encourages instant naming of a word (rather than the letter-by-letter sounding which can occur if there is strong emphasis on phonic analysis). This may lay the foundation of fluent reading.

Disadvantages

(i) It provides no help with writing and spelling.

(ii) It imposes an enormous burden on visual memory.

(iii) English words are not well differentiated visually; in ordinary prose, 80 per cent of all words begin with only ten different letters; 70 per cent of all words end in only six different letters (Baddeley *et al.*, 1960).

(iv) It gives no method of attacking unfamiliar words.

(v) It may encourage the child to pay attention to gross physical differences in words, such as ascending or descending letters, and to ignore finer detail. This can cause the formation of bad reading habits.

(vi) Eye-movement studies by Taylor *et al.* (1960) suggest that children do not take in a whole word at a single eye-fixation until the age of ten.

7.4.3 *Language-experience approach*

This approach does not use printed materials for initial instruction. Rather, the child's own writing (either written down from his dictation by the teacher or composed with *Breakthrough to Literacy* cards—see 7.3.2 above) provides the first reading material. In this way, it is certain that the language the child reads will be within his own level of language development, in terms of both grammar and vocabulary. Also, the child is less likely to experience cognitive confusion about the purpose of reading than if he were reading a book written in language he does not use about children whose interests and experiences are remote from his own. However, by itself the method does not explicitly or systematically reveal anything about the relationships between letters and sounds. (For a fuller account, see Goddard, 1974.)

7.4.4 *Eclectic approach*

This approach is probably the one most widely used in Great Britain. A survey of teaching methods in British primary schools conducted by the Bullock committee (D.E.S., 1975) revealed that most teachers used a combination of several methods. Ninety-seven per cent of all teachers questioned used both phonics and the whole-word method. Generally, the first words are taught using a whole-word or language-experience approach, so that the problem of phonemic analysis does not arise until the child has some insight into the reading process. Phonics is introduced gradually so that the child can induce phoneme–grapheme correspondences and develop a method of independent word-attack. This mixed-method approach recognises the nature of the English writing system—fundamentally alphabetic but complex in its grapho-phonemic correspondences.

7.5 *The language of reading materials*

At the beginning of this chapter it was suggested that one of the key issues in the teaching of reading may be the way in which written language is simplified for the beginner. There are various ways in which this is done.

Some early reading materials are printed in the initial teaching alphabet. To a large extent, this regularises English spelling. There are forty-four graphemes, twenty-four of them letters from the traditional alphabet, the remaining twenty mostly consisting of amalgamations of traditional letters to form composite symbols. The use of materials written in i.t.a. obviously emphasises the alphabetic nature of the writing system, since the grapho-phonemic correspondences are regular enough for children to be able to induce the relationships for themselves. Elementary i.t.a. reading books can employ a larger and more varied vocabulary than books written in traditional orthography because the regularity of the script gives the reader a reliable method for tackling unfamiliar words. Another form of special orthography (used by only 6 per cent of primary teachers) is a colour-coded script. The system devised by Jones (1967) uses the traditional alphabet but varies the colour of each letter according to its phonemic value within a word, so the <a> in *made* is printed in red and the <a> in *mad* is printed in green. Only three colours are used in addition to black, so not all the complexities of the orthography can be eradicated, but the beginning reader is given more aid in independent decoding than is afforded by the conventional writing system.

Teachers relying on a phonic method of teaching use books written as far as possible with regularly spelt words such as *cat*, *cup*, *bed*, *pin*, *pen*, *pan*, etc. Once the child has mastered phoneme–grapheme correspondences he is able to analyse words he has not met before if they are regular in spelling. So the language of phonic reading schemes is characterised by quite a large vocabulary and by rather a jerky rhythm which arises from the use of so many monosyllabic words.

The whole-word method requires a different form of simplification. There is no need for an exclusive use of short, monosyllabic words—indeed, they are too visually similar to each other to be used extensively in this approach—but it is necessary for the vocabulary to be as limited as possible so that too great a burden is not placed on the child's visual memory. When a writer tries to repeat a small number of words in as many different combinations as possible it is not surprising that this results in stilted, unnatural language, e.g. *John, see my kitten play*.

In recent years there has been a great deal of criticism of the unnatural and sometimes ungrammatical language found in elementary reading books. (There is a summary of these criticisms in Crystal, 1976.) Many people stress that, when children come to the reading task, they need to be able to utilise the language skills they have already acquired. They have already learnt to speak fluently in well formed sentences and to understand what is said to them. Their knowledge of language structure can be of benefit to them only if what they read accords with their linguistic expectations. The Bullock Report (D.E.S., 1975) comments, 'Unless there is a close match between the syntactic features of the text and the syntactic expectancies of the reader, there will be a brake on the development of word-identification. . . . There are schemes in widespread use whose language is stilted and unnatural and far removed from anything the child ever hears in real life or uses himself' (p. 105). The error-analysis studies referred to in 7.2.3 above certainly show that children are able to predict what might come next in a sentence; if the language is unnatural, then obviously prediction is no longer one of the tools available to the reader and his task is made that much harder.

The corollary of the desire for predictable language, however, is sometimes held to be that early reading books should use the sentence patterns of children's speech (Strickland, 1962; Reid, 1970). There are several problems in this approach. Firstly, there is not a great deal of information on the language patterns school-age children do use in speech. Secondly, it is not clear at what level the correspondence between spoken and written patterns is important. For example, Strickland (*ibid.*) shows that the sentence pattern: Subject—Verb TO BE—Adjective (e.g. *John is tall*) occurs frequently in children's speech. The following sentence from *Racing to Read* (Tansley, 1962) has that pattern: *The roof and chimney of my house are red*. And yet the long, conjoined noun phrase in subject position seems unlikely to occur in a young child's speech. Is it sentence structure, or phrase structure, or both, that should be matched in some way to children's oral language? (Although Strickland analyses both the phrase structure and the sentence structure of early reading books in her study, she uses only overall sentence patterns in her comparison with oral language.) Thirdly, it is by no means certain that finding a written counterpart for a child's spoken language would necessarily make reading easier for him. For example, Reid (1970) suggests that, as children use long sentences in speech, reading schemes should include longer sentences than they have done in the past. But the slowness of the reading process in the early stages and the limitations on short-term memory may well mean that children cannot process long *written* sentences, although they have no problem interpreting long *spoken* ones.

It seems reasonable to suggest that children will find it difficult to read language they would never use, but that they will not necessarily be able to read with ease all the sentences that they might say.

A mother is able intuitively to simplify her language to her young child (see 3.8 above) so that at each stage in his linguistic development he hears speech which is simple enough for him to understand yet advanced enough for him to gain new grammatical understanding. Although many attempts have been made to simplify written language, it seems unlikely that the ideal way has yet been found of helping the child to take the step forward from his oral competence to the mastery of reading and writing.

Glossary *Some basic terms in phonetics and linguistics*

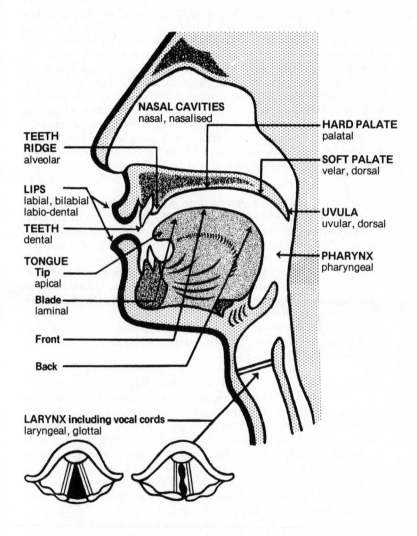

NASAL CAVITIES
nasal, nasalised

HARD PALATE
palatal

SOFT PALATE
velar, dorsal

TEETH RIDGE
alveolar

LIPS
labial, bilabial
labio-dental

TEETH
dental

UVULA
uvular, dorsal

TONGUE
Tip
apical

PHARYNX
pharyngeal

Blade
laminal

Front

Back

LARYNX including vocal cords
laryngeal, glottal

ORGANS OF SPEECH and related adjectives

This glossary is intended as a short guide to some technical terms in phonetics and linguistics. The descriptions should not be taken as formal definitions, partly because in some cases no short definition is possible without making use of other technical terms (or their formal symbols), and partly because definitions are rarely agreed on in linguistics, e.g. the term *phoneme* can be given a physical, psychological, or functional definition (and some people may deny the relevance of this sort of unit altogether). Some terms are not included at all because it is assumed readers will have at least some understanding of them, e.g. *syllable*, *vowel*, and *consonant*. It is not particularly helpful to introduce the reader to more technical definitions of these terms in a short glossary. Nor is any attempt made to explain too many technicalities associated with various grammatical theories, since the use of such technicalities is very limited in the body of the book. For more detailed discussion of technical terms the reader is referred to Gimson (1970), Lyons (1968), and Quirk *et al.* (1972). Where phonetic exemplification is used in the glossary, the examples are from educated southern British English, traditionally known as Received Pronunciation (R.P.).

Accent   in this book this term is used synonymously with *stress* to indicate the making prominent of (a) certain syllable(s) in a word or utterance and is generally marked ', e.g. un'*fortunately*. This prominence may be achieved by pitch, loudness or length. Other books vary considerably in the way they use these words. Some use *accent* to mean 'made important by having a syllable made prominent'; some limit *stress* to syllables made prominent by loudness. The meaning of *accent* discussed here must not of course be confused with the word used when we are talking of a *regional accent*.

Affricate   a plosive sound (*q.v.*) in which the release stage is performed slowly so that friction occurs at the same place of articulation, e.g. the first sounds in *cheese* and *judge*.

Allophone   a variant of a phoneme (*q.v.*). Allophones may be in *complementary distribution*, that is, where one allophone occurs the other does not. Thus /p/ is always aspirated before a vowel in an accented syllable, as in *pin*, but usually unaspirated at the end of a word, e.g. *ship*. Alternatively, allophones may be in *free variation*, that is, they may freely vary within one position. Thus the phoneme /r/ in *very* may be either a voiced post-alveolar (i.e. just behind the teeth ridge), friction-less continuant (*q.v.*) or a voiced alveolar (*q.v.*) flap (*q.v.*).

Alveolar   made by a narrowing or closure between the tip or blade of the tongue and the teeth ridge (see diagram of the organs of speech), e.g. the first sounds in *tip*, *dip*, *sun*, *zoo* and *no*.

Anaphora   reference by means of a pronoun to something or somebody which has already been mentioned in the conversation, e.g. *I've just seen John. He said that* . . . Anaphora should be compared with *exophora*, by which reference is made to something or somebody present in the situation, e.g. *I don't like the look of that*, where *that* is referring to something which has just been brought into the room.

Apical   made with the tip of the tongue. In English this covers sounds which are usually classified as dental (/θð/), alveolar (/tdnsz/), and palato-alveolar (/ʃtʃdʒ/). The term *coronal* is sometimes used in the literature in a nearly equivalent way.

Assimilation   the changing of one sound to another under the influence of a neighbouring sound, e.g. *in parliament* /in pɑ :ləmənt/ changing to /im pɑ :ləmənt/ in which, under the influence of the bilabial plosive /p/, the alveolar nasal /n/ has changed to the bilabial /m/. Assimilation may be *regressive*, when a later sound influences an earlier sound, as in the example just given; or *progressive*, when the earlier sound influences the later sound, e.g. *it is* /it iz/ > /its/, whereby /z/ > /s/ under the influence of the proceding /t/ after /i/ has been elided. Assimilation usually involves a change from voiceless to voiced or vice versa (as in the last example) or a change of place of articulation (as in the first example).

Bilabial   made by a narrowing or closure between the two lips (see diagram of the organs of speech), e.g. the first sounds in *pea* and *booth*.

Cardinal Vowels   a set of auditory reference points, commonly used by British phoneticians, for describing vowel qualities. The original set of Cardinal Vowels were recorded by Daniel Jones and the reader is referred to Jones (1956) for further explanation.

Case grammar   such a grammar suggests that underlying all (surface) sentences is a deep structure which consists basically of a proposition plus a modality. The modality component contains elements that modify the proposition as a whole. The proposition 'consists of a verb and one or more noun phrases, each associated with the verb in a particular case relationship' (Fillmore, 1968). The original list of case relationships proposed by Fillmore was agentive, instrumental, dative, factitive, locative, and objective. Each verb is associated with a particular selection from this list, and there are rules which determine how the various underlying cases are realised in terms of subject, direct object, indirect object, and so on.

Clefting   a construction designed to give special prominence to one element of a clause by dividing the clause into two separate sections. So *John hit Peter in the eye* can be altered to give special prominence to *John* by clefting it to *It was John who hit Peter in the eye*. A similar construction is *pseudo-clefting* in which a *wh-* clause fills the subject position. So the sentence *We want Watney's* can be pseudo-cleft to *What we want is Watney's* (compared with ordinary clefting to *It's Watney's that we want*).

Click   see under *Velaric ingressive airstream*.

Complementary distribution see under *Phoneme*.

Dental   made by a narrowing between the tip of the tongue and the upper teeth (see diagram of the organs of speech), e.g. the first sounds in *thorn* and *that*.

Determiner see under *Noun phrase.*

Digraph see under *Grapheme.*

Distinctive feature a feature which distinguishes two phonemes. Thus a feature of manner of articulation (plosive v. fricative) distinguishes *tea* from *sea*. The same distinctive feature may distinguish several pairs of phonemes. Thus /t/ and /d/, /p/ and /b/, /k/ and /g/ are obviously distinguished by the same distinctive feature. In this case, however, a difficulty arises, since this one distinctive feature actually varies somewhat according to the position in the syllable in which the sound occurs; voicing, aspiration, the effect on preceding sounds (consider the length of the /n/ in *lent* and *lend*), and the energy of articulation may all play a varying important part. The distinctive difference between these pairs is generally labelled by the feature which is most consistently present; in this case some consider it to be voicing, others energy of articulation (fortis v. lenis, *q.v.*).

In recent years several different sets of distinctive features have been postulated as universal, notably in the field of generative phonology, where such distinctive features are generally binary. In this book, however, more traditional articulatory features are used, largely following Trubetzkoy (1939) and Gimson (1970).

Dorsal made by a narrowing or closure involving the back of the tongue (see diagram of the organs of speech), e.g. the first sounds in *keen* and *gate* (for English this term is used synonymously with *velar*).

Double articulation (also called *Duality*) the combining of a number of sound-units to make words (or, more strictly, morphemes) and the further combining of words to make phrases and sentences. This is one of the basic facts about the structure of all human languages.

Ellipsis the omission of elements which are in some way necessary to make a sentence grammatically complete and which are easily supplied by the listener. A speaker might say *Have you seen John today?*, to which a second speaker might reply *Yes, I have*. The first speaker interprets this sentence as *Yes, I have seen John today*.

Embedding the use of a higher linguistic unit to fulfil a function in sentence structure normally filled by a lower linguistic unit. Most commonly this refers to nominalisation (*q.v.*).

Extraposition a construction designed to shift an element which would normally occur first in a sentence to a position towards the end of a sentence. So a sentence like *To get upset about it is foolish* becomes by extraposition *It is foolish to get upset about it*.

Exophora see under *Anaphora.*

Flap (also called *Tap*) a sound produced by rapidly flapping the tip of the tongue against the teeth-ridge, or the uvula (see diagram of the organs of speech) against the back of the tongue.

Fortis/Lenis made with a high amount of breath-force and muscular tension (*fortis*) or a low amount of breath-force and muscular tension (*lenis*).

Free variation see under *Phoneme.*

Fricative (also called *Spirant*)   a narrowing at some point in the vocal tract which causes fricative noise as the air passes through, e.g. the first sounds in *fat, view, think, that, sound, zoo, shoe* and the second consonant in *measure*.

Frictionless continuant (also called *Approximant*)   a sound in which, although there is a narrowing of the vocal tract which affects the quality of the sound, the narrowing is not sufficient to produce a fricative. All vowels are of this sort, although in practice the term is usually applied to those consonants which are not plosive, fricative, or affricate, e.g. the first sounds in *rat* and *last*.

Function words (sometimes called *grammatical words*)   words which have little lexical content and whose function is mainly grammatical, e.g. *to* as used in *I want to paint*. Function words contrast with *content words* (or *lexical words*) which do have lexical content. A simplistic way of dividing words into the two categories is to regard all nouns, lexical verbs (i.e. not auxiliaries and modals), adjectives, and adverbs as content words and words from all other grammatical classes as function words. But the dividing line is not really an easy one to make and is theoretically dubious, although sometimes useful in practice.

Glottal   made by a narrowing or closure of the *glottis*, the space between the vocal cords (see diagram of the organs of speech).

Grapheme   minimum distinctive unit of orthography. One grapheme may have several variants. So the grapheme <g> may occur in at least three variants g, g, and *G*. The first two variants concern handwriting v. print; the third is the capital letter used at the beginning of sentences. In English the relationship between phonemes and graphemes is inconsistent: one phoneme may in different contexts be represented by different graphemes, e.g. /i/ by <i> and <y>, while one grapheme may at times represent different phonemes, e.g. <s> may represent either /s/ or /z/. The term *grapheme* is very close in meaning to what is generally understood by *letter*, although in some cases two letters may constitute one grapheme, e.g. <qu> in English. The term *digraph* is sometimes used of a grapheme consisting of two or more letters, when it is necessary to emphasise the compound nature of the symbol.

Ideational   the term is taken from Halliday (1970) and is to be compared with *interpersonal*. The ideational aspect of language might also be called cognitive: it is concerned with the speaker's experience and knowledge of the world and with concepts like actor, affected, events, states etc. These notions are conveyed in the adult language by internal grammatical form (e.g. what the speaker decides to make the subject and object of the verb). The interpersonal aspect of language is concerned with the relationship between speaker and listener and with concepts like statement, question, and command. Such concepts are conveyed in the adult language by external grammatical form (e.g. whether the speaker decides to invert subject and verb to form a question).

Interpersonal   see *Ideational*.

Intonation   the pitch pattern of an utterance. There are three important divisions in the study of intonation. Firstly, how words are grouped together by the use of intonation, e.g. *The first person I saw/was John*. Secondly, where the main accent, or nucleus, occurs in an intonation-group, cf. *John didn't `do it* and *`John didn't do it*. The nucleus is generally indicated by the main pitch change in the group. Thirdly, the contour of the pitch pattern; here we are principally concerned with the contour from the nucleus to the end of the intonation-group, which is sometimes called the *nuclear tune*. Falling nuclear tunes are marked by `, e.g. *Didn't you `know?*. Rising tunes are marked by, e.g. *Didn't you know?* Falling–rising tunes are marked by ˇ, e.g. *Didn't you `know?*.

Labial   made by a narrowing or closure between the two lips (= *bilabial*) or between the lower lip and the upper teeth (= *labio-dental*) (see diagram of the organs of speech), e.g. the first sounds in *fast, vase, pork, bottle* and *wing* (see also labio-dental, bilabial, and labio-velar).

Labio-dental   made by a narrowing or closure between the lower lip and the upper teeth (see diagram of the organs of speech), e.g. the first sounds in *fast* and *vase*.

Labio-velar   made by a narrowing both at the lips and between the back of the tongue and the soft palate (see diagram of the organs of speech), e.g. the first sound in *west*.

Lateral   a sound in which a closure is made somewhere in the middle of the mouth, but in which air escapes round one or both sides of this closure, e.g. the first sound in *leaf*.

Lenis   see under *Fortis*.

Metathesis   the interchanging of two sounds, e.g. *remember* >/mərembə/, *car park* >/pɑ :kɑ :k/.

Morpheme   the smallest grammatical and lexical unit; the minimal unit of meaning, e.g. *cat, dog, horse, to, the*; *cat* and *fish* in *catfish*; and the plural morpheme {-Z} represented by /s/ in *cats*, /z/ in *dogs*, and /iz/ in *horses* (these variants of a morpheme as exemplified in the plural morpheme are called *allomorphs* and the set of variants is referred to as *morphophonemic variation*). *Cat, fish, dog* and *horse* are called free morphemes because they can stand as words on their own. The plural morpheme {-Z} is called a bound morpheme because it cannot stand on its own. Bound morphemes may either be largely grammatical in function like the English plural morpheme or largely lexical in function (*derivational*) like the ending *-let* involved in *droplet*. Derivational morphemes may involve no change in word-class, as in the preceding example (both *drop* and *droplet* are nouns), or they may involve a change of word-class, e.g. *perform/performer* (verb to noun).

Nasal   a sound in which there is a complete closure somewhere in the mouth, but the soft palate is lowered, allowing air to escape through the nose (see diagram of the organs of speech), e.g. the first sounds in *nose* and *mouth*, and the last sound in *sing*.

Neutralisation   the non-existence of a contrast between two sounds in one context when they are generally in contrast in other contexts. Thus

/p/ and /b/ are generally in contrast in English, e.g. *pea* v. *bee*, but after /s/ there is no contrast, e.g. there are not two words /spin/ and /sbin/. The contrast between /p/ and /b/ is said to be neutralised after /s/.

Nominalisation   the use of a whole sentence to fulfil a function in another sentence which is usually filled by a noun phrase e.g. *he knew what he ought to do*. Here *what he ought to do* has a subject and a verb of its own, i.e. it is like a sentence, but nevertheless functions as the object of *knew* in the higher sentence.

Noun phrase   this is the unit which may fulfil the functions of subject and complement (including object) in sentence structure (*q.v.*). At its simplest a noun phrase may consist of a noun on its own or with a *determiner* (most commonly *a* or *the*), e.g. *John*, *bread*, or *a pen*. Noun phrases may be expanded with various types of premodification (e.g. *all the books*, *all the pretty books*, *a car-hire company*, *the King of Spain's daughter*) and postmodification (e.g. *the man on the moon*, *the man controlling the operation*).

Object   see under *Sentence structure*.

Palatal   made by a narrowing or closure between the front of the tongue and the hard palate (see diagram of the organs of speech), e.g. the first sound in *yacht*.

Phoneme   the 'minimal contrastive unit of sound', made up of a bundle of *distinctive features* (*q.v.*), e.g. the phonemes /p/ and /b/ in *pin* and *bin*. Phonemes may have different *allophones* (*q.v.*), e.g. the /p/ in *pin* is aspirated, whereas the /p/ in *ship* is unaspirated.

Pseudo-clefting   see under *Clefting*.

Plosive (sometimes called *Stop*)   a sound made by a complete closure at some point in the vocal tract, e.g. the first sounds in *pot*, *born*, *tea*, *dark*, *cup*, *gate*. Plosive sounds have three stages: (i) the closing stage of the relevant place of articulation, e.g. bilabial in *pot*; (ii) the compression of air behind this closure; (iii) the sudden release of the closure with an explosion.

Prosodic   this term covers all aspects of sound systems above the level of segmental sounds, e.g. *accent* (*q.v.*), *rhythm*, and *intonation* (*q.v.*).

Received Pronunciation (or R.P.)   the type of British English pronunciation which is generally regarded as 'standard' and which is described in most British textbooks on phonetics and pronunciation. The educated speech of the south-east of England is nearest to this 'standard'. Of course many people speak some sort of mixture between a regional accent and R.P.

Reduplication   a syllable and its immediate repetition, e.g. [dada], [mama].

Reference   the relationship between words and the 'things' they name or stand for. Reference is a relationship easier to study when the 'things' referred to are physical objects like dogs and cars than when they are abstract qualities like happiness or pain. See Lyons (1968).

Roll   see *Trill*.

Semantic feature   one of the components of the meaning of a word. Thus various combinations of the features *temporal*, *simultaneous*, and *prior* might be involved in some of the occurrences of *after*, *before*, and *when* (see E. V. Clark, 1971). Some linguists have recently suggested that all word-meanings can be broken down into combinations from a universal set of such features and that languages differ in the way they combine these features into words; but such an all-embracing claim is at least dubious. As has been pointed out many times, the relationship between the meanings associated with a single word is often such that it is difficult to find any one feature which they all share (e.g. Wittgenstein's, 1963, example of *game*). More recently a 'prototype' theory of word-meaning has been suggested according to which there is one basic meaning for a word from which other meanings radiate out. This viewpoint is difficult to maintain for abstract items in the adult language (e.g. what is the prototype *animal*?) but may be helpful in the study of child language, since children often learn a word-meaning in a special environment (e.g. *dog* may be learnt as referring to the dog in the house). See full discussion of semantic features in Lyons (1968).

Sense 'By the *sense* of a word we mean its place in a system of relationships which it contracts with other words in the vocabulary' (Lyons, 1968). Sense relationships have generally been studied in a particular *semantic field*, e.g. colour-terms. It has, for example, been hypothesised that the meaning of a colour-term in a language is partly determined by the total number of colour-terms which divide the spectrum in that language. In acquisition studies it is useful to look at all the terms in a particular semantic field (e.g. dimensional adjectives) and see how the child gradually acquires an interconnected set of meanings.

Sentence 'an independent linguistic form, not included by virtue of any grammatical construction in any larger form' (Harris, 1946). Such a definition may be helpful for the adult language; but is difficult to apply to early child utterances, because it is not at all clear how to determine that a grammatical construction is present. Child language seems to demand an approach from intonation: if a unified intonation contour is present over a number of words, we can assume we are dealing with one sentence. Thus intonation can determine the presence of one or two sentences, e.g. *No lorry*. 'There isn't a lorry (in the box).' *No/lorry*. 'I don't want a car. I want a lorry.'

Sentence structure the model of sentence structure used in this book largely follows Quirk *et al*. (1972). Thus the major type of sentence has a structure of the sort *subject–verb–complement–adverbial*, in which both the complement (which includes the notion object) and the adverbial may or may not be present. The positions of subject and complement are generally filled by a *noun phrase* (*q.v.*) and the position of verb by a *verb phrase* (*q.v.*). In some other grammatical descriptions verb and complement are grouped together as *predicate*.

Sibilant the term is used for those sounds (e.g. English /szʃʒtʃdʒ/) which are characterised by a particular type of friction (sibilance) produced by making a groove in the tip and/or blade of the tongue.

Stop   see under *Plosive*.

Stress   see under *Accent*.

Stress-timed/syllable-timed   different languages use different types of rhythm. The two extremes are *syllable-timed*, when an approximately equal amount of time is taken over each syllable (as in French); and stress-timed, when there is a tendency to take an equal amount of time between stressed syllables (as in English). Thus in a sentence like *There's a 'terrible 'noise 'coming from 'Dan's 'workshop, 'Bill*, a roughly equal amount of time is taken for *noise*, which is one syllable, *workshop*, which has two syllables, and *coming from*, which consists of three syllables. Regardless of the type of rhythm used in the adult language, early child language tends to be syllable-timed.

Subject   see under *Sentence structure*.

Syllable-timed   see under *Stress-timed*.

Transformational-generative grammar   it is impossible to put an adequate short gloss on this type of grammar, which, since the publication of Chomsky's *Syntactic Structures* in 1957, has, in several major and many minor variants, dominated linguistic theory. The model proposed by Chomsky in *Aspects of the Theory of Syntax* (1965) has become known as the 'Standard Theory'. It is this version which has been used to describe early child syntax in several influential books (notably Bloom, 1970). The syntactic component of this type of grammar is itself divided into two parts: a base component, which consists primarily of phrase-structure rules; and a transformational component which maps the *deep structures* of the base component into *surface structures* by processes of deletion, addition and permutation. It is the most basic phrase-structure rules which have been utilised in applications of the *Aspects* grammar to child language: S (Sentence) is made up of (or, technically, 'rewritten as') NP + VP (VP here equals predicate, since it includes any object or complement); VP then (when a transitive verb is present) splits into V + NP (V is what Quirk *et al.*, 1972, and this book, call VP). The *Aspects* model uses a purely grammatical deep structure (although of course this grammatical base is used in any semantic interpretation of the sentence), whereas a case grammar (*q.v.*) uses semantic notions like agentive and dative in its base.

Trill   a sound made by a number of rapid taps of the tip of the tongue against the teeth-ridge (as in Spanish *perro*) or by the uvula against the back of the tongue (as in stage pronunciations of the French *r* sound).

Uvular   made by a narrowing or closure between the back of the tongue and the uvula (the small appendage hanging down at the back of the soft palate—see diagram of the organs of speech), e.g. the first sound in French *rare*.

Velar   made by a narrowing or closure between the back of the tongue and the soft palate (see diagram of the organs of speech), e.g. the first sounds in *keen* and *gate*.

Velaric ingressive airstream   most speech sounds are made by interfering in some way with air which is being pushed out of the lungs (i.e. the airstream is *pulmonic egressive*). Sounds using other airstreams occur as phonemes in other languages and also extra-linguistically in English. Among such sounds are the *clicks* which are made by making a closure between the back of the tongue and the soft palate (i.e. they are *velaric*). After another closure has been made somewhere further forward in the mouth, the cavity between the two closures is enlarged by muscular action. When the forward closure is then released, air rushes in (i.e. the airstream is *ingressive*), producing a click, e.g. the sound in 'tut-tut' or 'gee-up'.

Verb phrase   this is the unit which fulfils the function of verb in sentence structure (*q.v.*). It may consist of a simple verb as in *He disappears* or it may be expanded in ways involving tense (e.g. *He disappeared*), aspect (e.g. *She is working hard*), mood (e.g. *She might go*), voice (e.g. *He was bitten by a snake*), negation (e.g. *He didn't go*), and other modifications of meaning. The basic verb itself may be of a phrasal kind, e.g. *The trouble blew over*.

Voiced   made with the voicing which is produced by the vibration of the vocal cords within the larynx. In English the consonant phonemes /ptkfθsʃhtʃ/ are most commonly *voiceless*, while all other consonant phonemes and the vowel phonemes are typically *voiced*.

Word   the 'minimum free form' (consisting of one or more morphemes), i.e. a form which cannot be further analysed without leaving some part which is incapable of standing on its own, e.g. *cat*, *dog*, *horses*, *disorganised*. This sort of definition enables us to divide sentences into words: it does not, however, limit words semantically. We would certainly wish to consider the same form with two obviously different meanings as two different words, e.g. *peace* and *piece* (both /piːs/), i.e. we consider the two words to be homonyms; whereas we might wish to consider *coat* in *a duffle coat* and *a coat of paint* as the same word with different but related meanings (polysemy). But the dividing line is not clear: are we to consider *bright* in *bright sunlight* and *bright child* as a case of homonymy or polysemy? For full discussion, see Lyons (1968).

References

Albrow, K. H. (1972) *The English writing system: notes towards a description*. Schools Council Programme in Linguistics and English Teaching Papers, Series II, Vol. 2. London: Longman.

Allerton, D. J. (1976) 'Early phonotactic development: some observations on a child's acquisition of initial consonant clusters'. *Journal of Child Language*, 3, 429–33.

Amidon, A. (1976) 'Understanding sentences with connectives'. *Journal of Experimental Child Psychology*, 22, 423–37.

Amidon, A., and Carey, P. (1972) 'Why five-year-olds cannot understand *before* and *after*'. *Journal of Verbal Learning and Verbal Behaviour*, 11, 417–23.

Anglin, J. M. (1970) *The growth of word-meaning*. Cambridge, Mass.: M.I.T. Press.

Anthony, A., Boyle, D., Ingram, T. T. S., and McIsaac, M. W. (1971) *The Edinburgh Articulation Test*. Edinburgh and London: E. S. Livingstone.

Antinucci, F., and Miller, R. (1976) 'How children talk about what happened'. *Journal of Child Language*, 3, 167–89.

Asch, S. E., and Nerlove, H. (1960) 'The development of double function terms in children: an exploratory study'. In Kaplan, B. and Wapner, S. (eds), *Perspectives in psychological theory: essays in honour of Heinz Werner*. New York: International Humanities Press.

Atkinson-King, K. (1973) 'Children's acquisition of phonological stress contrasts'. University of California at Los Angeles: Working Papers in Phonetics, 25.

Atkinson, K., MacWhinney, B., and Stole, C. (1969) 'An experiment in the recognition of babbling'. University of California at Berkeley: Language Behaviour Research Laboratory, Working Paper No. 15.

Baddeley, A. D., Conrad, R., and Thomson, W. E. (1960) 'Letter structure of the English language'. *Nature*, 186, 414–16.

Baldie, B. J. (1976) 'The acquisition of the passive voice'. *Journal of Child Language*, 3, 31–48.

Bar-Adon, A., and Leopold, W. F. (eds) (1971) *Child language: a book of readings*. Englewood Cliffs, N. J.: Prentice-Hall.

Barrie-Blackley, S. (1973) 'Six-year-old children's understanding of sentences adjoined with time adverbs'. *Journal of Psycholinguistic Research*, 2, 153–65.

Bartlett, E. J. (1976) 'Sizing things up: the acquisition of the meaning of dimensional adjectives'. *Journal of Child Language*, 3, 205–19.

Bashaw, W. L., and Anderson, H. E. Jr (1968) 'Developmental study of the meaning of adverbial modifiers'. *Journal of Educational Psychology*, 59, 111–18.

Beaken, M. (1972) 'Speech-sound discrimination and developing speech'. *Journal of the International Phonetic Association*, 2, 48–57.

Bellugi, U. (1967) 'The acquisition of negation'. Unpublished doctoral dissertation, Harvard University. [Cited in McNeill, D. (1970).]

Bellugi, U., and Brown, R. (eds), *The acquisition of language. Monographs of the society for research in child development*, 29. Chicago: Chicago University Press.

Bellugi, U., and Klima, E. S. (1968) 'Linguistic mechanisms underlying child speech'. In Zale, H. (ed.), *Proceedings of the conference in language and language behaviour*. New York: Appleton-Century-Crofts.

Berdiansky, B., Cronnell, B., and Koehler, J. (1969) *Spelling-sound relations and primary form-class descriptions for speech-comprehension vocabularies of 6–9-year-olds*. Southwest Regional Laboratory for Educational Research and Development, Technical Report No. 15. [Cited in Smith, F. (1973).]

Bereiter, C., and Engelmann, S. (1966) *Teaching disadvantaged children in the preschool*. Englewood Cliffs, N.J.: Prentice-Hall.

Berko, J. (1958) 'The child's learning of English morphology'. *Word*, 14, 150–77. [Reprinted in Saporta, S. (ed.), *Psycholinguistics: a book of readings*. New York: Holt, Rinehart & Winston.]

Bernstein, B. (1971) *Class, codes, and control*. Vol. 1: *theoretical studies towards a sociology of language*. London: Routledge & Kegan Paul.

Bever, T. G., Fodor, J. A., and Weksel, W. (1965a) 'On the acquisition of syntax: a critique of contextual generalisation'. *Psychological Review*, 72, 467–82. [Reprinted in Jacobovits, L. A., and Miron, M. S. (eds), *Readings in the psychology of language*.]

Bever, T. G., Fodor, J. A., and Weksel, W. (1965b) 'Is linguistics empirical?' *Psychological Review*, 72, 492–500. [Reprinted in Jacobovits, L. A., and Miron, M. S. (eds), *Readings in the psychology of Language*.]

Blasdell, R., and Jensen, P. (1970) 'Stress and word position as determinants of imitation in first-language learners'. *Journal of Speech and Hearing Research*, 13, 193–202.

Bloom, L. (1970) *Language development: form and function in emerging grammars*. Cambridge, Mass.: M.I.T. Press.

Bloom, L. (1971) 'Why not pivot grammar?' *Journal of Speech and Hearing Disorders*, 36, 40–50.

Bloom, L. (1973) *One word at a time*. The Hague: Mouton.

Bloom, L. (1976) 'An integrated perspective on language development'. *Papers and Reports on Child Language Development*, 12, 1–22.

Bloom, L., Hood, L., and Lightbown, P. (1974) 'Imitation in language development: if, when, and why'. *Cognitive Psychology*, 6, 380–420.

Bowerman, M. (1973) *Early syntactic development with special reference to Finnish*. Cambridge: Cambridge University Press.

Braine, M. D. S. (1963a) 'On learning the grammatical order of words'. *Psychological Review*, 70, 323–40. [Reprinted in Jakobovits, L. A., and Miron, M. S. (ed), *Readings in the psychology of language*.]

Braine, M. D. S. (1963b) 'The ontogeny of English phrase structure: the first phase'. *Language*, 39, 1–14.

Braine, M. D. S. (1965) 'On the basis of phrase structure: a reply to Bever, Fodor, and Weksel'. *Psychological Review*, 72, 483–92. [Reprinted in Jakobovits, L. A., and Miron, M. S. (eds), *Readings in the psychology of language*.]

Brewer, W. F., and Stone, J. B. (1975) 'Acquisition of spatial antonym pairs'. *Journal of Experimental Child Psychology*, 19, 299–307.

Brown, R. (1958a) 'How shall a thing be called?' *Psychological Review*, 65, 14–21. [Reprinted in Oldfield, R. C., and Marshall, J. W. (eds), *Language*.]

Brown, R. (1958b) *Words and things*. Glencoe, Ill.: Free Press.

Brown, R. (1970) 'The first sentences of child and chimpanzee'. In Brown, R., *Psycholinguistics: selected papers*. New York: Free Press.

Brown, R. (1973) *A first language: the early stages*. Cambridge, Mass.: Harvard University Press.

Brown, R., and Bellugi, U. (1964) 'Three processes in the child's acquisition of syntax'. In Lenneberg, E. H. (ed.), *New directions in the study of language*.

Brown, R., Cazden, C., and Bellugi, U. (1969) 'The child's grammar from I to III'. In Hill, J. P. (ed.), *Minnesota symposia on child psychology*. Vol. II. Minneapolis: University of Minnesota Press. [Reprinted in Ferguson, C. A., and Slobin, D. I. (eds), *Studies of child language development*.]

Brown, R., and Fraser, N. (1963) 'The acquisition of syntax'. In Cofer, N., and Musgrave, B. S. (ed), *Verbal behaviour and learning: problems and processes*. New York: McGraw-Hill.

Brown, R., and Hanlon, C. (1970) 'Derivational complexity and order of acquisition in child speech'. In Hayes, J. R. (ed.), *Cognition and the development of language*. New York: John Wiley.

Bruce, D. J. (1964) 'The analysis of word sounds by young children'. *British Journal of Educational Psychology*, 34, 158–69.

Bruner, J. S. (1975) 'The ontogenesis of speech acts'. *Journal of Child Language*, 2, 1–19.

Bullowa, M., Jones, L. G., and Duckert, A. R. (1964) 'The acquisition of a word'. *Language and Speech*, 7, 107–11.

Carroll, J. B. (1972) 'The case for ideographic writing'. In Kavanagh, J. F., and Mattingly, I. G. (eds), *Language by ear and by eye*.

Carrow, M. A. (1968) 'The development of auditory comprehension of language structure in children'. *Journal of Speech and Hearing Disorders*, 33, 99–111.

Cazden, C. (1968) 'The acquisition of noun and verb inflections'. *Child Development*, 39, 433–8. [Reprinted in Ferguson, C. A., and Slobin, D.

I., *Studies of Child language development*.]

Cazden, C. (1972) *Child language and education*. New York: Holt, Rinehart & Winston.

Chall, J., Rosewell, F. G., and Blumenthal, S. H. (1963) 'Auditory blending ability: a factor in success in beginning reading'. *The Reading Teacher*, 17, 113–18.

Chomsky, C. (1969) *The acquisition of syntax in children from five to ten*. Cambridge, Mass.: M.I.T. Press.

Chomsky, C. (1971a) *Linguistic development in children from six to ten*. Final Office of Education report. [Cited in Atkinson-King, (1973).]

Chomsky, C. (1971b) 'Write first, read later'. *Childhood Education*, 47, 296–9.

Chomsky, N. (1957) *Syntactic structures*. The Hague: Mouton.

Chomsky, N. (1959) Review of Skinner, B. F. (1957) In *Language*, 35, 26–58.

Chomsky, N. (1964) Formal discussion of Miller, W., and Ervin, S. (1964).

Chomsky, N. (1965) *Aspects of the theory of syntax*. Cambridge, Mass.: M.I.T. Press.

Chomsky, N. (1968) *Language and mind*. New York: Harcourt Brace.

Chomsky, N. (1970) 'Phonology and reading'. In Levin, H., and Williams, J. P. (eds), *Basic studies on reading*.

Chomsky, N., and Halle, M. (1968) *The sound pattern of English*. New York: Harper & Row.

Clark, E. V. (1971) 'On the acquisition of the meaning of *before* and *after*'. *Journal of Verbal Learning and Verbal Behaviour*, 10, 266–75.

Clark, E. V. (1973) 'What's in a word? On the child's acquisition of semantics in his first language'. In Moore, T. E. (ed.), *Cognitive development and the acquisition of language*.

Clark, H. H. (1970) 'The primitive nature of children's relational concepts'. In Hayes, J. R. (ed.), *Cognition and the development of language*.

Clark, H. H. (1973) 'Space, time, semantics, and the child'. In Moore, T. E. (ed.), *Cognitive development and the acquisition of language*.

Clark, R. (1974) 'Performing without competence'. *Journal of Child Language*, 1, 1–10.

Clay, M. M. (1969) 'Reading errors and self-correction behaviour'. *British Journal of Educational Psychology*, 39, 47–56.

Cleary, C. J. D. (1976) 'A developmental study of the syntax and semantics of recurrence words'. Unpublished M. A. dissertation, University of Manchester.

Coker, P. L. (1975) 'On the acquisition of temporal terms: *before* and *after*'. *Papers and Reports on Child Language Development*, 10, 166–75.

Compton, A. J. (1970) 'Generative studies of children's phonological disorders'. *Journal of Speech and Hearing Disorders*, 35, 315–39.

Conrad, R. (1972) 'Speech and reading'. In Kavanagh, J. F., and

Mattingly, I. G. (eds), *Language by ear and by eye*.

Corrigan, R. (1975) 'A scalogram analysis of the development of the use and comprehension of "because" in children'. *Child Development*, 46, 195–201.

Cromer, R. F. (1970) ' "Children are nice to understand": surface structure clues for the recovery of deep structure'. *British Journal of Psychology*, 61, 397–408.

Cruse, D. A. (1977) 'A note on the learning of colour names'. *Journal of Child Language*, 4, 305–11.

Cruttenden, A. (1970) 'A phonetic study of babbling'. *British Journal of Disorders of Communication*, 5, 110–17.

Cruttenden, A. (1974) 'An experiment involving comprehension of intonation in children from 7 to 10'. *Journal of Child Language*, 1, 221–32.

Crystal, D. (1975) Review of Brown, R. (1973). In *Journal of Child Language*, 1, 289–307.

Crystal, D. (1976) *Child language, learning and linguistics*. London: Edward Arnold.

Crystal, D., Fletcher, P., and German, M. (1976) *The grammatical analysis of language disability*. London: Edward Arnold.

Curtiss, S., Fromkin, V., Krashen, S., Rigler, D., and Rigler, M. (1974) 'The linguistic development of Genie'. *Language*, 50, 528–54.

Dale, P. S. (1972) *Language development: structure and function*. Hinsdale, Ill.: Dryden Press.

Department of Education and Science (1975) *A language for life*. Report of the Committee of Inquiry under the Chairmanship of Sir Alan Bullock. London: Her Majesty's Stationery Office.

De Villiers, J. G., and De Villiers, P. A. (1973) 'Development of the use of word-order in comprehension'. *Journal of Psycholinguistic Research*, 2, 331–41.

Doman, G. (1965) *Teach your baby to read*. London: Cape.

Donaldson, M. (1963) *A study of Children's thinking*. London: Tavistock.

Donaldson, M., and Balfour, G. (1968) 'Less is more: a study of language comprehension in young children'. *British Journal of Psychology*, 59, 461–71.

Donaldson, M., and McGarrigle, J. (1974) 'Some clues to the nature of semantic development'. *Journal of Child Language*, 1, 185–94.

Dore, J. (1975) 'Holophrases, speech acts, and language universals'. *Journal of Child Language*, 2, 21–40.

Downing, J. (1969) 'How children think about reading'. *The Reading Teacher*, 23, 217–30.

Downing, J. (1973) *Comparative reading. Cross-national studies of behaviour and processes in reading and writing*. New York: Macmillan.

Downing, J., and Oliver, P. (1973) 'The child's conception of a "word" '. *Reading Research Quarterly*, 9, 568–82.

Drach, K. M. (1969) 'The language of the parent: a pilot study'.

University of California at Berkeley: Language Behaviour Research Laboratory, Working Paper No. 14.

Dunn, L. (1965) *Peabody Picture Vocabulary Test*. Minneapolis: American Guidance Service.

Edwards, A. D. (1976) 'Speech codes and speech variants: social class and task differences in children's speech'. *Journal of Child Language*, 3, 247–65.

Edwards, M. L. (1974) 'Perception and production in child phonology: the testing of four hypotheses'. *Journal of Child Language*, 1, 205–19.

Eilers, R. E., Kimbrough Oller, D., and Ellington, J. (1974) 'The acquisition of word-meaning for dimensional adjectives: the long and short of it'. *Journal of Child Language*, 1, 195–203.

Eimas, P. D. (1974) 'Linguistic processing of speech by young infants'. In Schiefelbusch, R. L., and Lloyd, L. L. (eds), *Language perspectives—acquisition, retardation, and intervention*. London: Macmillan.

Eimas, P. D. (1975) 'Auditory and phonetic coding of the cues for speech discrimination of the [r–1] distinction by young infants'. *Perception and Psychophysics*, 18, 341–7.

Eimas, P. D., Siqueland, E. R., Jusczyk, P., and Vigorito, J. (1971) 'Speech perception in infants'. *Science*, 171, 303–6.

Entwistle, D. R. (1966) 'Form class and children's word association'. *Journal of Verbal Learning and Verbal Behaviour*, 5, 558–65.

Entwistle, D. R., Forsyth, D. F., and Muuss, R. (1964) 'The syntagmatic–paradigmatic shift in children's word associations'. *Journal of Verbal Learning and Verbal Behaviour*, 3, 19–29.

Ervin, D. (1961) 'Changes with age in the verbal determinants of word association'. *American Journal of Psychology*, 74, 361–72.

Ervin, S. (1964) 'Imitation and structural change in children's language'. In Lenneberg, E. H. (ed.), *New directions in the study of language*.

Ervin, S. M., and Foster, G. (1960) 'The development of meaning in children's descriptive terms'. *Journal of Abnormal and Social Psychology*, 61, 271–5.

Ferguson, C. A. (1964) 'Baby talk in six languages'. *American Anthropologist*, 66, 103–14.

Ferguson, C. A. (1973) 'Fricatives in child language acquisition'. *Papers and Reports on Child Language Development*, 6, 61–85.

Ferguson, C. A., and Farwell, C. (1975) 'Words and sounds in early language acquisition'. *Language*, 51, 419–39.

Ferguson, C. A., and Slobin, D. I. (eds) (1973) *Studies of child language development*. New York: Holt, Rinehart & Winston.

Fillmore, C. (1968) 'The case for case'. In Bach, E., and Harms, R. T. (eds), *Universals in linguistic theory*. New York: Holt, Rinehart & Winston.

Fillmore, C. (1971) 'Types of lexical information'. In Steinberg, D. D., and Jakobovits, L. A. (eds), *Semantics: an interdisciplinary reader in philosophy, linguistics, and psychology*. Cambridge: Cambridge University Press.

Flores d'Arcais, G. B., and Levelt, W. J. M. (1970) *Advances in psycholinguistics*. New York: Elsevier.

Fraser, C., Brown, R., and Bellugi, U. (1963) 'Control of grammar in imitation, comprehension, and production'. *Journal of Verbal Learning and Verbal Behaviour*, 2, 121–35. [Reprinted in Oldfield, R. C., and Marshall, J. W. (eds), *Language*, and in Ferguson, C. A., and Slobin, D. I. (eds), *Studies of child language development*.]

French, M. A. (1976) 'Observations on the Chinese script and the classification of writing-systems'. In Haas, W. (ed.), *Writing without letters*. Manchester: Manchester University Press.

Fry, D. B. (1966) 'The development of the phonological system in the normal and the deaf child'. In Smith, F., and Miller, G. A. (eds), *The genesis of language*.

Fudge, E. C. (1969) 'Syllables'. *Journal of Linguistics*, 5, 254–80.

Furth, H. C. (1966) *Thinking without language: the psychological implications of deafness*. Glencoe, Ill.: Free Press.

Gardner, B. T., and Gardner, R. A. (1971) 'Two-way communication with an infant chimpanzee'. In Schrier, A., and Stollnitz, F. (eds), *Behaviour of nonhuman primates: modern research trends*. Vol. IV. New York: Academic Press.

Garnica, O. K. (1973) 'The development of phonemic speech perception'. In Moore, T. E. (ed.), *Cognitive development and the acquisition of language*.

Garnica, O. K. (1977) 'Some prosodic characteristics of speech to young children'. Ohio State University: Working Papers in Linguistics, 22, 11–72.

Gibson, E. J., Gibson, J. J., Pick, A. D., and Osser, R. (1962) 'A developmental study of the discrimination of letter-like forms'. *Journal of Comparative and Physiological Psychology*, 55, 897–906.

Gimson, A. C. (1970) *An introduction to the pronunciation of English*. Second edition. London: Edward Arnold.

Gleason, J. B. (1973) 'Code-switching in children's language'. In Moore, T. E. (ed.) *Cognitive development and the acquisition of language*.

Goddard, N. (1974) *Literacy: language-experience approaches*. London: Macmillan.

Goodglass, H., Gleason, H. A., and Hyde, M. R. (1970) 'Some dimensions of auditory comprehension in aphasia'. *Journal of Speech and Hearing Research*, 13, 584–94.

Goodman, K. S. (1969) 'Analysis of oral reading miscues: applied psycholinguistics'. *Reading Research Quarterly*, 5, 9–30.

Goodman, K. S. (1972) 'Orthography in a theory of reading instruction'. *Elementary English*, 1254–61.

Greenfield, P. M., and Smith, J. H. (1976) *The structure of communication in early language development*. New York: Academic Press.

Grégoire, A. (1937) *L'apprentissage du langage*. Vol. 1. *Les deux premières années*. Paris: Droz.

Guillaume, P. (1927) 'Les debuts de la phrase dans le langage de l'enfant'. *Journal de Psychologie*, 24, 1–25.

Haas, W. (1976) 'Writing: the basic options'. In Haas, W. (ed.), *Writing without letters*. Manchester: Manchester University Press.

Hall, R. M. R., and Hall, B. D. (1965) 'The child's learning of noun modification'. Paper read to Linguistic Society of America meeting in Chicago. [Cited in Rosenberg, S., and Koplin, J. H., *Developments in applied psycholinguistics research*.]

Halliday, M. A. K. (1970) 'Language structure and language function'. In Lyons. J. (ed.), *New horizons in linguistics*. Harmondsworth: Penguin.

Halliday, M. A. K. (1975) *Learning how to mean: explorations in the development of language*. London: Edward Arnold.

Harris, Z. S. (1946) 'From morpheme to utterance'. *Language*, 22, 161–83. [Reprinted in Joos, M. (ed.) (1957). *Readings in linguistics*, Vol. 1. Chicago: Chicago University Press.]

Hayhurst, H. (1967) 'Some errors of young children in producing passive sentences'. *Journal of Verbal Learning and Verbal Behaviour*, 6, 634–9.

Henzl, V. M. (1975) 'Acquisition of grammatical gender in Czech'. *Proceedings and Reports on Child Language Development*, 10, 188–99.

Herriot, P. (1969) 'The comprehension of tense by young children'. *Child Development*, 40, 103–10.

Huey, E. B. (1908) *The psychology and pedagogy of reading*. New York: Macmillan. Reprinted 1968, Cambridge, Mass.: M.I.T. Press.

Hunt, K. W. (1965) *Grammatical structures written at three grade levels*. Champaign, Ill.: National Council of Teachers of English.

Hutcheson, S. (1968) 'Some quantitative and qualitative criteria in articulation test scoring'. *British Journal of Disorders of Communication*, 3, 36–42.

Huttenlocher, J. (1974) 'The origins of language comprehension'. In Solso, R. L. (ed.), *Theories in cognitive psychology*. Hillsdale, N. J.: Erlbaum.

Huxley, R. (1970) 'The development of the correct use of subject personal pronouns in two children'. In Flores d'Arcais, G. B., and Levelt, W. J. M. (eds), *Advances in psycholinguistics*.

Ingram, D. (1974) 'Phonological rules in young children'. *Journal of Child Language*, 1, 49–64.

Ingram, D. (1975) 'Surface contrast in children's speech'. *Journal of Child Language*, 2, 287–92.

Irwin, O. C. (1947a) 'Infant speech: consonantal sounds according to place of articulation'. *Journal of Speech Disorders*, 12, 397–401.

Irwin, O. C. (1947b) 'Infant speech: consonantal sounds according to manner of articulation'. *Journal of Speech Disorders*, 12, 402–4.

Irwin, O. C. (1948) 'Infant speech: development of vowel sounds'. *Journal of Speech Disorders*, 13, 31–4.

Jakobovits, L. A., and Miron, M. S. (1967) *Readings in the psychology of language*. Englewood Cliffs, N. J.: Prentice-Hall.

Jakobson, R. (1941) *Kindersprache, Aphasie, und allgemeine Lautgesetze*. Uppsala: Almqvist & Wiksell. [English translation, 1968, by Keiler, A. R., under the title *Child language, aphasia and phonological universals*. The Hague: Mouton.]

Jeffrey, W., and Samuels, S. J. (1967) 'Effect of method of reading training on initial learning and transfer'. *Journal of Verbal Learning and Verbal Behaviour*, 6, 354–8.

Johansson, Bo. S., and Sjölin, B. (1975) 'Preschool children's understanding of the coordinates *and* and *or*'. *Journal of Experimental Child Psychology*, 19, 233–40.

Jones, D. (1956) *An outline of English phonetics*. New edition. Cambridge: Heffer.

Jones, D. (1967) *An English pronouncing dictionary*. Thirteenth edition, edited by Gimson, A. C. London: Dent.

Jones, J. K. (1967) *Colour story reading*. London: Nelson.

Kaplan, E. L. (1969) 'The role of intonation in the acquisition of language'. Unpublished doctoral dissertation, Cornell University. [Cited in Menyuk, P., *The development of speech*.]

Katz, E. W., and Brent, S. B. (1968) 'Understanding logical connectives'. *Journal of Verbal Learning and Verbal Behaviour*, 7, 501–9.

Kavanagh, J. F., and Mattingly, I. G. (eds) (1972) *Language by ear and by eye: the relationships between speech and reading*. Cambridge, Mass.: M.I.T. Press.

Keenan, E. (1974) 'Conversational competence in children'. *Journal of Child Language*, 1, 163–83.

Keenan, E., and Klein, E. (1975) 'Coherency in children's discourse'. *Journal of Psycholinguistic Research*, 4, 365–80.

Keller, H. (1958) *The story of my life*. New, revised and enlarged edition. London: Hodder & Stoughton.

Kenyon, J. S., and Knott, T. A. (1944) *A pronouncing dictionary of American English*. Springfield, Mass.: Merriam.

Kessell, F. S. (1970) 'The role of syntax in children's comprehension from six to twelve'. *Monographs of the Society for Research in Child Development*, 139. Chicago: Chicago University Press.

Kirk, L. (1973) 'An analysis of speech imitations by Ga children'. *Anthropological Linguistics*, 15, 267–75.

Klima, E. S., and Bellugi, U. (1966) 'Syntactic regularities in the speech of children'. In Lyons, J., and Wales, R. J. (eds), *Psycholinguistic papers*. Edinburgh: Edinburgh University Press.

Kobashigawa, B. (1969) 'Repetition in a mother's speech to her children'. University of California at Berkeley: Language Behaviour Research Laboratory, Working Paper No. 14.

Krashen, S. (1975) 'The development of cerebral dominance and language learning: more new evidence'. In Dato, D. P. (ed.), *Developmental psycholinguistics: theory and applications*. Georgetown University Round Table on Languages and Linguistics, 1975. Washington, D.C.:

Georgetown University Press.

Kuczaj II, S. A. (1975) 'On the acquisition of a semantic system'. *Journal of Verbal Learning and Verbal Behaviour*, 14, 340–58.

Kuczaj II, S. A., and Maratsos, M. P. (1975) 'On the acquisition of *front*, *back*, and *side*'. *Child Development*, 46, 202–10.

Labov, W. (1969) 'The logic of non-standard English'. *Georgetown monographs on language and linguistics*, 22, 1–31.

Lenneberg, E. H. (1962) 'Understanding language without ability to speak: a case report'. *Journal of Abnormal and Social Psychology*, 65, 419–25.

Lenneberg, E. H. (ed.) (1964) *New Directions in the study of language*. Cambridge, Mass.: M.I.T. Press.

Lenneberg, E. G. (1966) 'The natural history of language'. In Smith, F., and Miller, G. R. (eds), *The genesis of language: a psycholinguistic approach*.

Lenneberg, E. H. (1967) *Biological foundations of language*. New York: John Wiley.

Lenneberg, E. H., and Lenneberg, E. (eds) (1975) *Foundations of language development*. Two volumes. New York: Academic Press.

Legum, S. E. (1975) 'The acquisition of adverbial noun complements'. *Papers and Reports on Child Language Development*, 10, 178–85.

Leopold, W. F. *Speech development of a bilingual child: a linguist's record*. Vol. 1. (1939) *Vocabulary growth in the first two years*. Vol. 2. (1947) *Sound learning in the first two years*. Vol. 3. (1949a) *Grammar and general problems in the first two years*. Vol. 4. (1949b) *Diary from age two*. Evanston, Ill.: Northwestern University Press.

Lesser, H., and Drouin, C. (1975) 'Training in the use of double-function terms'. *Journal of Psycholinguistic Research*, 4, 285–302.

Levin, H., and Williams, J. P. (eds) (1970) *Basic studies on reading*. New York: Basic Books.

Lewis, M. M. (1936) *Infant Speech*. London: Routledge Kegan Paul.

Li, C. N., and Thompson, S. A. (1977) 'The acquisition of tone in Mandarin-speaking children'. *Journal of Child Language*, 4, 185–99.

Lieberman, P. (1967) *Intonation, perception, and language*. Cambridge, Mass.: M.I.T. Press.

Limber, J. (1973) 'The genesis of complex sentences'. In Moore, T. E. (ed.), *Cognitive development and the acquisition of language*. New York: Academic Press.

Loban, W. D. (1963) *The language of elementary children*. Champaign, Ill.: National Council of Teachers of English.

Lorenz, K. (1953) *King Solomon's ring*. London: Methuen.

Lovell, K., and Dixon, E. M. (1967) 'The growth of the control of grammar in imitation, comprehension, and production'. *Journal of Child Psychology and Psychiatry*, 8, 31–39.

Lumsden, E. A., and Poteat, B. W. S. (1968) 'The salience of the vertical dimension in the concept of "bigger" in five- and six-year-olds'. *Journal of Verbal Learning and Verbal Behaviour*, 7, 404–8.

Luria, A. R. (1959) 'The directive function of speech in development and dissolution'. *Word*, 15, 341–52 and 453–64.

Luria, A. R., and Yudovitch, F. Ia (1971) *Speech and the development of mental processes in the child*. Harmondsworth: Penguin.

Lyons, J. (1966) 'Towards a "notional" theory of the "parts of speech" '. *Journal of Linguistics*, 2, 209–36.

Lyons, J. (1968) *An introduction to theoretical linguistics*. Cambridge: Cambridge University Press.

McCarthy, D. (1930) *The language development of the pre-school child*. Minnesota: University of Minnesota Press.

McCarthy, D. (1954) 'Language development in children'. In Carmicheal, L. (ed.), *Manual of child psychology*. Second edition. New York: John Wiley.

McGrath, C. O., and Kunze, L. H. (1973) 'Development of phrase-structure rules involved in tag questions elicited from children'. *Journal of Speech and Hearing Research*, 16, 498–512.

MacKay, D., Thompson, B., and Schaub, P. (1970) *Breakthrough to literacy*. London: Schools Council/Longman.

McNeill, D. (1966a) 'The capacity for language acquisition'. *Volta Review*, 68, 5–21.

McNeill, D. (1966b) 'Developmental psycholinguistics'. In Smith, F., and Miller, G. A. (eds), *The genesis of language*.

McNeill, D. (1970) *The acquisition of language: the study of developmental psycholinguistics*. New York: Harper & Row.

McNeill, D., and McNeill, N. B. (1968) 'What does a child mean when he says "no"?' In Zale, H. (ed.), *Proceedings of the conference in language and language behaviour*. New York: Appleton-Century-Crofts. [Reprinted in Ferguson, C. A., and Slobin, D. I., *Studies of child language development*.]

MacWhinney, B. (1976) 'Hungarian research on the acquisition of morphology and syntax'. *Journal of Child Language*, 3, 397–410.

Major, D. (1974) *The acquisition of modal auxiliaries in the language of children*. The Hague: Mouton.

Maratsos, M. P. (1973) 'Decrease in the understanding of the word "big" in preschool children'. *Child Development*, 44, 747–52.

Maratsos, M. P. (1974) 'Preschool children's use of definite and indefinite articles'. *Child Development*, 45, 446–55.

Maratsos, M. P. (1976) *The use of definite and indefinite reference in young children*. Cambridge: Cambridge University Press.

Marchbanks, G., and Levin, H. (1965) 'Cues by which children recognize words'. *Journal of Educational Psychology*, 56, 57–61.

Martin, S. E. (1972) 'Nonalphabetic writing systems: some observations'. In Kavanagh, J. F., and Mattingly, I. G. (eds), *Language by ear and by eye*.

Martinet, A. (1960) *Eléments de linguistique génŕale*. Paris: Armand Colin.

Massaro, D. W. (1975) 'Primary and secondary recognition in reading'.

In Massaro, D. W. (ed.), *Understanding language*. New York: Academic Press.

Mattingly, I. G. (1972) 'Reading, the linguistic process, and linguistic awareness', In Kavanagh, J. F., and Mattingly, I. G. (eds), *Language by ear and by eye*.

Menyuk, P. (1963) 'Syntactic structures in the language of children'. *Child Development*, 34, 407–22.

Menyuk, P. (1964) 'Syntactic rules used by children from preschool through first grade'. *Child Development*, 35, 533–46.

Menyuk, P. (1969) *Sentences children use*. Cambridge, Mass.: M.I.T. Press.

Menyuk, P. (1971) *The acquisition and development of language*. Englewood Cliffs, N.J.: Prentice-Hall.

Menyuk, P., and Anderson, S. (1969) 'Children's identification and reproduction of /w/, /r/, and /l/'. *Journal of Speech and Hearing Research*, 5, 39–52.

Menyuk, P., and Bernholtz, N. (1969) 'Prosodic features and children's language production'. Quarterly Progress Report No. 93, M.I.T. Research Laboratory of Electronics, April 1969, 216–19. [Cited in Cazden, C., *Child language and education.*]

Miller, W. R., and Ervin, S. (1964) 'The development of grammar in child language'. In Bellugi, U., and Brown, R. (eds), *The acquisition of language*. [Reprinted in Ferguson, C. A., and Slobin, D. I. (eds), *Studies of child language development.*]

Moore, T. E. (ed.) (1973) *Cognitive development and the acquisition of language*. New York: Holt, Rinehart & Winston.

Morse, P. A. (1974) 'Infant speech perception: a preliminary model and review of the literature'. In Schiefelbusch, R. L., and Lloyd, L. L. (eds), *Language perspectives—acquisition, retardation, and intervention*. London: Macmillan.

Mowrer, O. H. (1950) *Learning theory and personality dynamics*. New York: Ronald Press.

Nakazima, S. (1962) 'A comparative study of the speech developments of Japanese and American English in childhood'. *Studia Phonologica*, 2, 27–39.

Neimark, E. D., and Slotnick, N. S. (1970) 'Development of the understanding of logical connectives'. *Journal of Educational Psychology*, 61, 451–60.

Nelson, K. (1973) 'Structure and strategy in learning to talk'. *Monographs of the Society for Research in Child Development*, 38. Chicago: Chicago University Press.

Nelson, K. (1974) 'Concept, wood, and sentence: interrelations in acquisition and development'. *Psychological Review*, 81, 267–85.

Nelson, K. E., Carskaddon, G., and Bonvillian, J. D. (1973) 'Syntax acquisition: impact of experimental variation in adult verbal interaction with the child'. *Child Development*, 44, 497–504.

O'Connor, J. D., and Arnold, G. F. (1973) *Intonation of colloquial*

English. Second edition. London: Longman.

O'Donnell, R. C., Griffin, W. J., and Norris, R. C. (1967) *Syntax of kindergarten and elementary school children: a transformational analysis*. Champaign, Ill.: National Council of Teachers of English.

Oldfield, R. C., and Marshall, J. W. (eds) (1968) *Language*. Harmondsworth: Penguin.

Olds, H. F. Jnr (1968) *An experimental study of syntactic factors influencing children's comprehension of certain complex relationships*. (Center for Research and Development of Educational Difficulties, Report No. 4) Cambridge, Mass.: M.I.T. Press. [Cited in Palermo, D. S., and Molfese, D. L. (1972). 'Language acquisition from age five onward'. *Psychological Bulletin*, 78, 409–28.]

Olmsted, D. L. (1966) 'A theory of the child's learning of phonology'. *Language*, 42, 531–5.

Olmsted, D. L. (1971) *Out of the mouth of babes*. The Hague: Mouton.

Omar, M. K. (1973) *The acquisition of Egyptian Arabic as a native language*. The Hague: Mouton.

Opie, I., and Opie, P. (1959) *The lore and language of schoolchildren*. London: Oxford University Press.

Oyama, S. (1976) 'A sensitive period for the acquisition of a nonnative phonological system'. *Journal of Psycholinguistic Research*, 5, 261–83.

Palermo, D. S. (1973) 'More about less: a study of language comprehension'. *Journal of Verbal Learning and Verbal Behaviour*, 12, 211–21.

Parisi, D., and Antinucci, F. (1970) 'Lexical competence'. In Flores d'Arcais, G. B., and Levelt, W. J. M. (eds), *Advances in psycholinguistics*.

Parry, P. G. (1976) 'Some aspects of the child's acquisition of *left* and *right*'. Unpublished M.A. dissertation, University of Manchester.

Pavlov, I. P. (1927) *Conditioned reflexes*. Translated by Anrap, G. V. London: Oxford University Press.

Piaget, J. (1923) Translated by Gabain, M., and Gabain, R. *The language and thought of the child*. London: Routledge & Kegan Paul.

Piaget, J. (1928) *Judgement and reasoning in the child*. London: Routledge & Kegan Paul.

Piaget, J. (1954) *The construction of reality in the child*. New York: Basic Books.

Piaget, J. (1967) *The child's concept of space*. New York: Norton.

Piaget, J., and Inhelder, B. (1969) *The psychology of the child*. London: Routledge & Kegan Paul.

Pike, E. G. (1949) 'Controlled infant intonation'. *Language Learning*, 2, 21–4. [Reprinted in Bar-Adon, A., and Leopold, W. F. (eds). *Child language, a book of readings*].

Premack, D. (1971) 'On the assessment of language competence in the chimpanzee'. In Schrier, A., and Stollnitz, F. (eds), *Behaviour of nonhuman primates: modern research trends*. Vol. 4. New York: Academic Press.

Preston, M. S., (1971) 'Some comments on the developmental aspects of voicing in stop consonants'. In Horton, D. L., and Jenkins, J. J. (eds), *Perceptions of language*. Ohio: Merrill.

Quirk, R., Greenbaum, S., Leech, G., and Svartvik, J. (1972) *A grammar of contemporary English*. London: Longman.

Raffler-Engel, W. von (1965) 'Die Entwicklung vom Laut zum Phonem in der Kindersprache'. In Zwirner, E., and Bethge, W. (eds), *Proceedings of the fifth International Congress of Phonetic Sciences, Munster, 1964*. Basel: Karger. [Translated in Ferguson, C. A., and Slobin, D. I. (eds), *Studies of child language development*.]

Raffler-Engel, W. von, and Lebrun, Y. (eds) (1976) *Baby talk and infant speech*. Lisse: Swets & Zeitlinger.

Ramer, A. L.H. (1976) 'Syntactic styles in emerging language'. *Journal of Child Language*, 3, 49–62.

Read, C. (1975) 'Lessons to be learned from the pre-school orthographer'. In Lenneberg, E. H., and Lenneberg, E. (eds), *Foundations of Language Development*, Vol. 2.

Reed, M. (1970) 'Deaf and partially hearing children'. In Mittler, P. J. (ed.), *The psychological assessment of mental and physical handicaps*. London: Methuen.

Reich, P. A. (1976) 'The early acquisition of word-meaning'. *Journal of Child Language*, 3, 117–23.

Reid, J. F. (1966) 'Learning to think about reading'. *Education Research*, 9, 56–62.

Reid, J. F. (1970) 'Sentence structure in reading primers'. *Research in Education*, 3.

Rheingold, H. L., Gerwitz, J. L., and Ross, H. W. (1959) 'Social conditioning of vocalizations in the infant'. *Journal of Comparative and Physiological Psychology*, 52, 68–78.

Richardson, K. (1977) 'The writing productivity and syntactic maturity of eleven-year-olds in relation to their reading habits.' *Reading*, 11, No. 2, 46–53.

Roeper, T. (1973) 'Theoretical implications of word-order, topicalization, and inflections in German language acquisition'. In Ferguson C. A., and Slobin, D. (eds), *Studies of child language development*.

Rosenbaum, P. S. (1967) *The grammar of English predicate complement constructions*. Cambridge, Mass.: M.I.T. Press.

Rosenberg, S., and Koplin, J. H. (1968) *Developments in applied psycholinguistics research*. New York: Macmillan.

Ross, A. S. C. (1937) 'An example of vowel-harmony in a young child'. *Modern Language Notes*, 52, 508–9.

Roussey, C. (1899–1900) 'Notes sur l'apprentissage de la parole chez un infant'. *La Parole*, 1, 870–80; 2, 23–40. [Cited in Ingram, D. (1974), 'Phonological rules in young children'. *Journal of Child Language*, 1, 49–64.]

Rozin, P., Poritsky, S., and Sotsky, R. (1971) 'American children with reading problems can easily learn to read English represented by

Chinese characters'. *Science*, 171, 1264–7. [Reprinted in Smith, F. (1973), *Psycholinguistics and reading.*]

Sachs, J., and Devin, J. (1976) 'Young children's use of age appropriate styles in social interaction and role-playing'. *Journal of Child Language*, 3, 81–98.

Sakamoto, T. (1975) 'Preschool reading in Japan'. *The Reading Teacher*, 29, 240–4.

Savin, H. B., and Bever, T. G. (1970) 'The non-perceptual reality of the phoneme'. *Journal of Verbal Learning and Verbal Behaviour*, 9, 295–302.

Schvachkin, N. Kh. (1966) Abstract by Slobin, D. I. In Smith, F., and Miller, G. (eds). *The genesis of language.*

Schvachkin, N. Kh. (1973) 'The development of phonemic speech perception in early childhood.' In Ferguson, C. A., and Slobin, D. I. (eds), *Studies of child language development.*

Schwenk, M. A., and Danks, J. H. (1974) 'A developmental study of the pragmatic communication rule for prenominal adjective ordering'. *Memory and Cognition*, 2, 149–52.

Seashore, R. H., and Eckerson, L. D. (1940) 'The measurement of individual differences in general English vocabularies'. *Journal of Educational Psychology*, 31, 14–38.

Shankweiler, D., and Liberman, I.Y. (1972) 'Misreading: a search for causes'. In Kavanagh, J. F., and Mattingly, I. G. (eds), *Language by ear and by eye.*

Shatz, M., and Gelman, R. (1973) 'The development of communication skills: modification in the speech of young children as a function of listener'. *Monographs of the Society for Research in Child Development*, 38. Chicago: Chicago University Press.

Sheridan, M. D. (1973) *Children's developmental progress. From birth to five years. The stycar sequences*. New, illustrated edition. Windsor: NFER Publishing Company.

Shipley, E. F., Smith, C. S., and Gleitman, L. R. (1969) 'A study in the acquisition of language: free responses to commands'. *Language*, 45, 322–42.

Sinclair-de Zwart, H. (1969a) 'Developmental psycholinguistics'. In Elkind D., and Flavell, J. (eds), *Studies in Cognitive development*. London: Oxford University Press.

Sinclair-de Zwart, H. (1969b) 'A possible theory of language acquisition within the general framework of Piaget's developmental theory'. In Elkind, D., and Flavell, J. (eds), *Studies in cognitive development*. London: Oxford University Press.

Skinner, B. F. (1938) *The behaviour of organisms: an experimental analysis*. New York: Appleton-Century-Crofts.

Skinner, B. F. (1957) *Verbal behaviour*. New York: Appleton-Century-Crofts.

Slobin, D. (1966a) Comments on McNeill, D., 'Developmental psycholinguistics'. In Smith, F., and Miller, G. A. (eds), *The genesis of language: a psycholinguistic approach.*

Slobin, D. (1966b) 'Grammatical transformations and sentence comprehension in childhood and adulthood'. *Journal of Verbal Learning and Verbal Behaviour*, 5, 219–27.

Slobin, D. (1966c) 'Soviet psycholinguistics'. In O'Connor, N. (ed.), *Present-day Russian psychology: a symposium by seven authors.* Oxford: Pergamon Press.

Slobin, D. (1966d) 'The acquisition of Russian as a native language'. In Smith, F., and Miller, G. A. (eds), *The genesis of language: a psycholinguistic approach.*

Slobin, D. I. (1968) 'Imitation and grammatical development in children'. In Endler, N. S., Boutler, L. R., and Osser, H. (eds), *Contemporary issues in developmental psychology*. New York: Holt, Rinehart & Winston.

Slobin, D. I. (1970) 'Universals of grammatical development in children'. In Flores d'Arcais, G. B., and Levelt, W. J. M. *Advances in pscycholinguistics.*

Slobin, D. (1971) *Psycholinguistics.* Glenview and London: Scott, Foresman.

Slobin, D. I. (1973) 'Cognitive prerequisites for the development of grammar'. In Ferguson, C. A., and Slobin, D. I. (eds), *Studies of child language development.*

Slobin, D. I., and Welsh, C. A. (1973) 'Elicited imitation as a research tool in developmental psycholinguistics.' In Ferguson, C. A., and Slobin, D. I. (eds), *Studies of child language development.*

Smith, F. (1973) *Psycholinguistics and reading.* New York: Holt, Rinehart & Winston.

Smith, N. V. (1973) *The acquisition of phonology: a case study.* Cambridge: Cambridge University Press.

Smith, F., and Miller, G. A. (eds), (1966) *The genesis of language. Proceedings of a conference on 'Language development in children'.* Cambridge, Mass.: M.I.T. Press.

Snow, C. E. (1972) 'Mothers' speech to children learning language'. *Child Development*, 43, 548–65.

Snow, C. E. (1976) 'The language of the mother–child relationship'. In Rogers, S., (ed.), *They don't speak our language.* London: Edward Arnold.

Snow, C. E. (1977) 'The development of conversation between mothers and babies'. *Journal of Child Language*, 4, 1–22.

Snow, C.E., and Ferguson, C. A. (eds) (1977) *Talking to children: language input and acquisition.* Cambridge: Cambridge University Press.

Söderbergh, R. (1971) *Reading in early childhood: a linguistic study of a Swedish pre-school child's gradual acquisition of reading ability.* Stockholm: Almqvist & Wiksell.

Southgate, V., and Roberts, G. R. (1970) *Reading—which approach?* London: University of London Press.

Spalding, R. B., with Spalding, W. T. (1957)   *The writing road to reading*. New York: Morrow.

Stampe, D. (1969)   'The acquisition of phonetic representation'. *Papers of the fifth regional meetings, Chicago Linguistics Society*, 443–54.

Strang, B. M. H. (1970)   *A history of English*. London: Methuen.

Strickland, R. (1962)   'The language of elementary school children: its relationship to the language of reading textbooks and the quality of reading of selected children'. *Bulletin of the School of Education*, No. 4, 38. Bloomington, Ind.: University of Indiana.

Tansley, A. E., and Nicholls, R. H. (1962)   *Racing to read*. Leeds: E. J. Arnold.

Tanz, C. (1975)   'Learning how *it* works'. *Papers and Reports on Child Language Development*, 10, 136–52.

Taylor, S. E., Franckenpohl, H., and Pette, J. L. (1960)   'Grade level norms for the components of the fundamental reading skill'. *EDL Information and Research Bulletin No. 3*. Huntington, N.Y.: Educational Developmental Laboratories. [Cited in Massaro, D. W. (ed.), *Understanding language*. New York: Academic Press.]

Templin, M. C. (1957)   *Certain language skills in children*. Minneapolis: University of Minnesota Press.

Terman, L. M., and Merrill, M. A. (1967)   *Stanford-Binet intelligence scale: manual for the third revision form L-M*. London: Harrap.

Thorndike, E. L., and Lorge, I. (1944)   *The teachers' word book of 30,000 words*. New York: Teachers' College, Columbia University.

Tinbergen, N. (1951)   *The study of instinct*. London: Oxford University Press.

Tonkova-Yompol'skaya, R. V. (1969)   'Development of speech intonation in infants during the first two years of life'. *Soviet Psychology*, 7, 48–54. [Reprinted in Ferguson, C. A., and Slobin, D. I. (eds), *Studies of child language development*.]

Tough, J. (1973)   *Focus on meaning: talking to some purpose with young children*. London: Allen & Unwin.

Trevarthen, C. (1974)   'Conversations with a two-month-old'. *New Scientist*, 62, 230–5.

Trubetzkoy, N.S. (1939)   *Grundzüge der Phonologie*, Travaux du Cercle Linguistique de Prague, 7. [Translated by Baltaxe, C. A. M. (1969), as *Principles of phonology*. Berkeley and Los Angeles: University of California Press.]

Trudgill, P. (1975)   *Accent, dialect and the school*. London: Edward Arnold.

Turner, E. A., and Rommeveit, R. (1967)   'The acquisition of sentence voice and reversibility'. *Child Development*, 38, 649–60.

Velten, H. V. (1943)   'The growth of phonemic and lexical patterns in infant language'. *Language*, 19, 281–92.

Vernon, M. D. (1957)   *Backwardness in reading*. London: Cambridge University Press.

Vygotsky, L. S. (1962)   *Thought and language*. Edited and translated by

Hanfmann, E., and Vakar, G. Cambridge, Mass.: M.I.T. Press.

Wales, R., and Campbell, R. (1970) 'On the development of comparison and the comparison of development'. In Flores d'Arcais, G. B., and Levelt, W. J. M. (eds), *Advances in psycholinguistics*.

Warburton, F. W., and Southgate, V. (1969) *i.t.a.: an independent evaluation*. London: Chambers.

Wasz-Höckert, O., Lind, J. Vuorenkoski, V., Partanen, T., and Valanne, E. (1968) *The infant cry: a spectrographic and auditory analysis*. London: Spastics International Medical Publications in association with William Heinemann.

Waterson, N. (1971) 'Child phonology: a prosodic view'. *Journal of Linguistics*, 7, 179–212.

Waterson, N. (1976) 'Perception and production in the acquisition of phonology'. In Raffler-Engel, W. von., and Lebrun, Y. (eds), *Baby talk and infant speech*.

Waterson, N., and Snow, C. (eds) (in press) *The development of communication: social and pragmatic factors in language acquisition*. New York: John Wiley.

Watts, A. F. (1944) *The language and mental development of children*. London: Harrap.

Weber, R. (1970) 'A linguistic analysis of first-grade reading errors'. *Reading Research Quarterly*, 5, 427–51.

Weeks, T. E. (1971) 'Speech registers in young children'. *Child Development*, 42, 1119–31.

Weeks, T. E. (1975) *The slow speech development of a bright child*. Lexington, Mass: D. C. Heath.

Weir, R. (1966) 'Some questions on the child's learning of phonology'. In Smith, F., and Miller, G. A. (eds), *The genesis of language*.

Wells, G. (1974) 'Learning to code experience through language'. *Journal of Child Language*, 1, 243–69.

Whitford, H. C. (1966) *A dictionary of American homophones and homographs*. New York: Teachers College Press.

Wijk, A., (1966) *Rules of pronunciation for the English language*. London: Oxford University Press.

Wittgenstein, L. (1963) *Philosophical investigations*. Translated by Anscombe, G. E. M. Oxford: Blackwell.

Wolff, P. H. (1969) 'The natural history of crying and other vocalizations in early infancy'. In Foss, B. M. (ed.), *Determinants of infant behaviour IV*. London: Methuen.

Zhurova, L. Ye. (1964) 'The development of analysis of words into their sounds by pre-school children'. *Soviet Psychology and Psychiatry*, 2, 11–17. [Reprinted in Ferguson, C. A., and Slobin, D. I. (eds), *Studies of child language development*.]

Index

accent
    received pronunciation, 7.1.1, 7.1.3
    regional, 7.1.1, 7.1.3
accent and stress, 2.10, 3.2, 3.9.1, 6.1
adverbials, 3.3.4, 3.9
Albrow, K. H., 7.1.2
Allerton, D. J., 7
alphabetic writing system, 7.1.1, 7.1.2,
    7.4.1, 7.4.4
Amidon, A., 4.5.3, 6.3
Anderson, H. E., Jr, 6.3
Anderson, S., 2.8
Anglin, J. M., 4.4, 6.3
Anthony, A., 2.1, 2.1.3, 2.1.4
Antinucci, F., 3.3.2, 5.4
Arnold, G. F., 7.1.3
Asch, S. E., 6.3
assimilation, 2.5., 2.7., 7.1.3
Atkinson (-King), K., 1.2, 6.1
awareness of language, 3.4, 4.4, 6.1

babbling, 1.2, 1.2.1, 2.1
Baddeley, A. D., 7.4.2
Baldie, B. J., 3.3.2, 3.6
Balfour, G., 4.5.2, 5.4
Barrie-Blackley, S., 4.5.3
Bartlett, E. J., 4.5.1
Bashaw, W. L. 6.3
Beaken, M., 2.8
behaviourist theories, 5.2
Bellugi, U., 2.10, 3.2, 3.2.1, 3.3.5,
    3.5.2, 3.6, 3.7, 3.8, 5.1, 5.2
Berdiansky, B., 7.1.2
Bereiter, C., 6.4
Berko, J., 3.4, 3.4.2, See also Gleason,
    J.B.
Bernholtz, N., 1.6
Bernstein, B., 6.4
Bever, T. G., 2.10, 3.8, 5.2.1, 7.1.1
Blasdell, R., 3.5.3
Bloom, L., introduction, 3.2, 3.2.1,
    3.2.2, 3.3.3, 3.7.1, 4.4
Bonvillian, J. D., 3.8
Bowerman, M., 3.2, 3.2.3, 3.3.3, 3.8
Braine, M. D. S., 3.2, 3.2.1, 5.2.1

Breakthrough to Literacy, 7.3.2, 7.4.3
Brent, S. B., 6.3
Brewer, W. F., 4.5.1
Brown, R., 1.2, 3.2, 3.2.1, 3.2.2, 3.3.1,
    3.4, 3.5.1, 3.5.2, 3.6, 3.7, 3.7.2,
    3.8, 4.2, 4.4, 5.1, 5.2
Bruce, D. J., 6.1
Bruner, J., 5.4
Bullock Report, 7.1.2, 7.2.4, 7.4.4, 7.5
Bullowa, M., 1.2.1

Campbell, R., 4.5.1, 4.5.2
Carey, P., 4.5.3
Carroll, J. B., 7.1.1, 7.2.4
Carrow, M. A., 3.6
Carskaddon, G., 3.8
case grammar, 3.2.3
categorical perception, 1.4
Cazden, C., 3.4, 3.6, 5.1, 5.2
Chall, J., 7.2.2
chimpanzees, 5.3
Chomsky, C., 6.1, 6.2, 7.3.2
Chomsky, N., introduction, 2.9.1,
    3.2.3, 3.8, 5.2, 5.3, 7.1.2, 7.2.2
Clark, E. V., 4.4, 4.5.1, 4.5.3
Clark, H. H., 4.5.1, 4.5.4, 5.4
Clark, R., 3.3.3, 3.5.2, 3.5.4, 3.7
classical conditioning, 5.2
Clay, M. M., 7.2.3
Cleary, C. J. D., 5.6
cognitive development, 3.5, 5.1, 5.4
Coker, P. L., 4.5.3
colour-coded script, 7.5
comprehension, 3.6, 3.6.1, 3.7.1, 6.2
Compton, A. J., 2.1.3
conditioned variation, mor-
    phophonemic, 3.4.2
Conrad, R., 7.2.1, 7.2.4
consonantal clusters, 2.3, 2.7, 6.1, 7
consonantal system, 2.1.1
consonant harmony, 2.5
content (or lexical) words, 3.2.1, 7.1.2
contextual generalisation, 5.2.1
conversation, introduction, 3.8, 3.9,
    3.9.1

cooing, 1.2
Corrigan, R., 6.3
Cromer, R. F., 6.2
Cruse, D. A., 4.5.1
Cruttenden, A., 1.2, 6.4
crying, 1.1, 1.3
Crystal, D., 3.3.1, 3.3.2, 7.5

Dale, P. S., v
Danks, J. H., 6.2
Department of Education and Science,
    7.1.2, 7.2.4, 7.4.4, 7.5
De Villiers, J. G., 3.6
De Villiers, P. A., 3.6
Devin, J., 3.9.2
discourse, introduction, 3.9, 3.9.1
Dixon, E. M., 3.6.1
Doman, G., 7.2.4
Donaldson, M., 4.5.1, 4.5.2, 5.4
Dore, J., 1.6
double articulation, 3.5
Downing, J., 7.2.1, 7.3.1
Drach, K. M., 3.8
Drouin, C., 6.3
Dunn, L., 6.2

Eckerson, L. D., 4.1
Edwards, A. D., 6.4
Edwards, M. L., 2.8
Eilers, R. E., 4.5.1
Eimas, P., 1.4, 2.8
elaborated/restricted codes, 6.4
Engelmann, S., 6.4
English writing system, 7, 7.1.2, 7.4.4
Entwistle, D. R., 6.2
Ervin, S., 2.10, 3.2.1, 3.7.2, 6.2, 6.3
expansions, 3.8

Farwell, C., 2.1.3, 2.2
feature synthesis, 2.3
Ferguson, C. A., introduction, 2.1.1,
    2.1.3, 2.1.4, 2.2, 3.8
Fillmore, C., 3.2.3
first meanings, 1.5
Fletcher, P., 3.3.2
Fodor, J. A., 2.10, 3.8, 5.2.1
Forsyth, D. F., 6.2
Foster, G., 6.3
Fraser, C., 3.2.1, 3.5.2, 3.6, 3.6.1,
    3.7.1, 3.7.2
French, M. 7.1.1
frequency, 3.4, 4.2, 4.5.1, 5.1
Freud, S., 5.4
Fry, D. B., 1.2.1
Fudge, E., 2.5

function (or grammatical) words, 3.2.1,
    3.5.3, 7.1.2, 7.1.3
Furth, H., 5.4, 6.4

Gardner, B. T., 5.3
Gardner, R. A., 5.3
Garman, M., 3.3.2
Garnica, O. K., 2.8, 3.8
Gelman, R., 3.9.2
generalisation,
    lexical, 4.4
    morphological, 3.4.1, 6.2
generative phonology, introduction
Gerwitz, J. L., 3.8
gesture, 1.6
Gibson, E. J., 7.2.2
Gimson, A. C., 7.1.3
given/new, 2.10, 3.9.1
Gleason, H. A., 4.5.4
Gleason, J. B., 3.8, 3.9.2, *See also*
    Berko, J.
Gleitman, L. R., 3.6.1
Goddard, N., 7.4.3
Goodglass, H., 4.5.4
Goodman, K. S., 7.2.2, 7.2.3
grammatical (or function) words, 3.2.1,
    3.5.3, 7.1.2, 7.1.3
grapheme-phoneme relationships,
    7.1.1, 7.1.2, 7.1.3, 7.2.1, 7.2.2,
    7.3.1, 7.3.2, 7.4.1, 7.4.3, 7.4.4, 7.5
Gray Oral Reading Test, 7.2.2
Greenfiled, P. M. 1.6, 3.2.3, 3.8
Grégoire, A., 1.2, 3.3.5, 3.5.3
Griffin, W. J., 6.2
Guillaume, P., 4.4

Haas, W., 7.1.1
Hall, B. L., 7.2
Hall, R. M. R., 6.2
Halle, M., introduction
Halliday, M. A. K., 1.3, 1.5, 1.6, 2.10,
    3.2.4, 3.3.3, 3.3.5, 3.5, 3.6, 3.9.1,
    5.2, 5.5
Hanlon, C., 5.1
Hayhurst, H., 3.3.2
Henzl, V. M., 3.9.2
Herriot, P., 3.6
Hood, L., 3.7.1
Huey, E. B., 7.2.4
Hutcheson, S., 2.1.4
Huttenlocher, J., 4.4
Huxley, R., 3.3.3
Hyde, M. R., 4.5.4

ideational component, 1.6, 3.2.4, 3.5
imitation, 3.7, 3.7.1, 3.7.2
Ingram, D., 2.7
Inhelder, B., 5.4, 5.5
initial teaching alphabet, 7.1.1, 7.1.2, 7.5
innatist theories, 3.8, 5.3
interpersonal component, 3.2.4
intonation, 1.3, 1.4, 1.5, 1.6, 2.10, 3.2.4, 3.8, 7.1.1, 7.1.3
Irwin, O. C., 2.1
item-learning, 3.1.3, 3.5, 3.6.1, 3.7

Jakobson, R., 2.1, 2.1.1, 2.1.2, 2.1.3
Jeffrey, W., 7.4.1
Jenson, P., 3.5.3
Johansson, Bo. S., 6.3
Jones, D., ix
Jones, J. K., 7.5

Kaplan, E. L., 1.4
Katz, E. W., 6.3
Kavanagh, J. F., 7.2.4
Keenan, E. O., 3.9.1
Keller, H., 5.3.1
Kessell, F. S., 6.2
Kirk, L. 1.3
Klein, E., 3.9.1
Klima, E. S., 2.10, 3.3.5
Kobashigawa, B., 3.8
Kol'tsova, M. M., 4.3
Kuczaj II, S. A., 4.5.3, 4.5.4
Kunze, L. H., 3.3.2
Krashen, S., 5.3.1

Labov, W., 6.4
language-experience approach to reading, 7.4.3, 7.4.4
language of reading materials, 7.5
Leach, E., 7.3.1
Legum, S. E., 6.3
Lenneberg, E. H., 3.6.1, 5.3.1
Lesser, H., 6.3
Levin, H., 7.4.1
Lewis, M. M., 1.2, 1.3, 1.4, 1.5
lexical diffusion, 2.1.3, 2.9.1
lexical (or content) words, 3.2.1, 7.1.2
Li, C. N., 1.3
Liberman, I. Y., 7.2.2
Lieberman, P., 1.3
Lightbown, P., 3.7.1
Limber, J., 3.3.5
Loban, W. D., 6.2
look and say, 7.4.2, 7.4.4, 7.5
Lorenz, K., 5.3.1

Lorge, E. L., 4.1
Lovell, K., 3.6.1
Lumsden, E. A., 4.5.1
Luria, A. R., 5.1
Lyons, J., 3.2.1, 3.5.1

McCarthy, D., 3.3.1, 4.1, 6.2, 6.4
McGarrigle, J., 4.5.2
McGrath, C. O., 3.3.2
MacKay, D., 7.3.2
McNeill, D., v, 3.2.1, 3.3.5, 4.4, 4.5.1, 5.3
McNeill, N. B., 3.3.5
MacWhinney, B., 3.5
Major, D., 3.3.2
manner of articulation, distinctions based on, 2.1.1
Maratsos, M. P., 3.6, 4.5.1, 4.5.4
Marchbanks, G., 7.4.1
Martin, S. E., 7.1.1
Martinet, A., 3.5
Massaro, D. W., 7.2.1
Mattingly, I. G., 7.1.1, 7.2.4
maturation, 5.3.1
mean length of utterance, 3.3.1
Menyuk, P., v, 1.6, 2.8, 3.3.3, 6.2
Merrill, M. A., 3.2
metathesis, 2.6
Miller, R., 3.3.2
Miller, W. R., 2.10, 3.2.1
morphology, 3.4, 3.5.3
Morse, P. A., 1.4
motor development, xii
Mowrer, O. H., 1.2.1
Muuss, R., 6.2

Nakazima, S., 1.3
negation, 3.3.5
Neimark, E. D., 6.3
Nelson, K., introduction, 3.8, 4.4
neonate, 1.1, 1.4
Nerlove, H., 6.3
noun phrase, 3.3.3
Norris, R. C., 6.2

O'Connor, J. D., 7.1.3
O'Donnell, R. C., 6.2, 7
Oliver, P., 7.3.1
Olmsted, D. L., 1.2.1, 2.1.4
Omar, M. K., 3.2, 3.3.5, 3.4.1
one-word stage, 1.6
operant conditioning, 1.2.1, 5.2
Opie, I., 3.9.2
Opie, P., 3.9.2

overgeneralisation
  lexical, 4.4
  morphological, 3.4.1, 6.2
Oyama, S., 5.3.1

Palermo, D. S., 4.5.2
parental speech, introduction, 3.8, 5.3, 7, 7.5
Parisi, D., 5.4
Parry, P. G., 4.5.4
Pavlov, I. P., 5.2
phoneme-grapheme relationships, 7.1.1, 7.1.2, 7.1.3, 7.2.1, 7.2.2, 7.3.1, 7.3.2, 7.4.1, 7.4.3, 7.4.4, 7.5
phonemic analysis in reading, 7.2.1, 7.2.2, 7.2.4, 7.4.1, 7.4.4
phonemic development, 1.6, 2.1, 2.9.1, 6.1
phonemic substitution, 2.2, 2.7
phonic method, 7.4.1, 7.4.4, 7.5
Piaget, J., 5.4, 5.5, 6.3, 6.4
Pike, E., 1.3
pivots, 3.2.1, 5.3
place of articulation, distinctions based on, 2.1.1
Poteat, B. W. S., 4.5.1
Premack, D., 5.3
Preston, M. S., 2.1.1
pronouns, 3.3.3, 6.2
punctuation, 7.1.3, 7.3.1

Quirk, R., introduction, 3.3.5

Racing to Read, 7.5
Raffler-Engel, W. von, 1.3
Ramer, A., introduction
Read, C., 7.2.2
reading
  abilities needed to learn, 7.2.1
  analysis of errors, 7.2.3, 7.5
  early stages of, 7.2
  for meaning, 7.2.2
  materials, language of, 7.5
  optimal age for learning, 7.2.4
  sources of difficulty in, 7.2.2
  speed, 7.1.2, 7.2.1
  teaching of, 7.2.4, 7.3.1, 7.4, 7.5
Reed, M., 5.4
Reich, P. A., 4.4
Reid, J. F., 7.2.1, 7.5
register, introduction, 3.9, 3.9.2
relationship between spoken and written language, 7, 7.1.3, 7.5
relational meanings, 4.5.1
Rheingold, H. L., 3.8

rhythm, 2.4
Richardson, K., 7
Roberts, G. R., 7.4
Roeper, T., 3.5.2
Rommetveit, R., 3.6
Rosenbaum, P. S., 6.2
Ross, A. S. C., 2.5
Ross, H. W., 3.8
Roswell-Chall Auditory Blending Test, 7.2.2
Roussey, C., 2.4
Rozin, P., 7.1.1

Sachs, J., 3.9.2
Sakamoto, T., 7.1.1, 7.1.2
Samuels, S. J., 7.4.1
Savin, H. B., 7.1.1
Schvachkin, N., Kh., 2.8
Schwenk, M. A., 6.2
Seashore, R. H., 4.1
semantic feature hypothesis, 4.5.1, 4.5.3, 4.5.4, 6.3
sentence functions, 3.2.4, 3.6
sentence processes, 3.3.5, 3.5.4
sentence structure, 3.3.5
Shankweiler, D., 7.2.2
Shatz, M., 3.9.2
Sheridan, M. D., xii
Shipley, E. F., 3.6.1, 3.8
short-term memory, 3.2, 7.2.1, 7.2.4, 7.5
Sinclair (-de Zwart), H., 3.4, 5.4
Sjölin, B., 6.3
Skinner, B. F., 1.2.1, 5.2
Slobin, D., 3.2, 3.3.5, 3.4, 3.4.1, 3.6, 3.7.1, 3.7.2, 3.8, 4.3, 5.3
Slotnick, N. S., 6.3
Smith, C. S., 3.6.1
Smith, F., 7.1.1, 7.2.1, 7.2.2
Smith, J. H., 1.6, 3.2.3, 3.8
Smith, N. V., 2.1.1, 2.1.2, 2.4, 2.8, 2.9.1
Snow, C. E., introduction, 3.8
social class, 6.4
Söderbergh, R., 7.2.4
Southgate, V., 7.1.2, 7.4
Spalding, R. B., 7.3.2
speech perception, 1.4, 2.8, 2.9.1, 7.1.1, 7.2.1, 7.2.2
spelling, 7.1.2, 7.1.3, 7.2.2, 7.3.2, 7.5
  rules, 7.1.2, 7.2.1, 7.3.1
  teaching of, 7.4.1
Stampe, D., 2.9.2
Stone, J. B., 4.5.1
Strang, B. M. H., 7.1.2

strategies, 3.5
stress and accent, 2.10, 3.2, 3.9.1, 6.1
Strickland, R., 7.5
style, 3.9, 3.9.2
syllable perception, 7.1.1, 7.2.2
syntagmatic-paradigmatic shift, 6.2

Tansley, A. E., 7.5
Tanz, C., 3.6
Taylor, S. E., 7.4.2
telegraphic speech, 3.2, 3.7, 3.7.1
Templin, M. C., 2.1, 3.3.1, 6.1, 6.2
Terman, L. M., 3.2
Thompson, S. A., 1.3
Thorndike, E. L., 4.1
Tinbergen, N., 5.3.1
Tonkova-Yampol'skaya, R. V., 1.3
traditional orthography, 7.1.2, 7.5
transformational-generative grammar,
    introduction, 3.2.3
Trevarthen, C., 3.8
Trubetzkoy, N. S., introduction, 2.1
Trudgill, P., 7.1.1
T-unit, 6.2
Turner, E. A., 3.6
two-word sentences, 3.2

variability in phonemic development,
    2.1.3
variation in language development,
    introduction
Velten, H. V., 2.9.2
verb phrase, 3.3.2
Vernon, M. D., 7.2.1

vocabulary, 1.6, 4.1
voicing, distinctions based on, 2.1.1
vowel system, 2.1.2
Vygotsky, L. S., 4.4, 6.3, 7.2.1

Wales, R., 4.5.1, 4.5.2
Warburton, F. W., 7.1.2
Wasz-Höckert, O., 1.1
Waterson, N., introduction, 2.5, 2.9.1
Watson, J. B., 5.2
Watts, A. F., 4.1, 6.3
weak forms in reading, 7.1.3
Weber, R., 7.2.3
Weeks, T. E., 2.1.1, 3.9.1
Weir, R., 1.2, 1.3
Weksel, W., 2.10, 3.8, 5.2.1
Wells, G., 3.2.3, 5.4
Welsh, C. A., 3.7.1
Whitford, H. C., 7.1.2
whole-word method, 7.4.2, 7.4.4, 7.5
Wijk, A., 7.1.2
Wolff, P. H., 1.1, 1.2
word order, 3.2, 3.5.2
writing
    abilities needed, 7.3.1
    early stages of, 7.3
    teaching of, 7.3.2, 7.4.1
written language, 7.1, 7.2.1, 7.3.1
writing systems, 7, 7.1.1, 7.1.2, 7.4.1,
    7.4.2, 7.4.4

Yudovitch, F. la., 5.1

Zhurova, L. Ye., 6.1, 7.2.2, 7.2.4